MW01130384

Fragile Families

PENNSYLVANIA STUDIES IN HUMAN RIGHTS

Bert B. Lockwood, Series Editor

A complete list of books in the series
is available from the publisher.

Fragile Families

Foster Care, Immigration, and Citizenship

Naomi Glenn-Levin Rodriguez

PENN

UNIVERSITY OF PENNSYLVANIA PRESS

PHILADELPHIA

Published by
University of Pennsylvania Press
Philadelphia, Pennsylvania 19104-4112
www.upenn.edu/pennpress

Printed in the United States of America
on acid-free paper

1 3 5 7 9 10 8 6 4 2

Library of Congress Cataloging-in-Publication Data
ISBN 978-0-8122-4938-5

CONTENTS

Introduction

It was Esperanza[1] Foster Family Agency's annual holiday party and I was sitting with Liliana, Bailey, and Emma's foster father, Trevor. We were eating enchiladas and listening to Trevor speak about the challenges and rewards of being a foster parent, the "high highs and the low lows." Emma, not quite two years old, had been leaning between the knees of her other foster father, Josh, while Trevor spoke. Partway through his speech she toddled over to Trevor and put her arms up. He reached down and scooped her up with one arm and she laid her head against his shoulder, one small hand on the back of his neck. The room was filled with a collective sigh—here was a perfect moment between father and daughter, an image of the sort of relationship that Esperanza Foster Family Agency stood for. I knew Trevor and Emma well and Trevor certainly felt like Emma's father to me. Emma's pending adoption would be finalized soon, and Trevor and Josh would be Emma's permanent family.

Yet as I sat watching them under the glow of the lanterns and the warm San Diego evening sky, I thought about all the other relationships in which Emma was embedded. Her biological mother and father meeting her at Chuckie Cheese the next week, still hoping for her return. Her grandmother who had wanted to take her in but felt too old to do so without help. Emma's older siblings, placed with various extended family. The broader social networks that connected her back to family in Honduras, a set of legal relationships that would be severed by her pending adoption and new legal birth certificate, which would list Trevor and Josh as her parents.

I tried to imagine how the scene would feel if Emma's biological parents and siblings were in the room. They had been neglectful and unstable, but they had not been violently abusive. Emma's social worker had eventually ruled out reunification with Emma's parents, but she had considered the possibility of placing Emma with her extended family right up until the last few months, when she determined that no relative was able to take in Emma permanently. So Emma had never been simply Trevor and Josh's child, and, in fact, had been in another foster home prior to placement with Trevor and Josh. She was removed from that home due to an allegation of physical abuse, which was later determined to have been unfounded. There were many ways her case could have gone, many lives she could have led. This is the case for all of us, but for foster children and families, the numerous trajectories one might experience are made more visible. And the traces of those other possible lives remain, shadowing families that are made through the awkward, fumbling, haphazard intervention of the state. The webs of social relatedness in which children and families are embedded, the networks that are interrupted, and the decisions that bring a child to one possible future while foreclosing others are the subject of this book. The central contention of this book is that in the context of child welfare, through relations that are ostensibly about protecting children and preserving families, vulnerability, inequality, and the contours of belonging, race, and citizenship are produced and reinforced.

Interventions

I initially met Trevor, Josh, and Emma, along with the other foster families, children, and social workers who are the primary subjects of this book, through Esperanza, a small foster family agency in San Diego that focused on Latina/o children and their families. Foster care, at its most basic level, is the site of one of the most concrete, heavy-handed state interventions into the private, intimate lives of families. Social workers are empowered to make decisions about whether children face a threat of danger, and if so, to remove them physically and legally from their parents' care. As I describe in more detail in Chapter 4, social workers are given broad latitude in enacting or deferring these forms of intervention—there is no protocol detailed enough to capture the complexity of family circumstances that bring children and their parents under the purview of child welfare authorities.[2] In the San Diego region, these interventions are deeply entangled with immigration policy and politics. Practices of detention and deportation, alongside racializing processes and structural violence, construct national boundaries as they position particular families as more likely to be subjects of state intervention. This book focuses on the everyday experiences of Latina/o families whose lives are shaped at the nexus of child welfare services and immigration enforcement.

"The state" is, of course, not a monolithic, faceless force but, in the context of child welfare services, is enacted through daily interactions among social workers, lawyers, judges, children, and families. Policy and political climate shape the terrain in which these interactions take place. But because social work, like many other fields in which the state operates, is a highly discretionary practice, foster care is also a means through which precariousness is produced for people's lives in ways that activate social relations of race, citizenship, and nationality. Social workers' assessments of a family's "fit-ness," their daily practices and budgetary constraints, alongside their sense of what a "good," "safe" home looks like, give force to the lived experiences of categories of race, class, and gender and demarcate boundaries of citizenship and nationality. Judicial determinations solidify these assessments and give them the force of law. As such, the impacts of social workers' and legal actors' decisions are profound and often permanent, though the social categories that inform these decisions, as I describe in Chapter 2, are shifting and unstable.

Many families come into contact with child welfare services because of the precariousness of their lives—unsafe housing, unstable employment, and the conditions of violence, drug use, and domestic violence made visible by the heightened police presence in impoverished communities. Yet the child welfare system itself, as I elaborate in the chapters that follow, is also a site where precariousness and vulnerability are produced. As social workers physically and legally sever relationships between parents and children, as they ask parents to meet goals that are outside the realm of parental capabilities due to economic or legal constraints, families teeter on the edge of dissolution, and often fall into the brink. Those families that are eventually reunited are brought back together after a period of extended separation, often filled with trauma, insecurity, and hardship for both parent and child. And few resources are available to help families heal and transition once the child welfare apparatus has receded from their lives.

To be clear, this book does not argue for the primacy of the biological family, nor does it call into question the biological family's centrality to current policy and law in the contemporary United States. The focus on the biological family as the de facto best place for children to be raised has been both lauded and critiqued in the realms of child welfare and immigration law (Bartholet 1999; Briggs 2012; King 2009; Yablon-Zug 2011; Zavella 2012). Rather than asking whether the biological family should be positioned in this manner, I accept this premise as a starting place. Throughout the chapters that follow, I argue that an inherent right to the integrity of a biological, or natal, family is not in fact equally extended to, and protected for, families with members who fall outside of the normative framework of "good" citizens. This may be due to a variety of factors that undermine an individual's belonging to the nation and their rights to full citizenship, including circumstances relating to race, class, nationality, legal citizenship, language use, or other mitigating factors.[3]

The research for this book was conducted in the San Diego-Tijuana region between 2008 and 2012. The cities of San Diego and Tijuana are deeply economically entangled and socially estranged.[4] They share a history of exchange through the recruitment of laborers from Tijuana to compensate for San Diego labor shortages, the use of Tijuana by U.S. citizens as a site for access to goods and entertainment during the Prohibition era, and particularly through the Border Industrialization Program and the implementation of NAFTA in the mid-1990s (Proffitt 1994).[5] The period from the establishment of NAFTA in 1994 to the present day has seen the tightening of business partnerships and explosive growth of the Tijuana population. Despite the fact that the Tijuana/San Diego area is the "busiest migration corridor in the western hemisphere" (Katsulis 2008:4), and thus an obvious site for considering the possibilities of binational collaboration and engagement, the two cities remain sharply separated by U.S. border enforcement and immigration policies.[6]

The social ties that do exist are largely constructed through individual family and social relations rather than facilitated through official government channels. Communities are formed across international lines through "transborder lives" (Stephen 2007), as individuals move across national, racial, and linguistic borders, suspended between, and participating in, multiple geographic spaces, living "neither here nor there" (Zavella 2011).[7] This lack of formal collaboration between governmental entities contributes to the absence of a clear protocol for navigating child welfare circumstances that engage individuals living on both sides of the border, as official means of collaboration would rely on an acknowledgment of connectedness that U.S. government officials are reticent to accept. As such, although the child welfare cases recounted throughout this book often draw in family members on both sides of the border, there is little protocol in place for formalized binational collaboration between the two social service or judicial systems.

Laura, a veteran social worker and head of a regional office in San Diego County, lamented to me at a fundraising event that many foster children perhaps only ten physical miles from their grandmother's home in Tijuana would be placed in a foster home with strangers in San Diego. Laura's view was that this resulted from the unnecessary difficulty of cross-border collaboration, not because a San Diego foster home was understood to be best for that particular child. As I discuss in Chapter 2, however, some social workers and legal actors did interpret the best interest of the child to be equated with "not Mexico," even if the child welfare system officially recognized family members as always preferable to a non-relative foster home, regardless of their country of residence. As such, the character of the relationship between these two cities, both connected and divided, established the conditions of possibility for shaping, and dividing, families in this region.

Esperanza Foster Family Agency was my starting point, and from there I connected with families, legal advocates, dependency court authorities, policy makers, and other small foster family agencies. I attended trainings and orientation sessions for foster parents, dependency lawyers, and legal advocates, as well as the monthly meetings of the San Diego network of foster family agencies. I conducted more than 60 formal and informal interviews with lawyers, judges, legal advocates, social workers, and current and former foster parents, and met with many of my interviewees multiple times. In Tijuana, I initially made contact with local orphanages through a network of San Diego donors. From there I was able to build relationships with a number of orphanage directors who connected me to social workers, lawyers, and medical staff at the Desarrollo Integral de la Familia (DIF), which provided child welfare services to Tijuana residents. Driving between Tijuana and San Diego each week, and tracking cases in both cities, gave me a view of the San Diego-Tijuana region, the ruptures and continuities, which few San Diego residents without ties to Tijuana experience. As I describe in further detail in Chapter 1, the child welfare systems in San Diego and Tijuana operated largely as distinct systems, rather than as a single, regional agency spanning the international border. However, numerous child welfare cases did involve family members, agencies, social workers, and legal actors from both cities, and mechanisms did exist, including the Mexican embassy and the International Liaison Office, staffed by San Diego County social workers, to facilitate communication between the San Diego child welfare agency and the DIF Tijuana.

I conducted participant observation as an intern at Esperanza Foster Family Agency, shadowing social workers and spending time with the foster families I met through the agency's daily operations. Although I was fortunate to interact with a number of state-employed San Diego County social workers and administrators, and to conduct a number of informal interviews and observations, I was not given official research access to the public child welfare agency.[8] This barrier shaped the material of this book in profound ways, and placed smaller agencies, legal actors, and foster families at the center of my analysis. Biological parents were primarily handled by the public agency, and for this reason my interactions with them were more limited than with the foster families, social workers, and other service providers involved in the child welfare system. And although I use the term "biological" throughout this book to refer to the parents from whom children are removed in the context of child welfare interventions, it should be noted that not all parents are necessarily "biological" in this context. Children may, of course, be removed from stepparents, adoptive parents, and other legal guardians. Social workers and legal actors commonly used the term "bio parents" to refer to the parents from whom foster children had been initially removed, regardless of the existence of a biological link between parent and child.

My role at Esperanza was complex. When interacting with foster children and families, my role was as a researcher. Though I accompanied Esperanza social workers on their official business, I was careful to make it clear that I was not in any way part of the decision-making processes that would shape the trajectory of any child's case. In the office, however, I participated as an intern in almost every aspect of social work practice—filing papers, fielding phone calls, typing case notes, organizing files, and preparing trainings and orientation sessions under the guidance of the head Esperanza social worker at the time. My relationship with Corinne, the Esperanza social worker who appears most frequently in the pages that follow, was the most intimate. Although there were five Esperanza employees at the beginning of my most extended research period in 2010, I worked with Corinne through an organizational transition that left her as the only Esperanza employee. She was a Mexican national, and fluent in Spanish and English. Her family had moved back and forth between San Diego and Baja California for years, primarily to enjoy U.S. schooling opportunities for Corinne and her siblings. Corinne had recently graduated from a local university, and was employed at Esperanza on a work visa while preparing to apply to graduate school. Many days I worked across from Corinne, on the edge of her desk, chatting and making our way through office tasks together throughout the day. Corinne left the agency in February 2010 because Esperanza had been merged with a broader social service organization and her new boss did not wish to renew the sponsorship that was necessary for her to maintain her U.S. visa. Alicia, who replaced her, was also the sole Esperanza employee until August 2011, when Esperanza operations were temporarily suspended. These conditions created an opportunity for me to be extremely useful to this small agency, which facilitated the research process in innumerable ways. Although I was initially unsure how eager busy social workers would be to share their experiences with me, and how willing foster and biological parents would be to discuss their intimate, sometimes painful experiences, I found that almost everyone I spoke with was quick to dismiss my concerns and generous in sharing their stories. Most of the individuals I spoke with felt that the foster care process was misunderstood or simply absent from public conversation, and that the problems were vast and needed to be discussed and addressed. Interviews were conducted in both Spanish and English; all translations are my own.

Children's experiences play a central role in the stories that follow, though their own voices and perspectives are notably, and intentionally, absent. Although many of the older children I spent time with, ranging from five to eight years old, had much to say about their experiences in foster care, the majority of children whose cases I followed were between infancy and five years old. Focusing on this young demographic limited children's ability to communicate about, and reflect on, their experiences, but also foreclosed the possibility of their being able to actively and willingly commit to participation in a research project. I wrote about children primarily in contexts where social workers were already actively documenting their experiences and during the course of my formal and informal interviews with foster parents. Voices of children are occasionally present in the text, but the majority of my analysis focuses on the way children were positioned as objects of intervention and of protection, rather than as active subjects participating in and shaping the contours of their lives.

A Temporality of Interruptions

I tell the stories of the children, parents, social workers, and legal actors who are introduced in this book through fragmented narratives. The cases themselves weave in and out, and often end abruptly, without resolution. Crucial details of many cases are missing and the end result for each child is often absent in the stories I tell in the pages that follow. In this way, the structure of the book and its stories mirror the experience of families embroiled within the child welfare system. As I recount, the actors and agencies involved often operate with partial information and constrained access. Cases are opened and closed according to the recommendations of social workers and lawyers and the determinations of judges. Decisions are often made based on incomplete case notes, and case files handed from social worker to social worker often go unread by overworked social workers who are regularly operating in crisis mode and constantly pressed for time. Social worker turnover is tremendous and children routinely interact with more than half a dozen case workers over the course of two years in foster care, which, at the time of this writing, is the average time a child spends in the system. Children and parents who have been legally separated often have difficulty locating each other, and obstructing this continued connection may, in some circumstances, be the goal of the child welfare agency, pursued in the name of child protection. Child welfare authorities operate in this realm of partial knowledge—it is a rare case that involves institutional actors who have a clear sense of what feels to them to be the "full story" from beginning to end. As a researcher, my access was similarly partial and fragmented, and there were few stories that I was able to track from start to finish. The gaps and omissions, however, are central to how this system operates, and are part of the story that needs to be told.

The temporality not only of the cases themselves, but also of parenthood and family, constitutes a strand that weaves throughout the text. The normative model of contemporary family formation is based on underlying assumptions about biology, blood, sameness, and permanence. These first three concepts—blood, biology, and sameness—have been thoroughly critiqued and eroded by the emergence of new kinship studies that began to gather force in the early 1990s (Ginsburg and Rapp 1991; Weston 1991; Franklin and McKinnon 2002). Permanence, however, has largely been left unaddressed in the scholarly literature, and temporary families, like foster families, continue to be positioned in popular discourse as "less than" (Wozniak 2001). Parenting, in many ways, is understood in popular discourse to be about both the everyday and the passage of time. Family invokes a sense of permanence; the birth or adoption of a child is understood to make a claim on the rest of that parent's life. I suggest in the chapters that follow that the experiences of foster families, and of biological families separated by state intervention, erode any easy linkages between experiences of family and assumptions about permanence.

Social workers and legal actors also confront the complexity of temporal limitations. Lawyers and judges, in making determinations about child removal, placement, and custody, must, in essence, predict the future. They ask themselves whether they think children will face future harm if they remain in the care of their natal families, and they must ask themselves whether that potential harm may be more or less impactful than the harm of dislocation, of the severance of kinship ties, of starting over again in a new family setting. Legal actors make these decisions in the context of inordinate caseloads of hundreds of foster children often during bi-annual court hearings that regularly take less than ten minutes from start to finish.

Social workers face similar predictive conundrums as well as a constant pull between short-term and long-term goals. The removal of a child for their short-term protection may be the best immediate solution while also being the intervention that may cause the most long-term damage. As Connolly (2000) reminds us, social services have roots in a charity model—one that expects short-term support to produce lasting consequences. Child Welfare Service interventions rarely offer adequate support to families with deeply rooted, complex problems informed by structural inequalities that shape their access to food, housing, employment, or mental health services (Lee 2016). Social workers routinely hand off cases every six months, a strategy that allows them to specialize in particular phases of the child welfare system, such as the initial investigation process, or the pursuit of an adoptive placement after family reunification has failed. This procedure narrows the necessary range of social worker expertise while also facilitating a focus on the short term, relieving them of having to consider the impacts of their decisions six months, or five years, down the line. Social workers know that the resources and supports the county provides are largely inadequate to address, in a substantial way, the challenges the families they work with face. Because they are unable to make substantial, systemic changes, they steel themselves for "frequent flyers," children and parents whom they expect to return again and again to state custody and state scrutiny. In this sense, the actors present in this book are enmeshed in fraught relations of temporality and power.

A Note on Violence

The child welfare system does the important work of intervening in circumstances where children may be experiencing extreme forms of physical, sexual, or emotional abuse. However, the vast majority of child welfare interventions in the United States involve concerns about neglect, often linked to conditions of poverty or to parental drug use. In the state of California in 2011, for example, 81.5 percent of children who entered foster care entered due to allegations of neglect, 9.8 percent for physical abuse, 2.4 percent for sexual abuse, and 6.3 percent for "other" reasons.[9] The news media draw the public's attention to foster cases that represent extreme, rather than typical, experiences of child abuse and of foster care. The cases I recount do not, in general, address the more extreme forms of violence and mistreatment from which child welfare services are tasked with protecting children. I avoid addressing these cases partly because they are the extreme minority of child welfare cases. Furthermore, my focus is on the discretionary processes and daily practices that constitute cases where the decision-making process is less clear, and where social workers, lawyers, and family members might be more likely to disagree about how to proceed. Regardless how categories of race, class, and citizenship might impact circumstances that are framed as instances of child abuse and neglect, it would be rare to question the decision to remove a child or to terminate parental rights in the face of extreme forms of violence. Cases that are unclear, and situations where one might imagine multiple possible outcomes, are cases that allow us to center the role of discretionary decision-making, and all the aspects that inform such a process. These, I suggest, are the richest sites for considering the way boundaries of citizenship, belonging, worthiness, race, and nation are produced through daily interactions between families and representatives of the state.

Boundaries of Belonging

As numerous scholars have noted (Dreby 2012; Chavez 2008; De Genova and Ramos-Zayas 2003), immigration enforcement and ideas about "illegality" impact most, if not all, Latina/os in the United States, regardless of their citizenship status. The framework of the "illegal immigrant" collapses categories of race, nationality, and citizenship to draw distinctions between who does and who does not belong within the boundaries of the state. At this particular historical moment, concerns about illegality, deportation, citizenship, and rights are center stage in popular and political discourse. Increased media coverage of parental deportations and the separation of families with young children alongside growing criticism of the rise in deportations under the Obama administration have raised humanitarian concerns about the contemporary U.S. approach to immigration. And, as I discuss in Chapter 1, the 2014 influx and subsequent deportation of a large number of Central American unaccompanied minors raises complex concerns about protections for children and families, and the broader question of the extension, or denial, of basic rights to non-U.S. citizens. Critiques of birthright citizenship, brought into mainstream political debate by Senator Lindsay Graham, ask the American public to consider how U.S. citizens are "made" and whether place of birth or parentage should be the primary factor in determining membership, belonging, and rights. Debates surrounding the DREAM Act have questioned the worthiness and the culpability of those referred to as the "1.5 generation," children born abroad who entered the United States without authorization, or who overstayed tourist visas, and have grown up attending U.S. schools, experiencing themselves as unquestionably American, although with severely restricted legal rights.[10] Finally, 2016 presidential candidate Donald Trump has garnered support for his candidacy through an immigration stance that includes banning all Muslims from legal entry to the United States, and building a wall on the U.S. border with Mexico. Taken together, these issues highlight contemporary struggles over the boundaries of belonging, tensions between social and legal forms of citizenship, and rising (though not novel) trends in anti-immigrant sentiment and xenophobia.

Numerous scholars have focused on the impacts of and responses to restrictive immigration policies on youth and families (Dreby 2010, 2015; Zayas 2015; Pallares 2015; Terrio 2015; Gonzales 2016, among others) and others have focused on the specific policies constraining immigrants' lives at the "systemic level" (Zatz and Rodriguez 2015:10; see also Heidbrink 2014; Bhabha 2014). I focus on the enactment of the policies themselves in the context of child welfare interventions—how the everyday interactions and decisions of social workers, family members, and legal actors breathe life into the policies and laws that shape child welfare and immigration in the contemporary United States. It is through daily interactions that the delineations that draw lines between citizen and "other" come to impact the intimate lives of Latina/o families. As Boehm (2012:9) reminds us, "the overlapping spheres of state power and intimate lives cannot be separated."

The ways in which ideologies of race, nation, and citizenship shape the expression of state power inform this book at a number of levels. At the most basic level, Latina/o parents who are in the U.S. without authorization are particularly vulnerable to the removal of their children through child welfare service intervention. As noted above, experiences of poverty, including presence in low-wage, unstable jobs, limited access to safe and affordable housing, and constrained ability to provide adequate childcare and medical care, are often translated into a language of "neglect." These forms of structural violence, where racialization and structural inequality come together, produce circumstances that increase the tenuousness of Latina/o family formations as that language of "neglect" both mobilizes and justifies child welfare interventions.

Second, social workers, lawyers, and judges who are authorized to make custody recommendations and determinations, and to effect the removal, placement, and adoption of children, are far from immune to the way conceptions of "good" parents and "safe" homes are shaped by categories of race, class, nationality, and language use. As described in Chapter 4, these circumstances complicate the role of discretionary decision-making practices among social workers and legal actors, and create the space for discriminatory patterns to take shape despite social workers' best intentions. And finally, the impacts of race, class, and citizenship categories take shape through the cross-border collaboration (or lack thereof) between social service agencies on both sides of the U.S.-Mexico border. As such, I explore the complexities of institutional systems and bureaucratic practices that span the border region. The conditions of "interlegality" (Santos 1995), where individuals are caught up at the nexus of overlapping legal systems, are fraught as different state systems confront questions of citizenship, belonging, and rights in distinct ways.

At all levels, the impact of ideologies of race, nation, and citizenship are profoundly shaped by current trends in immigration policy and enforcement, and the politicization of the U.S.-Mexico border in the wake of 9–11. Much as Walters (2002:267) approaches deportation as "*constitutive* of citizenship," I suggest that child welfare interventions into Latina/o families are constitutive of the production of the "good" family and, in turn, the "good" citizen. Importantly, the boundaries of belonging that are drawn throughout this book are not generally drawn under conditions of overt racism or explicit violence. Instead, I emphasize the ways the quotidian workings of the child welfare system serve as a site that illuminates how minute decisions ripple out to shape whole populations—primarily through gaps in institutional knowledge, discretionary decision-making, and processes of translation.

The child welfare system operates through categories such as "good" or "bad" parent, "stable" or "unstable" home, "abuser," "abandoner," and so on. The immigration system similarly operates through legal categories of the detainee, the deportee, the legal permanent resident, the citizen, and the criminal "alien." As parents and families live their lives amid these agencies, their individual actions and decisions are congealed and solidified, frozen into the operative agency categories. Not only do these categories work to reduce an individual to a single frame, but they also haunt the individual in the future. Despite their future actions, traces remain and color the way institutions interact with them and shape their path forward from the initial incident that pulled them into the agency's gaze. The existence and implementation of these categories compels parents to contend with interpretations of their actions within these categories, since parents are rarely in a position to contest their categorization. These categorization processes also enable institutional authorities to understand their own decisions as simply applying the appropriate, ostensibly objective label to a parent based on an institutional definition. Thus categories of "fit" or "unfit," "good" or "bad," trump other designations such as "under-resourced" or "impoverished" that are not codified within the child welfare system and might undermine clear categories of "good" or "bad" parenting. In this sense, categorization practices serve as a mode of cultural production in which "bad" parents come into existence through institutional processes and discourses.[11]

In this approach, I take inspiration from Bowker and Star, whose work *Sorting Things Out* (1999) offers a comprehensive analysis of the politics of categorization and the ways that categories are experienced as natural even while they operate as potent sites of political and social struggle.[12] For Bowker and Star, classification systems, while understood to be a necessary feature of social interaction, can never be merely descriptive. These classifications are productive of hierarchies of value, serving as key technologies for excluding certain subjects while framing others as normative and natural. As such, I ask how the interactions between social workers and families might facilitate the equation of illegality with "unfit" parenting or translate instances of involuntary deportation into the institutional category of "child abandonment."

Although the interactions I detail throughout this book are not always across languages, they are always across hierarchies of power and authority. Legal actors, social workers, and parents enact their relationships through language, among other modes of exchange and communication. Their employment, or reworking, of one another's terms and ways of speaking serve to construct, reproduce, and occasionally undermine the power relations that mark the terrain of child welfare. My approach to translation, as I detail below, is thus not limited to cross-border or cross-language exchanges.

Rather, I engage translation as a practice through which boundaries of citizenship, worthiness, and belonging are produced and reinforced, and as a framework for understanding complex interactions among myriad institutional authorities and the families entangled with the child welfare system.

I employ the concept of translation not only to make sense of how categories operate but also to make sense of the inter-institutional engagement that occurs at the juncture of the multitude of organizations that constitute the child welfare system. As legal organizations, government institutions, and nonprofit agencies come together, they do so through their own sets of agency protocols, employing the jargon, acronyms, and legalese that constitute their users as members of particular institutions. Terms such as "biomom" or "TPR'd" (shorthand for saying that someone's parental rights were terminated, as in "We TPR'd her") serve to demarcate the expert from the nonexpert.[13] Yet while these terms may be employed across institutions, they have different meanings for different actors, and figure into their daily practices in varied ways.

Translational processes give shape to interactions, where an ongoing and strategic struggle for "imperfect equivalences" (Clifford 1997) is, in a sense, a defining characteristic of engagement among differently situated people. As such, the mode of translation, as I employ it, attends to how meaning is constituted through movement across contexts and how a single referent takes on different meanings and facilitates different actions and interpretations in such contexts as a family's home, a social worker's file, or a courtroom exchange. Following Brenneis (2004), who considers translational processes in the institutional context of funding agencies, I explore the way "key terms and phrases move and circulate across various domains and of how their meanings and prescriptive implications are transformed and negotiated in new settings" (582).[14] I examine not only the processes through which the messy lives of individuals are translated into concrete legal categories but also how modes of translation and analogy-making enable engagement among disparate agencies and actors. The language through which these institutions interact enables the various agencies that constitute the child welfare system to come together, facilitating exchanges among individuals who use overlapping terms and referents, such as "unfit parent" or "best interest of the child," but with vastly different meanings. These exchanges necessarily engage asymmetrical power relations, as the usage of these terms by different agencies and actors—judges, lawyers, social workers, and family members—carries different degrees of weight.

Organization of the Book

The book begins with an exploration of the politics of worthiness and the boundaries of belonging, with a focus on the political relationship between the United States and Mexico in the context of anti-immigrant sentiment and legislation. Chapter 1, "Worthy" Migrants, is built around an examination of the cases of two children, both born in Tijuana and entangled in child welfare agencies on both sides of the border. This chapter charts how the boundaries of citizenship and state responsibilities for minors are carved out through narratives, advocacy work, and institutional processes that make only some children legible as deserving of state protection.

Chapter 2, Belonging and Exclusion, takes a historical perspective to consider the separation of Latina/o children and families alongside other histories of child removal in the United States, each of which illuminates historical concerns about race, citizenship, and normative family forms that continue to inform the present. I foreground an examination of the "best interest" principle, a legal framework that has been mobilized to justify the removal of children from a number of marginalized communities and is currently deployed in U.S. immigration and dependency courtrooms to justify the separation of children from parents who are categorized as "deportable." This chapter examines the discretionary decision-making processes through which circumstances of poverty and other forms of structural violence are translated into institutional categories of "fit" and "unfit" parents through the framework of "best interest."

The processes that position some families as "unfit" are complicated by the gaps and overlaps between immigration enforcement and child welfare policy. Chapter 3, Working the Gap, turns to the dual sets of obstacles and opportunities that arise at the juncture of these two overlapping legal systems. Through an exploration of the way child welfare and immigration enforcement systems each affect the other while proceeding on parallel tracks, I explore two main sets of outcomes. The first set involves problematic interactions between these two systems—court negotiations, documentary practices, and legal constraints—that create profound obstacles to family reunification for those caught up simultaneously in both systems, regardless of the intent of individual social workers, lawyers, advocates, and judges. The second set of outcomes concerns the production of possibilities for creative maneuvering, whereby legal advocates work within the gap between the two systems, using unexpected avenues to pursue citizenship and reunification strategies that do not, at first glance, appear to be within the realm of the intent of the law. I emphasize the translational processes through which immigration enforcement actions, such as detention and deportation, become reworked into child welfare categories of "unfit" parents. This chapter considers the ways the impact of legal systems exceeds their official mandate as discrete systems interact with each other in unexpected and unintended ways. In the case of child welfare and immigration enforcement, these interactions increase the precariousness and vulnerability of Latina/o families, an issue heightened in border regions where these two legal systems frequently come together.

Chapters 4 and 5 examine the production of boundaries of belonging on a more intimate scale. Rather than working at the level of legal systems, institutional practices, and nation-state relationships, these chapters ask about the decision-making processes and intimate interactions that shape the trajectory of children and families entangled in these institutional contexts. Chapter 4, Decisions, Decisions, focuses on interactions among social workers, children, and families. This chapter argues that the making and unmaking of families happens on an intimate, everyday scale where social workers are required to make decisions about child custody in the context of limited time, budgetary constraints, and lack of knowledge and protocol about how best to proceed in any particular case. I emphasize social worker discretionary decision-making practices as a form through which state authorities shape Latina/o families and the boundaries of belonging in the contemporary United States. Individual decisions become solidified and routinized through everyday agency practice in a manner that obscures the subjective and often discriminatory assessments of Latina/o families and Spanish-speaking nation-states that give shape to child welfare practice. Chapter 5, Intimacies, focuses on the perspectives of biological and foster parents embroiled in the child welfare system while performing the everyday tasks of caring for and about their children. This chapter emphasizes the fragility of parent-child relationships in the face of state intervention, and explores the ways biological and foster parents defer to, resist, and navigate social worker authority as they struggle to maintain connections with their children. The conclusion draws these themes together and asks how an examination of the experiences of Latina/o families in foster care might illuminate quotidian processes and intimate relations through which the boundaries of belonging, worthiness, citizenship, race, and nation are produced and remade.

CHAPTER 1

"Worthy" Migrants

I first met Alba in 2008 as she ran into the living room of her parents' home, followed by her father, who was waving a hairbrush playfully at her head of tangled curls. The social worker I was accompanying had explained to me on our drive over that Alba's foster parents were technically Alba's cousins. They were in the process of adopting Alba, a process slowed by her status as a non-U.S. citizen. Alba was born in Tijuana to two parents who were both heavily addicted to methamphetamines. Her mother disappeared shortly after Alba's birth. Alba was a little over a year old when her father, purportedly for drug money, agreed to sell her to Esther, a Guatemalan woman with U.S. citizenship, for $400. Esther then brought Alba into the United States using her own biological daughter's birth certificate. Alba's extended family, aghast at these events, managed to locate Esther, who was living in San Diego. Tatianna, Alba's cousin, who also lived in San Diego, went to find Alba, and eventually was able to initiate the process of adopting her through the child welfare system.

As I learned more about Alba's case over the next three years, it became clear that she was a child about whom many stories could be told. She was at once an adopted child and an abandoned child, a smuggled child, a trafficked child, a stateless child, and a migrant child.[1] As Boehm (2008) notes, the legal categories that define an individual's status in the United States serve as a central node for the assertion of state power that shapes migrant families in profound ways. As such, Alba was poised at the brink of multiple possible futures. The path eventually chosen for her, as I discuss below, both shaped her future and reworked her past.

In this chapter, I consider the force of these narrative frames, and the ways they shape differential outcomes for children in seemingly similar circumstances. Outcomes are affected not only by the stories that are told but also by the positionality of the (adult) advocate who tells the story and successfully reframes the child. The frameworks available and the impact they have on a child's trajectory are, of course, historically contingent. They are shaped by economic conditions, geopolitical relations, and the political moments in which they emerge. As Kelly (2004:97) notes, government efforts to keep people "in place" are central to state-making processes. Demarcations about which children are eligible to cross into the United States and eventually pursue a path to citizenship are shifting and unstable, changing in response to economic and political circumstances. Yet these boundaries are central to the production of the nation, and the limits of U.S. citizenship.

As such, the categories that confront a child like Alba become key sites for situating citizens and noncitizens, for making and unmaking racially marginalized families, and for policing the fragile boundary between deserving children in need of protection and threatening young criminals who do not merit the state's care.[2] And although the granting or denial of citizenship is experienced as a profound and permanent response, the production of these boundaries is tentative, fragile, and always in process, as policy and judicial rulings shift the landscape. I juxtapose divergent framings of child migrants to examine the strategies through which some children are categorized as worthy of protection and citizenship, while others are not. I consider the way the extension of humanitarian intervention, through the provision of citizenship for particular children, is enacted not in relation to the specific suffering of an individual child. Rather, pathways to citizenship are mobilized through the advocacy work of well-positioned adults who draw on powerful narratives to frame children as worthy of humanitarian protection.

The cases I describe in this chapter involve children caught up in overlapping institutions and geopolitical relations that shape ongoing interactions between the United States and Mexico. These relationships delimit the terrain on which claims to protection and to citizenship can be made. Mexican minors who migrate to the United States are typically seen as children who are not qualified for refugee status and are assumed to be primarily "economic" migrants. The category "economic" is used in the contemporary moment to delineate "deserving" migrants from "undeserving" migrants.[3] In the contemporary United States, framing migrants as an expense and a burden on the mythical "tax payer" is a key political strategy for facilitating an avoidance of the complex conditions that promote migration. Thus, legal immigration agreements between the two nations allow U.S. immigration officials to return Mexican citizens to Mexico through expedited procedures, denying them many of the legal protections available to other immigrants who are believed to have potentially valid claims for remaining in the United States.

These issues could not be illuminated more clearly than by the influx of unaccompanied minors from Central America across the Texas-Mexico border in 2014, ongoing at the time of this writing.[4] In response to an overwhelming number of young children arriving in Texas from Honduras, El Salvador, and Guatemala, lawmakers' concerns focused on the William Wilberforce Trafficking Victims Protection Reauthorization Act of 2008 (H.R. 7311), a provision that "gave substantial new protections to children entering the country alone who were not from Mexico or Canada by prohibiting them from being quickly sent back to their country of origin" (Hulse 2014). In other words, the perceived "crisis" of a surge of unaccompanied minors in the United States highlighted that children escaping dangerous situations in Central American countries could not be summarily deported as their Mexican counterparts could be, because of the potential that they might possess "valid" claims to protection, such as claims to political asylum (Rodriguez and Menjívar 2014).

Congressional reactions to these circumstances demonstrated that concerns about taxation and government spending were sufficient to override broad concerns about Central American children fleeing circumstances of poverty and violence. Claims to political asylum are based on the presence of a well-founded fear of persecution in relation to particular protected categories, such as religious or political affiliations. Notably, asylum claims rule out victims of structural violence, such as those facing widespread conditions of poverty or violence that cannot be said to target a specific individual, including, for example, the generalized violence that accompanies gang activity and drug trafficking. This specificity of victimhood is necessary to make an individual migrant legible as deserving of citizenship. It is on these grounds that legislators lobbied for the return of these minor migrants, without concern for the specifics of their individual circumstances. As I discuss below, the particularities of each child's experience and specific needs become subsumed into state-based categories; Mexican or Honduran affiliation determines a child's reception at the border, rather than do the specifics of their potential claims to immigration relief.[5] It is the translation of an individual's story into broad categories of "worthy victim" or "economic migrant" within a legal state framework that drives the extension or denial of citizenship on humanitarian grounds.

In my analysis, I focus on what I call "narratives of worthiness," the stories told about Latina/o children on either side of the U.S.-Mexico border that have the potential to position them as eligible for legal protection and U.S. citizenship. These narratives bring together conceptions of humanitarianism, tropes of children as innocent victims, and racialized visions of immigrants and their sending countries. These narratives contain elements of what Natalia Molina (2014) refers to as "racial scripts," the stories we tell to situate various racialized groups across time and space. Such scripts work to situate racialized groups in relation to others, in ways that shape their experiences, rights, and access to resources and to citizenship status. These scripts are imbued with a force that helps to locate particular subjects in a broader racialized milieu. The stories told about child migrants both draw on and depart from racial scripts as they situate children within the economic and political landscape that shapes the contours of citizenship and protection. Children, as I explore below, are caught up in particular narratives while also uniquely positioned, in some cases, to transcend them through the work of an effective advocate. In the stories that follow, I attend not just to the narratives themselves but also to the actors who put these stories to work for child migrants.

In exploring the ways these narratives are mobilized, I examine the cases of two children, Alba and Tommy, both of whom were born into precarious family circumstances in Tijuana. Using a detailed examination of their cases as a starting point, I consider what sorts of children, under what sorts of circumstances, are positioned as deserving of U.S. citizenship or safe harbor. This approach, I suggest, enables us to glimpse one of the processes through which the boundaries of citizenship are produced via determinations about child citizenship and child custody. Finally, I consider how social axes such as race and nationality both inform and are produced through these determinations.

The cases of Alba and Tommy include circumstances that appear to be sensational or extreme. Both children, at first glance, seem to have strong grounds for protection due to the particular conditions into which they were born. These circumstances, I argue, highlight the centrality of narratives to the outcomes of their cases, a feature particularly foregrounded in these examples, but that was a crucial element of every case I observed throughout my research.[6] Before examining the cases of Alba and Tommy, I begin with a discussion of migration and the politics of worthiness.

Child Migrants

The image of a child in need of rescue exerts a powerful pull. Images of abandoned, dirty, hungry, and needy children animate human rights campaigns, war efforts, philanthropic organizations, and trends in international adoption, shifting, to some degree, the anti-immigrant discourse that surrounds the plight of adult migrants. Yet children occupy a complex position in relation to U.S. immigration law. With the exception of international adoptees, child migrants have not generally been treated distinctly from adult migrants—they have been similarly subject to detention and deportation, and, until a class action law suit in 1996, were held in detention conditions along with adults and those with criminal convictions.[7] Children who are categorized as "economic" migrants are routinely detained and deported without any special rights to representation or counsel to support their ability to apply for immigration relief.[8]

It is not the circumstances of a child's migration experience alone that make that child legible within a framework of humanitarian rescue. Rather, this framework is constructed through a complex process of translation, a narrativization co-produced among immigrants, lawyers, and advocates (McKinley 1997; Cabot 2014). It is also shaped in profound ways by the circumstances of the children's arrival, and the agencies—immigration authorities, homeless shelters, or social service providers—with which they come into contact. Through the work of an effective advocate, international adoptees, child refugees, and children labeled as victims of trafficking appeal to universalist notions of suffering and of the innocence and desirability of children in a manner that circumvents the economic and racialized discourses that so often guide immigration policy and practices.[9] These children who are categorized as worthy of "rescue" include both international adoptees and some child migrants and refugees who are positioned as victims. The question of what sorts of children, from what nation-states, in what sorts of circumstances, shifts year-to-year and case-to-case in response to political events, legal climate, and global pressures. These actions occur even in the context of increasingly polarized contemporary debates about the worthiness of child migrants. However, as Orellana and Johnson note in relation to the political discourse surrounding the DREAM act, "there is evidence of a shift away from a view of all children as deserving of protection and care and toward one in which children must prove that they are deserving, either by birthright or by merit" (2011:20).[10] Geopolitical relations, national political climate, and narratives of worthiness position only particular children as subject to a story that supersedes the anti-immigrant sentiment directed at those perceived to be "economic" or "voluntary" migrants.

Care, Worthiness, and the Immigrant as "Victim"

In the case of child welfare services in both the United States and Mexico, protection is extended to children regardless of their citizenship status. That is, each state takes responsibility for child "victims" within its borders, regardless of their citizenship status or country of origin. However, as the case of the Central American minors recounted above demonstrates, children who are caught up in the immigration system, rather than child welfare services, and get framed as "economic" migrants, are often not extended protection.

These policies for child "victims" are driven by a universalist notion of human suffering and the unique vulnerability of children that supersedes the details of each particular case.[11] This was made evident in Alba's case, where her framing as a trafficked child through her initial "sale" to Esther was more important to her legal case for citizenship than any details about her actual treatment while in Esther's care. This vision of humanitarian intervention necessitates a moral obligation on the part of the receiving country. Here, humanitarian intervention draws on a notion of human suffering that separates those who are legitimate victims from those who suffer economic hardship.

Children are not exempt from this maneuvering.[12] Yet the distinction between economic migrants and "rights-worthy" migrants, and the disentangling of economic factors from those circumstances recognized as legitimate forms of persecution, is an increasingly impossible endeavor.[13] Of course infants and very young children, like Alba and Tommy, cannot be easily framed as economic laborers, but the presence of young, unauthorized migrant children in the United States is often explained through the economic needs of their parents in a way that narrates young children as present in the

United States primarily due to economic need. These sorts of narratives evade the story of a rights-worthy child by focusing on the narrative of the undeserving economic migrant that surrounds the parents' migration. Children as young as eight years old are effectively framed as "economic" migrants and summarily deported to their countries of origin. The cases of Alba and Tommy, and other children in similar circumstances, suggest that the mobilization of a narrative of worthiness may hinge on the action of a U.S. citizen adult positioned to compel the state in a way that a non-U.S. citizen, or a U.S. citizen child, is not equipped to do, a point to which I return below.

State Interactions with Citizen and Non-Citizen Children

The cases recounted below, and throughout this book, involve institutions, families, and legal systems that span both sides of the U.S.-Mexico border. Although both Tijuana and San Diego have well-established child welfare support systems, they are each structured differently and emphasize different sorts of programs. The child welfare system in San Diego County provides support services to families with children who have experienced, or have been alleged to have experienced, abuse, neglect, or abandonment. Children typically enter the system through a call to the child abuse hotline, often made by a concerned neighbor, teacher, medical authority, or anonymous third party. A child abuse hotline call prompts an investigation by a county social worker, which may lead to the provision of family maintenance services, such as parenting classes, therapy, or regular social worker visits. Alternatively, in cases where the child is determined to be in "imminent danger," the social worker may remove the child from the home, making the state the child's temporary legal parent. In these cases the child typically resides in a foster home or in the care of an agency-approved relative while the parent pursues a "case plan," designed by the social worker, that may involve drug treatment programs, anger management counseling, or separation from an abusive partner, among other possible requirements. Eventually, the social worker makes a recommendation to the court about whether the child should return to the parent's custody or be placed in a guardianship arrangement or an adoptive home. A dependency court judge makes a final ruling.

In Mexico, child welfare services are provided by Desarrollo Integral de la Familia (commonly referred to as "el DIF"), a system that provides a variety of support services including nutrition programs, legal services, a temporary shelter for children, and a network of private orphanages, many of which are run by religious organizations and supported by U.S. donors, volunteers, and staff. Although the vast majority of Tijuana orphanages are privately run, they are certified and overseen by the DIF Tijuana agency. Children are placed in orphanages and out for adoption by DIF social workers. Although DIF social workers do visit private orphanages, because there are only a small number of DIF Tijuana social workers—eight during the time of my research for the entire city—their oversight of the daily care and medical needs of the children is infrequent at best. As one orphanage director, Carlota, told me, "El DIF es como el Papá, y nosotros como mamá" (The DIF is like the father and we [the orphanage] are like the mother).[14] Carlota, who had grown up herself in the very orphanage she was directing, went on to explain that the orphanage provides the daily care, keeping the DIF informed and asking for permission for issues regarding schooling, placement, or medical treatment. She clarified, though, that unlike a traditional "papá," when a child needs expensive surgery or school fees the orphanage goes to donors rather than to the DIF for funding.

Because concerns in Mexico about child abuse or neglect must be made by a public "denuncio," as opposed to the option of making an anonymous call as in the U.S. child welfare system, many observers of child maltreatment are understandably hesitant to involve themselves. For this reason, many children are put under DIF's protective custody by the extended family when concerns about abuse or ongoing parental drug use become too extreme to ignore. It is also quite common for family members simply to provide care for children without involving the state agency in any way. Abandoned children, or children living on the street, are often brought to orphanage shelters by concerned neighbors. Although DIF offers parenting classes and reunification plans for parents, orphanage directors reported to me that reunification was a rare occurrence in Tijuana. Many children were regularly visited by their parents but did not return to their custody. Instead, they completed their youth and their schooling within the orphanage system, leaving at age fourteen of their own accord, often to live with extended family members with whom they had stayed in touch, once they were old enough to contribute to maintaining the household through their labor.

The child welfare systems in both Tijuana and San Diego took shape through extensive public-private partnerships. In Tijuana, this took the form of privately funded orphanages, often run by U.S. church groups and staffed

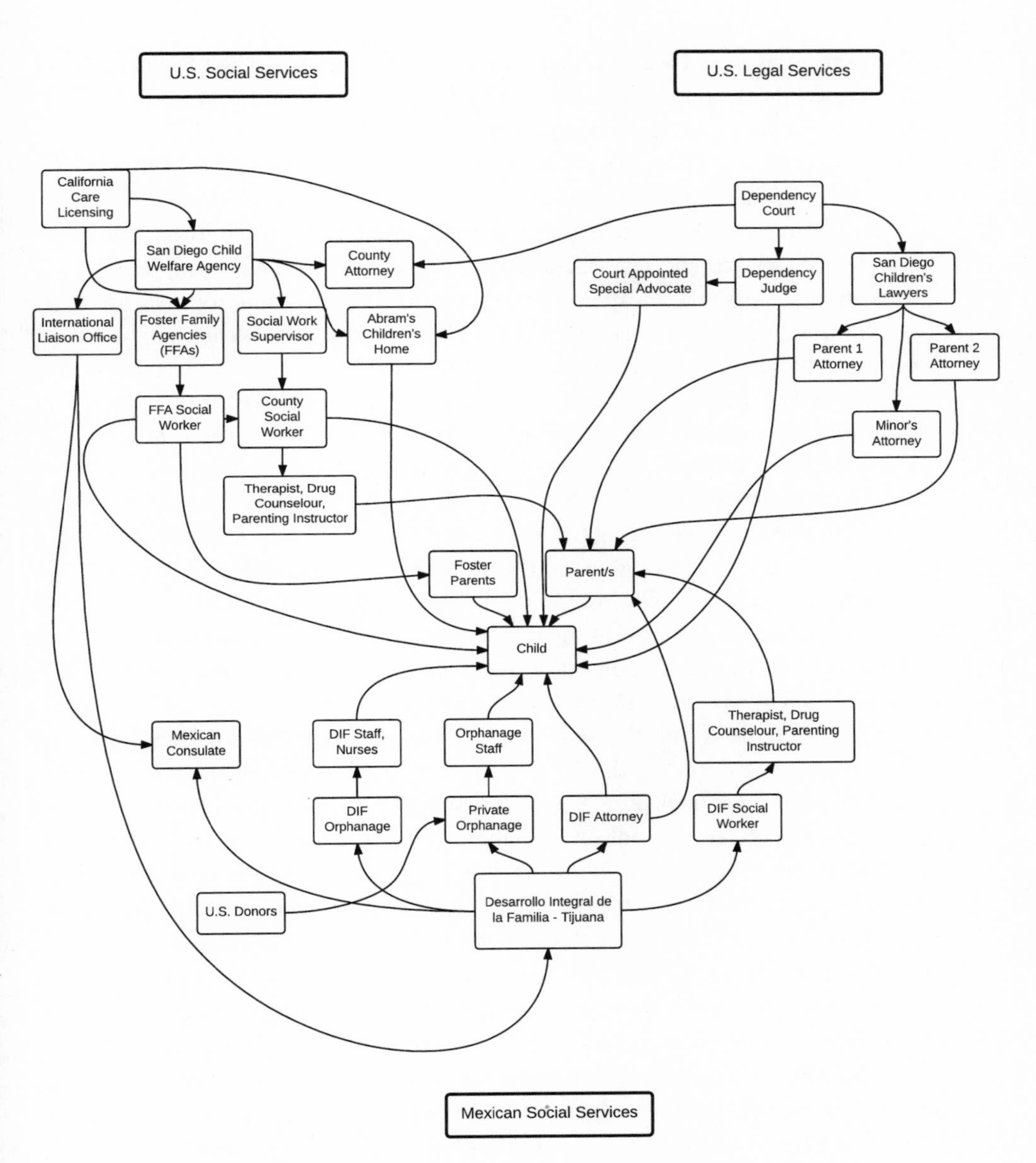

Figure 1. The child welfare system: key agencies and actors.

by a mixture of local Tijuana residents and U.S. volunteers. In San Diego, it took the form of nonprofit foster family agencies (FFAs). FFAs recruited and trained foster parents, and supervised the placement of foster children, through a subcontracting relationship with the county-run child welfare system. As in the Tijuana system, the public system in San Diego retained exclusive control over the initial intervention and removal of children, the selection of a placement option, and the court process associated with decisions about reunifying families, terminating parental rights, and pursuing adoptions for children.[15] Foster family agencies took on some of the county's workload by providing and overseeing additional foster homes, but they did not replace the work of the county social workers or reduce the number of children on a county worker's caseload. Furthermore, while the subcontracting relationship was monitored through a formal contract process, the financial relationship was complicated. Nonprofit FFAs, like Tijuana orphanages, received no funding from the county system for the services they provided. Although each foster family received monthly government funds for the provision of food, clothing, and other incidentals for their foster child, none of this money went to the agency itself.[16] Recruitment and training of families, program maintenance, building rental, and staff salaries were all underwritten by private donors or grant funding.

Esperanza, the agency through which I met Alba and where I conducted the bulk of my research on the San Diego foster system, was one such FFA. Esperanza's mission incorporated a focus on children under age five with the primary goals of keeping siblings together, addressing the specific needs of Latina/o foster children, maintaining small social worker case loads, and obsessively pursuing the goal of "one home for one child" to counteract the trend of foster children moving through multiple homes in the first few years of their lives. Esperanza aimed to provide specialized care for Latina/o foster children through the provision of bilingual social workers, specialized training for foster parents about "Hispanic cultural needs," and recruitment strategies that targeted Latina/o families through media campaigns on local Spanish-speaking TV and radio stations, as well as Mexican grocery stores and other such venues. When I asked Esperanza social workers and staff members to speak more explicitly about what they saw as "Hispanic cultural needs," their responses focused on the importance of bilingual social workers, service providers, and therapists who could work with both child and family, maintaining the ability of a foster child to communicate with biological parents even after a substantial period of separation.

Esperanza social worker Corinne explained to me, "As a bicultural social worker, being raised on both sides of the border, I just get things. The [foster] parents sometimes imply things to me that I don't think an English speaker would get." Corinne went on to note that this was important to county social workers who placed children from Spanish-speaking families at Esperanza. When I asked whether this was primarily to preserve their native language skills, she replied, "I think it's more practical than that. They want the kids to keep up the same language practices as they do at home so that it eases the transition back home and doesn't create more work for the bio[logical] parent."[17] Esperanza staff also mentioned such things as understanding the importance of extended family in the Latino community as well as the sorts of foods children would likely have been exposed to in their natal home or the language-based challenges they might face in school. The official Esperanza mission statement outlined the following goals for foster parent training around the issue of the specific needs of Latina/o foster children:

- Assure each child's healthy identity development by connecting him/her to her heritage, language and culture.
- Orient parents about the importance of home language development especially as it relates to school success in English.
- Offer families strategies for dual language development.
- Infuse concepts and strategies for achieving cultural and linguistic continuity into other topics of training.
- Acknowledge and celebrate the funds of knowledge, skills, and resources the families already have and can share with their foster and/or adoptive child.
- Every effort will be made to secure culturally and linguistically appropriate services when referring families for additional social, support, health, and educational services.

Esperanza's founder, Becky, contended that the county system repeatedly failed to address these sorts of specific needs for the Hispanic population. She took the position that "private money allows for better recruitment, screening, training, and support,"[18] and gave her the flexibility to address these concerns without the restrictions and cumbersome bureaucratic procedures of the public county agency.

Importantly, children were brought into these public/private partnerships, and provided with services including food, shelter, schooling, and medical care, by the child welfare systems in Tijuana and San Diego without regard for citizenship status. While each system was expected to alert the other to the presence of minor citizens across the border, they were not authorized to reclaim their own citizen children without express authorization by the other state or to repatriate noncitizen children of their own accord. In the U.S. context repatriation was not typically pursued for children within the child welfare system, and thus under state guardianship. However, children who were apprehended by border patrol authorities were frequently repatriated across the border into DIF custody, where they would commonly reside in temporary shelters while their family members in Mexico were located and contacted to collect them. Adults, and older youth who could pass as adults, were simply returned to the border and released into Mexico. The cases I turn to below involved Alba, a Mexican citizen child entangled in the San Diego child welfare system, and Tommy, a U.S. citizen sheltered in a Tijuana orphanage. The divergent trajectories of their two cases illuminate the ways that narratives of worthiness, under particular conditions, are mobilized to compel state actors to address the citizenship status of a child migrant. I argue that in that process the ever-shifting boundaries of the nation are reworked and reinforced.

Alba's Story

I first met Alba and her foster mother and biological cousin, Tatianna, in the summer of 2008, when Tatianna and her husband were still in pursuit of adoption and U.S. citizenship for Alba. Alba's story was unique because it had largely been resolved outside the law enforcement and federal bureaucracies typically involved in trafficking cases. According to Tatianna, this was partly because after arriving in the United States with Alba, Esther, who had allegedly "purchased" Alba, managed to register Alba under her legal guardianship and was able to receive some support services for food and housing through the social service system without raising any red flags about Alba's origins.[19] This meant that Alba was already enmeshed in the child welfare system, a circumstance that did not protect her from the threat of deportation but did enable her to sidestep the immigration bureaucracy that would normally attend to the circumstances of a child migrant or a trafficked child.

Children who are under the custody of the child welfare system are technically vulnerable to detention and deportation if they are not U.S. citizens. However, in practice it is quite unusual for children in foster care to be detained or deported while in care, and they are formally eligible for the same treatment and services provided to citizen foster children. Undocumented parents and family members attempting to regain custody of their children did experience profoundly differential treatment within the child welfare system; these distinctions form one of the central concerns of the chapters that follow. However, during my research I never observed undocumented foster children being treated differentially or denied access to services available to U.S. citizen foster children during their time in state custody. Although foster children were almost never detained or deported, it was much more likely that this might happen once they aged out of the foster care system at eighteen, particularly given high rates of homelessness, incarceration, and unemployment for former foster youth, and thus the likelihood of their increased visibility to law enforcement officers.[20]

Alba's story, as I recount it here, is full of gaps, unanswered questions, and inconsistencies. The depiction I present is primarily Tatianna's narrative, supplemented by my own observations while Alba's case was open, conversations with two Esperanza social workers involved in the case, case notes in Alba's file, and documents Tatianna shared with me, including a written exchange from Alba's biological father to Esther. However, substantial gaps in the story do remain, and without access to the county social worker's version of events, the story is partial at best.

Tatianna, Alba's cousin, was living in San Diego, where she had attended college. She lived in the city with her husband, with whom she co-owned a business, and their three-year-old daughter. Tatianna's extended family, living in Tijuana, did not initially know what had happened to Alba when she disappeared. However, they were hesitant to involve law enforcement in their family circumstances, concerned that Alba might be placed in a Tijuana orphanage instead of with her extended family. Tatianna's involvement in Alba's case began when one of Tatianna's aunts discovered a letter from Alba's father to Esther, requesting more money than the funds that had already been exchanged for Alba. Based on the name and address, Tatianna's aunt managed to locate Esther, who was living in San Diego. With this new information, Tatianna went to check up on Alba. She explained, "Look, I wanted to adopt Alba. But I would have been content to leave her there, with Esther, if things had seemed okay. But I just wasn't comfortable."[21]

When Tatianna arrived at Esther's house she was not happy with Alba's circumstances—she didn't feel that the home had enough room for the whole family, she didn't like that Esther said she was relying on welfare payments, and she wasn't comfortable with the fact that though Esther had told Alba's father she was married, she in fact lived in San Diego with an undocumented boyfriend. Tatianna felt that Esther had misrepresented her situation to Alba's father and that Alba was not as well cared for as she could be. When Tatianna explained who she was and refused to leave Esther's home without Alba, Esther called the police. Officers soon arrived, hands on their guns, to evict Tatianna from the property. Tatianna explained to the police that Esther had illegally smuggled Alba into the country, but they told her the situation was beyond their jurisdiction and would have to be settled in family court. Tatianna was then escorted off Esther's property.[22]

Tatianna then began the long, arduous process of petitioning for Alba's custody. She explained how surprised she had been that the social worker for Alba's case did not seem concerned by Alba's circumstances and the lack of clarity about how she had come to be in Esther's care. Even Tatianna explained, however, that Esther's intentions seemed good: "I really do think she just wanted another daughter," Tatianna told me, "She wasn't really trying to exploit her, I don't think. It wasn't a money situation."[23] I was never able to speak to the county social worker involved in this case, so I do not know what her perspective was on Alba's condition and Tatianna's claims. From Tatianna's perspective the social worker was dismissive of what amounted to human trafficking and did not feel she had any reason to be concerned about Alba's situation. Tatianna, for this reason, appeared to be nothing more than a hassle the social worker was forced to deal with in the context of an otherwise relatively straightforward, unproblematic case. Tatianna initiated a letter-writing campaign to Alba's social worker and her supervisor, eventually pressuring the social worker to move Alba to a foster home while the case was pending in dependency court. Tatianna realized she needed help navigating the legal complexities of the child welfare system. She happened to see an ad for the Court Appointed Special Advocate (CASA) program in San Diego, an agency that provided volunteer advocates empowered by the court to make recommendations on behalf of foster children. Tatianna requested an advocate for Alba, and was connected with a CASA without whom she felt she would not have been able to navigate the complex legal obstacles to gaining custody of Alba.

CASAs could be requested by anyone involved in a child's case, or by foster children themselves. They were charged with representing the interests of the child to the court, because children, according to the view of social workers and legal actors, were often not able to distinguish between what they wanted and what might be best for them in the long term. The role of the CASA was to get to know and to advocate for the child, effectively bringing the "voice" of the child into the courtroom. As the recruitment director at a CASA organization explained during an orientation session:

> It is not that the paid professionals are at fault it is just that they don't have the time, and this is why CASA volunteers are so important. You'll be given a badge and a court order to have access to legal, medical, educational records as well as social worker and judge's files. . . . [We] receive referrals for kids who need CASAs through teachers, social workers, foster parents, attorneys or even kids themselves. But, you cannot be a CASA if you work with any aspect of foster care or dependency court due to conflict of interest; the key to a CASA is that you are serving no one but the child.[24]

CASAs were officially appointed by the court to the cases of foster children who were determined to be the most in need. This typically included children who had experienced more placements than usual, children who were separated from siblings, children who were experiencing severe educational or emotional difficulties, and children involved in cases in which various parties disagreed about how the case should proceed. As noted above, CASAs were unique in that they had court-ordered access to all information pertaining to the child's case, including county social worker and FFA documents, medical files, psychological assessments, and school reports. Furthermore, county social workers were compelled by formal policy to respond to any inquiries from CASAs within 48 hours. Additionally, CASAs were volunteers, not limited by time, institutional resources, or government regulations. In Alba's case, her CASA worked with Tatianna to navigate the complexity of Alba's legal circumstances and to advocate for her eventual adoption by Tatianna.

The legal process was complicated by the fact that Alba had no birth certificate. This missing document posed two distinct problems. First, it affected Tatianna's ability to prove herself to be Alba's kin. Tatianna pushed for a DNA test that the county of San Diego did not pursue. Tatianna never received an official reason why her request for a DNA test was rejected but she told me that she assumed it was due to the expense of the procedure. She would have pushed the issue farther if the county agency had not eventually recognized her as Alba's kin, largely due to Esther's acknowledgment of Tatianna as Alba's relative. Tatianna explained "If she [Esther] hadn't admitted to the [social] worker, if she had just said 'I don't know who this crazy woman is' then I don't think I would have ended up with Alba."[25] Tatianna noted wryly to me that this was one favor Esther had done for the family. Second, Alba's lack of a legal birth certificate complicated her citizenship status and unsanctioned entry into the country. The pursuit of legal status for Alba was exacerbated by the fact that she was not legally recognized as a citizen in either the United States or Mexico. Particularly because she was located by family outside the bounds of a legal investigation of child trafficking, Alba's story exemplifies the difficult circumstances of non-U.S. citizens entangled in the child welfare bureaucracy, one in which families must doggedly pursue a legal solution to a series of illegal or unsanctioned circumstances. Thus began Tatianna's long engagement with child welfare services, law enforcement, and immigration authorities, in an effort to gain legal custody of Alba.

Paper Trails

Although the sale of a young child followed by that child's migration across an international border is an event unlikely to be accompanied by concrete documents, the provision of official documents for Alba, including a birth certificate and passport, was crucial to her case. Identity documents such as passports and birth certificates occupy a relationship to their holders that is partial and unstable at best.[26] Documents may be entirely at odds with an individual's lived experience and sense of self and place, and they may erase prior nationalities, birth dates, and parentage. They may be constructed in error or intentionally forged. Nevertheless, they are foundational to an individual's claim to recognition as a citizen of a nation-state and a crucial element in making claims for protection, such as for those in pursuit of asylum or refugee status.[27] Alba's existence as a trafficked child, a child worthy of protection, could not be validated if a formal paper trail could not establish her as a resident of Mexico. In other words, Alba had to be trafficked from somewhere in order to be granted protection, in the form of citizenship, by the U.S. state. This circumstance is one that Jacqueline Bhabha (2011:1–2) refers to as "effectively stateless," a situation where a child may in fact be a citizen of a specific nation but lacks the paperwork to prove it. As Bhabha asserts, effective statelessness is necessarily accompanied by a reduction of enforceable rights. In this sense, Alba's ability to call on her rights as a Mexican citizen, which was a necessary precondition to be recognized as a victim of trafficking, were inhibited by her paperless status.

Eventually, with the help of the Mexican consulate, it was determined that Alba had not been born in a hospital and thus there was no legal record of her existence. This complicated both Tatianna's claim that Alba had been trafficked and the possibility of Alba applying for U.S. citizenship—both claims hinged upon her recognition as a citizen of another nation. After some effort on Tatianna's part, the Mexican government issued Alba a certificate for unregistered births, a document Tatianna referred to as a "retrospective birth certificate." The Mexican consulate in San Diego also worked on Alba's case to verify that there were no missing person searches out for Alba within Mexico. This was necessary in order for the U.S. dependency court to terminate parental rights without the presence of Alba's parents, as neither parent could be located by Mexican authorities despite the cooperation of Alba's extended family in the search. The court eventually determined that Alba's presence in Esther's custody, and the lack of missing person inquiries, were sufficient to establish that she had been abandoned by her parents.

The determination that Alba had been abandoned was central to Tatianna's ability to frame her as a child both eligible for, and worthy of, citizenship. I suggest that it was through Tatianna's advocacy work to narrate Alba's abandonment and her subsequent trafficking experience, that Alba was effectively positioned as a victim of mistreatment. As such, she belonged to a broad category of children in need of protection, a category that was distinct from the care or treatment she may have actually received under Esther's custody. Once Alba's position as a victim was established, she was eligible, via Tatianna's advocacy, to be salvaged from the precarious status of statelessness (Kerber 2007) through a retrospective assertion of Mexican citizenship. Tatianna described the period during which Mexican authorities searched for Alba's biological parents as a time of great anxiety for her, as she held the erroneous belief that the Mexican government would want Alba to be returned to Mexico. However, Tatianna came to understand that the Mexican government not only lacked the authority to repatriate Alba but was also not inclined to intervene in a situation where a child's care was being addressed by her country of residence. As I discuss below, this is not a circumstance particular to the Mexican government. Rather, it reflects the limits of repatriation and nation-states' abilities to intervene extraterritorially on behalf of their citizens.

Statelessness

It was not Alba's position as a Mexican citizen that made her the responsibility of a specific nation-state or government agency. It was, rather, her status as a child in need of protection, officially due to "abandonment" by her father, and her physical presence within U.S. borders that made her potentially eligible for the protection of U.S. child welfare services.[28] As such, the territoriality of state protection, activated through Alba's physical presence within U.S. borders and compelled by Tatianna's efforts, came together with universal principles of humanitarianism and the generalized state responsibility to protect "vulnerable" children. Ironically, Alba's ability to take full advantage of this form of protection ultimately hinged on the Mexican state formally recognizing her as a citizen. In this way, Alba's worthiness seemed to rely upon circumstances that were outside the bounds of citizenship, yet Mexican membership was central to her ability to advance these claims.

Alba's status as a child in need of state protection, coupled with her position as a Mexican citizen abandoned in the United States, made her eligible for further protection through immigration relief. Because of the uniqueness of Alba's history, she in fact had several possible paths by which she could qualify for U.S. citizenship. Because she had allegedly been sold to Esther and then brought into the United States, she was potentially eligible under the Trafficking Victims Protection Reauthorization Act (TVPRA) as a victim of human trafficking. This act, established in 2000 and reauthorized in 2008, was intended to decrease the number of individuals being returned to their home country without assessment of whether they had been victims of trafficking or had legitimate claims to asylum.[29] With respect to children, it provided for the transfer of minors from Customs and Border Patrol (CBP) custody to the Office of Refugee Resettlment (ORR) within 72 hours and specified procedures for assessing claims for protection. However, a narrow definition of trafficking and uneven application of interview and assessment protocols have limited the reach of this provision.[30]

A second available pathway was Special Immigrant Juvenile Status (SIJS), a provision created in 1990 and expanded to its present form in 2008. Referred to as the "J-visa," it provided the most readily available path to citizenship for children who were dependents of the state or victims of abuse, provided they were unable to reunify with at least one of their parents and that it was deemed in their "best interest" to remain in the United States. Though SIJS is notable for centering the "best interest" of the child and the right to protection from abuse, this provision is not without its limitations.[31] SIJS is complicated by the fact that it relies on coordination between state and federal courts—state courts make the initial dependency ruling before federal immigration courts approve or deny the SIJS application. There is confusion among child welfare authorities and legal actors in terms of the initiation and coordination of the SIJS application, which has drastically reduced the number of children benefiting from this unique form of relief.[32] Alba could qualify for this status due to her "abandonment," her presence in state custody, and her likely history of neglect due to parental drug use. Or she could simply immigrate, though, of course, she was already present in the country, as the adoptee of U.S. citizen parents. Tatianna and her husband, in consultation with Alba's CASA and attorney, chose citizenship through adoption for Alba because it was the simplest and quickest route, primarily because an adopted child experiences the shortest wait time to U.S. citizenship.

Adoption Narratives

Adoption of non-U.S. citizen children such as Alba privileges the citizenship status of the adopting parents while erasing the former citizenship of the adopted child (Yngvesson and Coutin 2006). These children are reframed, through such processes as reissuing of a new legal birth certificate, as nonimmigrants.[33] Yet this reframing elides the similarities in the trajectories and lived experiences of children who move from one country to another as the children of labor migrants or as the international adoptees of citizen parents.[34] Though these two categories of child migrants may have similar questions about their national belonging, their official reception and the ideologies that surround their presence could not diverge more drastically. The children of labor migrants are all too frequently categorized as dangerous, unruly threats, while adopted migrants are held up as redemptive and celebratory instances of multicultural inclusion. Yet the absorption of these international adoptees requires an explicit framing of them as "not-migrants." The divergent discourses that surround adoptees as opposed to other migrants separate international adoption from labor migration. This delineation enables a narrative of humanitarian rescue to surround international adoption even in the context of blatant xenophobia and racism in relation to an immigrant labor community from the same sending nation.[35] In this way, adoption circumvents the narratives that can be mobilized to frame even young children as "economic," and thus "unworthy," migrants.

The migration pathway of international adoption is not primarily based on the worthiness of the child's own claim to citizenship status. Rather, inherent in these adoptive practices is the valuation of children as coveted items, who should not be held accountable for the circumstances that they were born into, and whose merit is based on their youthfulness and value to U.S. citizen parents.[36] As such, the state authorizes international adoptees to enjoy full citizenship rights in a manner not readily available to children who migrate through other avenues. The economic conditions that may frame the context in which children become "adoptable" do not, in this case, erode their worthiness or impact their reception in the United States, perhaps largely because any future economic needs they may have are expected to be a burden on their adoptive family, not on the state. An explicit distinction between "adoptees" and "migrants" justifies the presence of one group while excluding the other.

Although the details of Alba's case would have supported a strong argument for framing her as a victim of trafficking, it was primarily through Tatianna's advocacy and her availability as a willing adoptive home that the case was set into motion. Alba's "rescue" and path to citizenship was not put into motion by outrage at her tale as a trafficked child. As noted above, it was quite unusual for a child from Mexico to be framed as anything other than an "economic" migrant. Only recently have such pathways as the Trafficking Victims Protection Reauthorization Act and the Violence Against Women Act been successfully claimed by Mexican citizens, who tend to be framed as "economic" migrants regardless of the specific circumstances of a given case. As such, these migration categories are shaped more forcefully by political trends and perceptions about which nations produce "legitimate" asylum-seekers and refugees than by the specific details of an individual's experience. Alba's framing as an adoptee positioned her as an object of value to her adoptive parents, and circumvented broader questions about the "worthiness" of her specific case.

Tommy's Story

When I told Alba's story to social workers in both Tijuana and San Diego, it often elicited tales of the dysfunction of the child welfare system, which focused on how the system's task was so extensive and sprawling that children would invariably "fall through the cracks." Yet underlying these reactions was a common perception, held by bureaucrats and lay people I spoke with on both sides of the border, that the Mexican state was less competent than the U.S. state—Mexico was, for example, the nation without documentation of Alba's existence, a nation where selling a child could seemingly happen without consequence. Both U.S. and Mexican nationals described the Mexican government as an inadequate bureaucracy. However, Tatianna's shock at the Mexican state's lack of interest in returning Alba to Mexico was echoed by the U.S. government's lack of efforts to repatriate U.S. citizen children in Mexico. Tijuana orphanage directors and staff introduced me to U.S. citizen children in their care and told stories of repeated calls to U.S. consulate workers who were responsible for collecting U.S. citizen children abandoned across the border. Those consulate workers never returned calls or appeared to claim these children. Thus, if Mexico was seen as disorganized and disempowered to make claims on their citizens' behalf, the United States was framed as capable but uncaring, empowered to ignore Mexican officials and its own citizens residing outside national borders.

I met Tommy during my weekly visits to a Tijuana orphanage, where I helped the staff through their busy days by soothing crying babies, reading books, and chasing toddlers around the small concrete patio where they played on sunny days. The orphanage was in the southern part of the city, at the top of a pothole-marked dirt road. The facility was almost entirely staffed by local Tijuana residents with the exception of the official director, who was a member of the U.S. church that funded the orphanage project. The buildings housed children from infancy to ages twelve to fourteen, and efforts were being made to create separate housing units that would allow older children to remain on site.[37] The infant room, where I spent most of my time during weekly visits, consisted of a playroom, a large kitchen, and an open room lined with twelve cribs and a single rocking chair. Children remained in the infant room under the watchful care of a rotating staff of female workers and U.S. volunteers until they transferred at school age to separate boys' and girls' dormitories on the other side of the main courtyard.

Each day I arrived at the orphanage and parked my aging Honda in the dusty front entrance. I'd forgo standing at the locked main entrance gate and head for the outer door to the kitchen, where I would lean my head on the metal bars and holler "Buenas Dias, Doña Mari!" until I heard a faint, "Mande?" from the kitchen and saw Mari moving over to the door with her large ring of keys. Mari was the main cook and spent her early morning hours chopping meat and vegetables for lunch for the children and staff, cooking big pots of soup or spaghetti. We got to know each other as I came and went through the kitchen. Mari was often working with donated ingredients and a chaotic assortment of groceries, and I'd often pause on my way out to help her decode some of these mystery goods. One afternoon we stood together as I translated the directions on a military-issue bag of sugar cookie mix, and I wondered how these packages had arrived in her kitchen and how she managed to feed so many children out of such an unpredictable jumble of ingredients. Usually Doña Mari let me out of the kitchen and left me to repeat my hollering procedure at the entrance to the nursery, but that day she walked me across the courtyard and unlocked that door as well, muttering, "Este hombre, todo cerrado!" (This guy, with everything locked up!).[38]

The "hombre" Mari referred to was the U.S. orphanage director. I had been told by various staff that there was some tension between him and the Tijuana staff—he was a good decade or two younger than most of them and had instituted policies, such as locking all the doors throughout the day, that many staff members felt made the place feel more institutional and less like home while also creating a huge nuisance for letting people in and out.[39] Part of the reason I entered through the kitchen was to align myself clearly with the staff and avoid being escorted to the infants' room by the director each day. Though he had been nothing but kind and welcoming to me I wanted to understand the space of the orphanage through the eyes of those who worked most closely with the children.

Tommy was the blond haired, blue-eyed terror of the infant nursery. He was four years old and almost ready to move into the boys' quarters, and had a lamentable habit of tearing the toys he was interested in out of the arms of younger and smaller children. I spoke often with Sonia, a veteran staff member who handled the intake of new children to the orphanage and mediated all contact with the state in her role as the DIF liaison at the orphanage. Sonia and I were chatting about the "adoptability" of the children currently in the infant room, and Sonia surprised me by stating that, in her opinion, Tommy would never be adopted. She explained that Tommy was not Mexican, but was in fact the child of a U.S. citizen. His mother had contracted HIV doing sex work in Tijuana, where Tommy had been born HIV positive. Sonia said, with a wave of her hand that his mother was likely "indigente, andando por las calles" (indigent, wandering the streets of Tijuana).[40] Tommy had arrived at the orphanage, like most children, without documents. He had been brought by a concerned neighbor, and it was from this neighbor that the basic circumstances of his life had been learned. This was quite common for children in Tijuana orphanages, and in fact, Sonia felt she had more information about Tommy than many of the children in her care. Although some children are brought to orphanages by relatives or concerned neighbors, others are simply abandoned at orphanage gates where young children, because they are unable to communicate with orphanage staff, are given names and assigned birthdays, their age roughly estimated by height, appearance, and basic skills. Sonia explained this process, miming measuring a child's height with her hand, saying "Me parece como seis" (He looks about six to me).[41]

Tommy, like Alba, was effectively stateless and assumed to be a citizen of a nation-state from which he did not possess formal documents. Like Alba, who was afforded the protection of the child welfare system in San Diego, Tommy was provided with the shelter of his Tijuana orphanage without concern about his citizenship status. He received the same food, shelter, and medical care, and would likely follow the path of his fellow orphanage residents—out to work on the Tijuana streets in his teenage years, provided that he continued to receive the medical care needed to manage his HIV.

Although Tommy ostensibly had a right to U.S. citizenship through his perhaps still living, but, according to Sonia, likely deceased mother, there was no known relative to make that claim for him. Sonia explained that there might in fact be relatives in the United States, but there was no way for the orphanage to find them. She had, in the past, made telephone calls based on the name of a child in her care but these attempts proved entirely unsuccessful. Sonia's institutional authority in Mexico did not translate into the leverage necessary to pursue U.S. citizenship for Tommy. Similarly, the U.S. consulate authorities had the right to make a citizenship claim on Tommy's behalf, and to bring him into the U.S. foster care system, but Sonia laughed at the idea that the consulate workers would go through the effort of repatriating an HIV positive orphan with no known relatives.

Had there been someone well positioned to advocate for Tommy, he would have been a clear candidate for framing as a victim, deserving of U.S.

citizenship on humanitarian grounds due to both his illness and his abandonment. The categories of an abandoned, neglected, or abused child would likely have been available to Tommy had he been found within U.S. boundaries. In that case, his physical presence would have necessitated the care of the state, likely resulting in Tommy being placed in a long-term foster care situation, locating any existing relatives, and attending to his medical needs. But because of his presence in Tijuana, and his lack of an empowered advocate, those categories did not have the force to move him into the United States or into a status that would enable him to draw on his ostensible claims to U.S. citizenship. Movement across state lines was theoretically possible, largely because Tommy was already assumed to be a U.S. citizen. However, unlike Alba, he lacked an advocate equipped to make those claims on his behalf. And, as discussed in further detail below, repatriation of Mexican citizens from the United States into Mexico was decidedly easier to facilitate than movement of U.S. citizen children from Mexico into the United States.

Enacting State Care

According to Sonia and other orphanage workers I spoke with in Tijuana, the challenge in addressing the circumstances of children with ambiguous citizenship claims like Tommy was not what the law allowed but rather the absence of an effective protocol for cross-border collaboration. Movement of children in social welfare systems is a complex problem due to the fragmentation of social service providers, which, in both Mexico and the United States, are governed directly at state, city, and, in the United States, county levels, and only loosely regulated at the federal level. Cross-border and cross-agency collaborations are challenging not only across international borders but also from state to state or county to county. This is due to varying protocols among local agencies as well as complex funding streams that do not transition well between regions. The net result of this variation is that regional authorities are hesitant to take on the expense of caring for a child who is already being provided for by another regional agency.

This fragmentation of service providers meant that there were substantial obstacles to considering the extensive network of relatives, friends, and neighbors in which children and their families might be enmeshed, since these networks, particularly for Latina/o children, often extended across not only county and state borders but international borders as well. It presented challenges to working with families whose daily lives and social networks extended across the U.S.-Mexico border due to the practical need for individuals to be traceable and locatable in order to be provided with services. Additionally, cross-border collaboration took time, and children would often establish strong relationships with temporary care providers while waiting for agencies to work across borders. Child Welfare authorities' prioritization of stability and permanency of relationships between children and their care providers often reduced the appeal of the lengthy process of working with family members and social service agencies across international boundaries. For children like Tommy, this fragmentation meant that his presence in Tijuana was placed solely within the purview of the Tijuana orphanage staff and the Tijuana social service agency, the DIF. His status as an alleged U.S. citizen did not in itself call forth the involvement of U.S. social service providers, nor was there a clear protocol for his care providers to collaborate with U.S. social workers to pursue other possible care options for him.

Orphanage directors had no recourse in the face of unresponsive U.S. state agents and state agents had no compulsion to be responsive. Notably, the impotence of state agents to act across borders on issues of child welfare extended in both directions. Ben, a former San Diego County social worker, told me the story of a teenage girl who had, due to allegations of abuse, been removed from her parents' care while they were living in San Diego. While in foster care she disappeared and was believed to have returned to live with her parents, who had moved back to Tijuana. The judge, lawyers, and social worker involved in the case were concerned but had no jurisdiction to intervene across the border. They convinced DIF officials to accompany U.S. consulate staff on a visit to the girl's Tijuana home. Ben, a native Spanish speaker, accompanied the group as the liaison between the San Diego child welfare agency and the DIF. Upon locating the girl, and speaking with her and some neighbors, the group determined that she was safe and well cared for. The U.S. consulate workers wanted to bring her back to the United States, but Ben and the DIF representatives felt satisfied she was safe from harm. Ben explained that had they found circumstances to be otherwise, there was nothing U.S. officials could have done, regardless of the girl's status as a U.S. citizen.

Arguably, the population of U.S. citizen children abandoned in Mexico was relatively small.[42] Yet while U.S. immigration law included a voluntary removal policy written expressly for contiguous states that consisted of driving unaccompanied, unauthorized minors to the border and releasing them into DIF custody in Mexico, a similar policy did not exist for Mexican authorities to send U.S. citizen minors back north across the border.[43] And, perhaps more important, there were no Mexican officials with the clout or cross-border authority to put such a process into motion. In general, perceptions on both sides of the border were that government agencies, regardless of available resources, would prefer not to take on extra dependents already being cared for by other governments, unless they were forced to do so. This was not due to a lack of care for the well-being of minors. Rather, it was due to a lack of motivation to intercede in the case of a child who was already under another government's care, and the lack of resources and state agents with the time to deal with the complexity of cross-border cases.

Contingent Worthiness

The cases of Alba and Tommy, and the cases of other children caught up in state custody in the United States and Mexico, raise questions about which children, in what sorts of circumstances, can be positioned as worthy of citizenship as a form of humanitarian protection. Here I take up Ticktin's (2006:44) call for an interrogation of the humanitarian regime. She states:

> I want to end by suggesting that in this emergent regime of humanitarianism, one must inquire into the consequences of its (often) arbitrary nature, asking what conditions evoke compassion and why and what hierarchies are reproduced by it. The ability of such a system to further a more just world must be seriously interrogated when humanitarianism acts as a form of policing, choosing exceptional individuals and excluding the rest.

Whether Alba or Tommy was individually deemed worthy of rescue was determined less by actual circumstances than by the stories that might be told about them, the advocates equipped to tell those stories, and the legal categories that were potentially available to translate these children into legible victims, worthy of protection. In this sense, at least in the U.S. context, it was not the exceptional circumstances of the individual alone but the way those circumstances were mobilized or silenced due to the presence or absence of an effective advocate, within a specific policy context and historic moment. A child's citizenship, and territorial presence, may compel the state to act in particular ways to extend protection to that child. However, as the cases of Alba and Tommy demonstrate, that provision of care is enacted not through the nature of a child's specific circumstances but through the compelling work of an advocate who is able to mold that child's narrative to adapt to a category that will extend the legal protection the child requires. Of course the force of the narrative was not in itself enough to complete a conversion of legal status—effective policies, legal categories, and institutional procedures had to be in place to support the translation of a child, such as Alba, from noncitizen to citizen.

International adoption, as Alba experienced, skirts these broader issues by positioning the adopting parents, rather than the adopted child, as central to the way the process is imagined and pursued. While international adoption is embedded in narratives of saving and rescue, the worthiness of individual children is determined not by their particular history alone but by their status as an object of desire for the adopting family. In this sense, Tommy's HIV status makes him seemingly worthy of "rescue" but at the same time unlikely to be an object of desire for adopting parents in the United States. In effect, one might argue that all international adoptees are understood to qualify for special care through their legal status as "abandoned" children or legal orphans, but it is through the desire of adoptive parents that this status is activated. It was at this juncture that the cases of Tommy and Alba most sharply diverged.

Children like Alba, categorized as abandoned, abused, or neglected, are ostensibly framed as particularly deserving of citizenship and protection, while other children are not. Yet, as Tommy's case demonstrates, children may be framed this way only when a well-positioned adult makes claims on their behalf. This status, which I call contingent worthiness, raises questions about a broader sense of international social obligation rooted in the perceived special vulnerability of children as victims of mistreatment. The social obligation to bestow citizenship as a protective measure is not extended to all children, and in this way the making of these categories of worthy children implicitly demarcates the boundaries of what constitutes a deserving migrant. Importantly, no one I spoke with in relation to Alba's case ever referred to her as a migrant or an immigrant. Rather, she was described as an adopted child, a smuggled or trafficked child, or an abandoned child.

Children who migrate to the U.S. due to "economic" motivations are regularly returned to their home countries. These children, understood in terms of stories of poverty and economic necessity, do not compel the same humanitarian reaction or the necessity to confront a national obligation to a child in need. At the same time, some children who are understood to be victims of abuse, not necessarily in their home country, are granted special pathways to citizenship. Thus, abused children with well-positioned advocates join those refugees and asylum seekers who are perceived to have legitimate claims, as drawing on social obligations for shelter and protection that are enmeshed in pathways to U.S. citizenship. I suggest here that these "worthy" child migrants are juxtaposed with the popular conception of the unworthy migrant, a symbolic reference to migrants who ostensibly seek to benefit from services and opportunities that they have not, through some broad category of suffering, such as abuse, abandonment, or trafficking, come to "deserve." As such, legal pathways to citizenship for minor migrants appeal to broader ideals about humanitarian intervention that are denied to migrants understood to be motivated primarily by economic aspirations rather than mistreatment. They are interpellated physically and legally into U.S. families at the same time that they are embraced by the national family in a broader sense. Yet through this selective process, the sense that childhood is a broad category populated by individuals necessarily worthy of protection is unsettled by children who are eliminated from the right to protection through their framing as "economic" migrants.[44] Children in need of protection are to be rescued, but only those about whom particular stories, and not others, are told by the right people, at the right time, and in the right place. In this way, minor migrants who are understood to be in need of protection are entangled in broader networks of social obligations, obligations that mobilize sentiments regarding human rights, children's rights, and the state's responsibility to protect minors from harm.

Yet as Tommy's case illuminates, being "deserving" does not, in itself, mobilize state action. Alba and Tommy were both framed as stateless children, without legitimate documents and without a legal presence in the nation in which they were residing. In each case, the government system in that nation initially responded to the child as it would respond to any child within the nation, providing shelter in Tommy's case, and social service support in Alba's case, without specific concern for that child's citizenship status.[45] It was only through the concerted efforts of Tatianna, a college-educated U.S. citizen, that Alba was retrospectively granted Mexican citizenship, recognized as a victim of trafficking, and then granted U.S. citizenship through her legal adoption. Tommy's assumed rights as a U.S. citizen child, and as a sick and abandoned child, were not realized, I argue, because there was no one positioned to make claims on his behalf, no one to force the gears of the state apparatus into motion. These cases thus highlight the contingent status of vulnerable child migrants, and their comparative voicelessness in efforts to construct and mobilize an effective narrative of worthiness.

The cases of Alba and Tommy illuminate the shifting boundaries of citizenship, and the contingent, tentative narratives through which individuals are placed inside or outside national boundaries. And while narratives of poverty and economic need are decidedly problematic for enabling children to move across borders and enter the U.S. national "family," in many cases decisions about child custody are based on a child's increased life chances in a certain setting. These "life chances" or "future opportunities," the subject of the following chapter, are often framed in terms of a child's "best interest," and serve as a gloss for the economic circumstances that differentiate one custody setting, one possible future, from another.

CHAPTER 2

Belonging and Exclusion

Esperanza foster parents Trevor and Josh were reflective about their experiences fostering four children over a period of three years and about the pending adoption of their current foster daughter, a petite Honduran toddler named Emma. They spoke frankly about their concerns and reservations with the fostering system. I had spoken casually numerous times with both of them and more extensively with Trevor, since he took charge during most home visits and functioned, in both their opinions, as the primary parent. But when I sat down to interview Josh formally he surprised me with his direct and open reflections on his experience as a foster father and adoptive father-to-be. Josh and I spoke about the shifts in Emma's case. Although it had never seemed likely to social workers involved in the case that Emma's mother and father would regain custody, due to ongoing mental health issues and general conditions of family instability, Emma's maternal grandmother had expressed interest in gaining custody of Emma, as she already had custody of some of Emma's older siblings. Because she was elderly, Emma's grandmother felt she could not care for the children on her own, and wanted to bring a daughter, Emma's aunt, from Honduras to help care for the children. It was for this reason that Emma's case had dragged on for some time. However, when Emma's grandmother could not procure the required visa for Emma's aunt, the county social worker felt she had waited long enough for a family placement, and focused her attention on finding Emma a permanent, adoptive home, in this case with Trevor and Josh, to whom Emma had grown quite attached.

Toward the end of our interview, once my notepad had been put away and we were speaking more casually, Josh looked down at his lap and said, "I just don't know if we are doing the right thing by taking Emma away."[1] Josh told me he wondered about what they were doing, explaining that he was happy to adopt but he worried that sometimes adoptions happened in cases where it was not truly the only option. Citing the case of Kyle, one of Josh's former foster children who had been reunified with his father only after the forceful intervention of Josh and Trevor, Josh asserted he was speaking not from conjecture but from experience.

Kyle's parents split up when his father was hospitalized for severe depression. Kyle's mother remained with him in San Diego while his father relocated to another state. Months later, two-year-old Kyle was placed in foster care, with Trevor and Josh, due to allegations of maternal drug use and neglect. When Kyle's mother's parental rights were terminated, Kyle's father continued to fight to regain custody. Josh and Trevor believed the social worker had written Kyle's father off as a good placement option because she didn't feel that he had a strong relationship with Kyle, and their "visits" over the phone were not going well. Though Kyle did display anger at his father and unwillingness to speak with him on the phone, Trevor felt that no two-year-old could rebuild a relationship through phone calls. He and Josh set up Skype communication with Kyle's father, and each week coached him through reading stories and playing with finger puppets, something Trevor and Josh had discovered that Kyle loved. Kyle was eventually reunified with his father, and while Trevor and Josh were thrilled with the result, they felt that the reunification had occurred largely through their efforts and in spite of, rather than because of, the actions of the social worker and the routine workings of the child welfare system. Their experiences with Kyle left them feeling that the system did not always work toward reunification as enthusiastically as it might and, as a result, split up families without legitimate cause to do so. Josh explained that he had raised these sorts of concerns with Emma's adoption social worker, wondering whether all avenues had been exhausted before termination of parental rights, if adoption was really in her best interest. She had responded that Emma was going to be adopted, and that if he and Trevor did not "open their arms" to her, another family would. When I asked Trevor whether the various case outcomes he and Josh had witnessed were, in his opinion, largely contingent on the social worker who happened to be assigned to the case, he responded, "One hundred percent, oh, absolutely." But he went on to say how amazed he was by social workers and impressed by the passion they give to their job regardless of the "gross underpay" they received. "I wouldn't do it for that money," he told me, "No way."[2]

The vast majority of foster parents I spoke with articulated a nuanced understanding of their foster child's biological parents as not "bad" parents, but as people caught up in bad circumstances. But none except Josh expressed such an explicit sense of discomfort with their own adoption of a foster child and with a concern about what they saw as a potentially unnecessary severance of family ties. Josh, based on his own experiences, expressed a belief that the foster care system made it difficult for parents to get their children back and that the system as a whole supported adoption over reunification. He felt that the county was not sensitive to transportation difficulties parents faced in attempting to get between work, therapy, and visitations with their children. This was particularly the case given the size of San Diego County, the lack of effective public transportation, and the likelihood that biological parents were without their own vehicles. He had also heard that parents had their "salaries cut" when their children were removed.

Josh was correct, in a sense, because parents whose children were removed from their care did often lose benefits such as food stamps and housing subsidies based on the number of people in their "family." They also often had difficulty qualifying for subsidized housing or childcare while they did not have physical custody of their children.[3] This was a substantial obstacle for parents who had to demonstrate their ability to provide stable housing and a childcare plan before their children could be returned to them. The concerns that Josh voiced were issues that impacted parents entangled in the child welfare system, regardless of their social position, by virtue of being subject to the regulations and expectations of the social worker assigned to their case. However, as I argue throughout this book, these difficulties disproportionately impacted low-income parents, particularly those who were racially marginalized and undocumented, due to the precariousness of their legal status, their network for social support, and/or their economic circumstances. This differential impact was, in some sense, the issue Esperanza was founded to address. Most other foster parents I spoke with seemed to carefully avoid consideration of the possibility that they might have been raising children who could have been safely and happily returned to their parents' care. Josh, on the other hand, was willing to articulate this problem out loud and to mark the circumstantial differences between those who lose their children and those who adopt them.

Josh's concern about the patterns of removal and what he perceived to be the agency's inclination toward adoption rather than reunification were also concerns about the means through which child welfare pursued its goals of child protection. His concerns raised questions about what the personal stakes were for foster parents who participated in the removal and subsequent adoption of children. As I discuss throughout this chapter, processes of child removal have commonly taken place through a framework of "best interest." This framework asserts that state interventions into families, including the removal of children from their parents' custody and termination of parental rights, are not about social control or the production of social norms governing family life. Rather, these interventions are framed as being a singleminded pursuit of the "best" possible lives for children. "Best interest" is a powerful framework for intervention precisely because it is seemingly beyond reproach—who wouldn't want children to have their best interests met? Yet "best interest" is a slippery, multivalent category, and ideas about what is best for particular children, and from whose perspectives, varies across time and space.

"Best interest" is a discretionary legal framework, privileging those who are positioned to speak authoritatively while silencing others. And, as I suggest below, this framework has historically been mobilized to remove children from families who were framed as "unworthy" citizens, or noncitizens, rather than to protect children from concrete instances of physical, sexual, or emotional abuse. As such, a "best interest" framework has the propensity to categorize entire communities as abusive or neglectful through their social position, positing, in many cases, that the trajectory children might pursue under the care of white middle-class Protestant citizen parents is more important to their well-being than remaining in the custody of their natal family. To be clear, I am not arguing here for the necessary primacy of biological connections. Rather, I am interested in the way the agency may nominally prioritize the natal family while pursuing this policy for some individuals and not for racially or otherwise marginalized others.

This chapter takes up an examination of the "best interest" framework through a historical perspective. I consider practices of child removal, institutions and policies that have positioned some parents as unfit throughout U.S. history, and contemporary structural forces that mark out particular individuals as objects of intervention. I examine what these historical moments reveal about the ways children and families have been positioned as central sites for the production of citizenship, race, and national belonging and explore how philanthropic agencies and government actors have been involved in both the promotion and the dissolution of particular families. I consider what sorts of families have been positioned, throughout various points in U.S. history, as ideal homes for children. And finally, I ask how "best interest" is mobilized in the contemporary context of child welfare.

Family, Population, and Nation

The child and the family have been positioned at the frontlines of an effort to police the racial categories and citizenship limits that mark the boundaries of the national body within the contemporary United States. From eugenics to national hygiene campaigns and public health interventions, mothers and children have been the primary targets of widespread efforts to shape the national citizenry (Molina 2006; Donzelot 1979; Stoler 2002). The framework of "family values" serves as a stand-in for a particular raced and gendered construction of the family that is equated with the health of the nation itself (Collins 1998). Although the idealized family form may shift over time, what remains constant is the way the privileged form of family is linked up with economic, legal, and social privileges in relation to the nation-state (Coontz 2000). Families who do not fit this idealized form have historically been vulnerable to a variety of interventions. As such, the formation and dissolution of families enacted primarily through child removal, adoption, and residential schooling have constituted a central ground for contestations about citizenship, racial hierarchy, and belonging throughout U.S. history.[4]

In considering practices and policies surrounding the history of family intervention and forms of child removal in the U.S. context I address two overlapping periods—the moral reform era, constituting the majority of the nineteenth century, and the progressive era, lasting roughly from 1890 to 1920.[5] I focus on the treatment of dependent children throughout these periods and the accompanying anxieties about morality and the general "health" of the nation in which these efforts were enmeshed. This time frame foregrounds widespread efforts to explicitly shape parenting practices and marks a shift in the role of children from wage-earners to innocents in need of care, love, and protection (Zelizer 1985). As I examine below, ideas about hygiene, child labor, nutrition, supervision, and religious values became grounds for determining whether parents were acting, or were capable of acting, in their child's "best interest." These sorts of criteria resonate with the focus of contemporary child welfare interventions that disproportionately intervene in working-class and impoverished families of color. Although the contours of "best interest" have shifted over time, the framing of custody determinations around a focus on "best interest" has remained strikingly stable.

Family Interventions and the Construction of the Dependent Child

During the early 1800s, in the United States, children who were destitute or orphaned were often taken into almshouses and housed alongside adults who were categorized as indigent or mentally ill (Platt 2009[1969]:108). Due to poor sanitary conditions, children faced high death rates in almshouses, and concern with this problem eventually contributed to the development of orphanages and boarding schools initially run by philanthropic organizations, most of which were associated with religious organizations. The 1830s saw a proliferation of these institutions, and by 1910 more than 110,000 children were housed in 1,151 institutions across the United States (Tiffin 1982:64). These practices were developed out of a sense of community responsibility for impoverished individuals, rooted in the British Poor Laws that influenced practices for approaching the "problem" of the poor during the colonial era. Although U.S. policy and practices developed out of this foundation, conceptions of and approaches to the poor, and particularly impoverished children, gradually adapted and responded to the specific circumstances that arose in relation to westward expansion, substantial waves of immigration, and, later, industrialization and urbanization processes in large U.S. cities.

During this era, the primary focus of intervention was on the children of new European immigrant families, primarily Irish and Italian Catholic families, living in urban settings. Some parents and relatives sought care for their children in an institutional setting themselves, while other children were placed in such institutions through the intervention of charity workers or the authority of a local court. The majority of family interventions were initially enacted not by the state or federal government but by religious, philanthropic efforts spearheaded primarily by upper-class white women.[6] The normative values these women promoted were enmeshed with their own class positions and the patriarchal authority of their religious institutions.[7] And while they were largely focused on child-rearing practices, they were intimately bound up with concerns about the shape of what the future U.S. population would look like.

Awareness of child abuse as a social problem gradually arose in the 1870s, marked by the founding of Societies for the Prevention of Cruelty to Children (Gordon 1989).[8] While earlier interventions had focused on homelessness, abandonment, or starvation, these later efforts placed an increased emphasis on neglect and cruelty toward children. This reorientation considered the child specifically within the context of the family. With a shift toward concern over the treatment of children, rather than only their poverty, the question of the category of maternal "neglect" became a salient issue as it was necessarily constructed against a norm of "proper" care (Gordon 1989:7). As such, concerns about mothers' knowledge and conduct in relation to norms of hygiene, nutrition, and care of infants, among other topics, were central to the production of a healthy and proper citizenry.[9] In this way, concern about the "neglected" child was a site for concern about the health of the nation itself.

The questions of who constituted a child in need of saving and what characteristics defined a dependent or neglected child are issues that continue to plague agents and agencies charged with the goal of child protection. Mapping these shifts sheds light on changing norms and anxieties. An 1899 definition of the "dependent" or "neglected" child, for example, included homelessness, neglect, cruelty, and depravity on the part of the parents, but also included any child "found living in any house of ill-fame" and "any child under the age of eight who is found peddling or selling any article or singing or playing any musical instrument upon the street or giving any public entertainment," highlighting anxieties about child labor and the presence of children on urban streets acting as wage earners for their families (Tiffin 1982:38). The vagueness of the definition, which left open interpretation of such terms as "proper care" or "ill-fame," positioned a wide range of families as potentially vulnerable to intervention.

In the context of the pre-industrial English language, as Fraser and Gordon (1994) argue, the term "dependency" was synonymous with subordination. Dependency encapsulated not so much the trait of an individual, as with the specter of the welfare dependent mother in the contemporary U.S. context, but a positive social relation between master and apprentice, employer and laborer. It is in this sense, Fraser and Gordon note, that phrases like "independently wealthy" indicate an individual free of the obligation to labor. It was thus only with the rise of industrial labor that wage labor became understood as symbolic of independence based on the idea that individuals were free to sell their labor as they chose. Wage labor was no longer understood primarily as a social relationship of dependence between employer and employee. Because independence was positively equated with wage labor, dependency became reframed as a dysfunctional relationship, a "psychological/moral register" (Fraser and Gordon 1994). Dependency became a problematic characteristic rather than an indication of a productive social relation. With this shift dependency was no longer suitable for white working men and became the terrain of women, encapsulated by the figure of the "housewife," as well as by both men and women of color.

This pejorative reading of dependency was heightened in a U.S. social context where the "absence of a hierarchical social tradition in which subordination was understood to be structural, not characterological, facilitated hostility to public support of the poor" (Fraser and Gordon 1994:320). It is in relation to these historical conditions that we might understand the framing of "welfare dependency" more broadly. However, children constitute a category that perpetuates the concept of dependency as a productive social relationship. As senator Daniel Moynihan (1973) stated, "[Dependency] is an incomplete state in life: normal in a child, abnormal in the adult."[10] Dependency, in this sense, is naturalized as a characteristic embedded in the term "child." Healthy children are, by definition, dependent. Yet the notion of a *dependent* child departs from this normative, positive sense of dependency. That is, children marked as dependent are not dependent on their parents, as is deemed natural, but rather are problematically dependent on the intervention of the state or the kindness of strangers. In this sense, a dependent child is reworked as a potential burden and a social problem, one who lacks properly reliable parents to depend upon.

From Child Savers to Professional Social Work

Child saving efforts were driven by concerns about the morality of, and care for, children and were deeply enmeshed in efforts to preserve white Protestant values against rising concerns about immigration and the "moral depravity" of the urban poor.[11] Child saving efforts were primarily promoted by wealthy philanthropists concerned about the influence of new European immigrant communities, whom they categorized as nonwhite, and by anxieties about the sanitation, immorality, criminality, and disease associated with urban communities during the industrialization era in the United States. These efforts were pursued by a variety of organizations and individuals, and were not regulated by state or federal government. Thus they took a variety of forms, from teaching parenting skills and distributing informational pamphlets to scouring the streets for "neglected" children who were placed in orphanages or other charitable institutions. The majority of these efforts were focused on large urban cities such as Boston, New York, and Chicago.

As the rapid expansion of large U.S. cities accompanied the rise of industrialization during the late nineteenth and early twentieth centuries, "anxieties over immigration, urban social problems, and child labor" grew (Swartz 2005:23). These concerns, coupled with a rising sentiment that families were preferable to institutions as a site for ameliorating the risks facing impoverished children, led to increasing intervention into poor, urban families during the progressive era (Schlossman 2005:72–73). Importantly, as practices in relation to urban poverty and immigrant families shifted from institutional remedies to a focus on the family, interventions into Native American families shifted from an explicitly genocidal project to a strategy of removing Native children to boarding schools, a process some have referred to as a form of "cultural genocide" (Abourezk 1977).[12] These distinct processes of child removal, with disparate aims and forms, delineated populations that were deemed absorbable and salvageable from those that were not. As such, ideas about who needed to be removed and what sorts of remedies were suitable drew varyingly on categories of race, religion, poverty, and urbanity to redefine the boundaries of citizenship and national belonging.

Child savers were not only, and perhaps not primarily, concerned with the upbringing and treatment of individual children. They were invested in both promoting and producing particular social norms and reinforcing gender and class divisions. Rather than simply removing children and deeming parents unfit, child savers increased efforts to reform parenting practices within the home. The preference for keeping children in the home as opposed to removing them to institutional settings was at least partly motivated by financial constraints.[13] The contemporary placement of children with foster or adoptive families, as opposed to large-scale institutions, continues to be a more cost effective strategy for child placement in the contemporary United States.

Because child saving efforts during the late nineteenth century were primarily undertaken by private organizations and lacked government organization or oversight, they took on a wide variety of forms. They ranged in practice from organizing campaigns or lobbying for legislation, running orphanages and homes for pregnant, unmarried women, visiting families in their homes, scouring streets for child vendors, and taking families to court in relation to accusations of negligence or child delinquency. Although child saving efforts were initially instigated by private organizations, the early twentieth century saw an increase in federal involvement marked by the establishment of the Federal Children's Bureau in 1912, increasingly restrictive child labor laws, and the establishment of compulsory education laws in 1918 (Tiffin 1982). As favor shifted to government regulation of dependent children, the support for private, religious organizations declined and the rise of professional social workers began. Although state and federal governments took more responsibility for regulating the placement and care of dependent children throughout the late nineteenth century, it was not until the 1935 Social Security Act that child protection was officially established as the responsibility of the federal government.[14]

In her work on interventions into the lives of unmarried mothers from 1890 to 1945, Kunzel (1993) suggests that there was a shift during this period from "benevolent reform work" carried out by evangelical women to "professional casework" by social workers. This shift was motivated by a variety of factors including concerns about the irregularity of charity work, the desire of women to professionalize their involvement in the community, and the increasing support for approaching the welfare of citizens, particularly children, as the terrain of the federal and state governments. This shift encompassed the transition of unmarried mothers as victims to "social problems," where these women were seen "not as endangered but as dangerous" (1993:51). This shift meant that mothers were predisposed to be understood as "unfit" and social workers were likely to recommend adoption as a matter of the "best interest" of the child. Previously, evangelical women running maternity homes had seen the child as a means to the salvation of the mother. In other words, by caring for her child, the mother would be led toward moral rightness. The secularization of social work involved the recoding of these mothers into a secular-legal problem. As social workers attempted to regulate and formalize their work in the name of fairness, science, and predictability, they limited the possibilities for maternal "redemption" while maintaining the focus on the reform of "bad" mothers and a clear moralizing framework of "fit" and "unfit" parenting.[15]

This framework points to broader shifts in the care of dependent children and intervention into families that saw increased medicalization and bureaucratization of these processes.[16] Such trends were not limited to the field of social work, but were part of a broader shift in the fields of health care, psychology, and nutrition, among others. The struggle of social workers to establish their field as a legitimate profession against a history of philanthropy, "do-gooding," and negative perceptions of "women's work" was addressed by an increasing reliance on scientific and medicalized interpretations and categorizations of family problems.[17] These circumstances were accompanied by an approach to casework that stressed continuity over time and allowed for establishing patterns and generating data on instances and indicators of abuse and neglect. The construction of social workers as experts entailed "a process of restriction and exclusion" (Kunzel 1993:141), limiting who was authorized to facilitate interventions into families and whose narratives would provide the rationale for particular families to become subject to government oversight. The primary objects of intervention shifted throughout the twentieth century, from immigrant, urban families contemporarily categorized unambiguously as "white" to racially marginalized families. It was through these processes that the narratives of unfit, deviant, or criminal parents—those who were not just misguided but potentially irredeemable—began to take hold.

Assimilation, Rescue, and the Civilizing Project

Interventions into families through practices of child removal and policing of family norms and habits were largely enacted in the name of the "best interest" of the child. In many cases, the interpretation of "best interest" was predicated on presumptions that categorized non-white families as inadequate sites for raising healthy children. For example, Linda Gordon's *The Great Arizona Orphan Abduction* (1999) retells the history of a group of Irish Catholic children sent from New York City on an orphan train and placed in the homes of Mexican Catholic families in the mining towns of Clifton and Morenci, Arizona, in 1904. The majority of children sent West on orphan trains were children of recent immigrants, and few were actually orphans. Most were the children of single mothers or impoverished parents, many of whom turned their children over to a charitable organization so they would receive adequate food or medical care.[18] The children sent to Clifton and Morenci were removed at gunpoint by white residents horrified at the placement of what they saw as "white" children in Mexican families. The New York Catholic orphanage that had placed the children positioned religion as the operative category. For town residents a "fit" family was an Anglo family; for the New York nuns a "fit" family was a Catholic one. The vigilante actions of the white residents, however, were predicated on an emergent conception of race that superseded most religious, class, and ethnic divisions. Although this vigilante act had no clear legal precedent, the U.S. Supreme Court eventually upheld the Arizona court's ruling that the white residents who had removed the children had done so in their "best interest" and the children should thus remain with those new "adoptive" families.

Similarly, generations of Native American children were removed from their families and communities in the United States, Canada, and Australia in the name of civilizing, salvage, and rescue.[19] Many of these efforts were legitimized through the rhetoric of "best interest" that child welfare agencies employed. As Abourezk notes, "public and private welfare agencies seem to have operated on the premise that most Indian children would really be better off to grow up non-Indian" (1977:12). In this sense, Native American parents were positioned as de facto neglectful parents, regardless of their individual actions.

These removals were often embedded in large-scale government projects, but they were also enacted through the discretionary decisions of individual do-gooders and social workers, often in contradiction to the letter of the law.[20] It was widely assumed that it was in every child's "best interest" to be removed from parents who were relegated to the margins of full citizenship in order to absorb them into the white middle-class Protestant majority. Thus "salvageable" children had their "best interests" met through education, "civilizing" processes, and their absorption into the modern nation, while their unsalvageable parents, not similarly redeemable, were expected simply to die (Read 1981; Rose 2004).

Furthermore, the vast majority of the removals were based on determinations of neglect, often stemming from the impoverished conditions Native American parents found themselves caught up in via life on a reservation, rather than allegations of abuse. In this way, the poverty Native American parents experienced vis-à-vis their social, economic, and political position in the United States was translated into the child welfare category "neglect" and constituted legal grounds for the removal of their children. In fact, critics of government policies toward tribal communities note that contemporary standards for income and quality of residence often disqualified native community members who resided in government housing on reservation land from being able to qualify as foster families for members of their own community (Fournier and Crey 1997; Strong 2001). The removal of children from undocumented parents in the contemporary United States is also largely based on allegations of neglect as opposed to abuse. Similar sorts of translations are at play in this context where poverty is produced in part through obstacles to food, housing, child care, and medical care and then categorized as neglect by child welfare authorities.

Child saving practices, and perhaps all forms of intervention into families, are fraught because intervention relies upon a normative sense of proper parenting (Gordon 1999:309). As I suggest in the chapters that follow, this vulnerability impacts not only impoverished women but racially marginalized, undocumented families as well, delineating boundaries of belonging through intervention practices. Custody in such cases is determined by the belief that all children should be placed with families who are members of the dominant social group, usually white and Christian families: those best equipped to satisfy the "best interest" of the children, at least under circumstances where poverty or an inferior position in an established racial hierarchy constitutes neglect and abuse. This form of intervention is not so much about reforming "bad" families as it is a mode of "rescue," where children are placed in communities, and with families, that are understood as superior homes for all children, regardless of the racial or cultural position of a particular child.

Reading Contemporary Citizenship Through a "Best Interest" Framework

The historical uses of "best interest" recounted above positioned the alignment of children's and state's interests as justification for disregarding the parental rights of marginalized peoples through privileging what they perceived to be "best" for children over the maintenance of family and community bonds. Despite the use of this policy to erode family integrity, and in the case of Native American communities, to undermine tribal sovereignty, the "best interest" principle has taken on increasing importance in the latter half of the twentieth century. The principle plays a central role in the 1959 Declaration of the Rights of the Child (Alston 1994) and has taken on increasing legal significance since the establishment of the 1989 Convention on the Rights of the Child.[21] The prevalence of the "best interest" principle in custody determinations gathered force during the 1990s in response to a rising interest in children's rights.[22] As Chang (2003) notes, the "best interest" standard gained primacy in U.S. family courts in an effort to disrupt gendered assumptions about which parent might be best equipped to care for a child in the case of a custody dispute. More recently, the confluence of immigration enforcement and child welfare decision-making has provided new terrain for the application of this principle.

The "best interest" of the child figures centrally in contemporary child welfare policy as an ambiguous notion that judges, lawyers, and social workers are all charged to address. As legal scholar Dalrymple recounts, the "best interest" principle involves three issues: "to determine the best interests of the child in domestic family law cases, courts consider the parents' interest for family integrity, the state's interest to protect the minor, and the child's interest for safety and for a stable family environment."[23]

The notion of "best interest" was commonly understood by child welfare and the dependency courts to incorporate stability and permanency. During the time of this research the dominant trend in child welfare policy incorporated what was termed "permanency planning." This term referred to the social worker's responsibility to construct a contingency plan for where a child would reside should reunification with one or both biological parents fail. The emphasis on permanency privileged placement of children either with local kin who were potentially interested in adoption or, if no such kin were available, with foster parents who were hoping to become adoptive parents, even though the initial aim of the placement was to last only until parents could regain custody. An emphasis on permanency all too often promoted the severance of parental rights, as even if a child was wrongfully removed, a judge might rule against reunification, citing the degree of bonding assumed to have taken place in the foster home (Briggs 2012:87–88). And, as I discuss in the following chapter, geographic restrictions on the placement of foster children often reduced the likelihood of placing children with extended family members who did not live close by, citing bonding with the foster family as a primary obstacle.

This focus on permanency was solidified by congressional legislation, signed into law by President Bill Clinton. This legislation, titled the Adoption and Safe Families Act, shortened the reunification clock for biological parents and aimed to increase adoptions in an effort to decrease the number of children who were purportedly languishing in the foster care system, moved from home to home, and destined to "age out" with no stable support system or long-term relationships to rely on.[24] Even with these commonly agreed upon aspects of "best interest," opinion as to what outcome might be in a child's "best interest" varied widely across child welfare cases and the social workers, parents, and legal actors involved.

It is important to note that there is no clear, legal definition of "best interest."[25] Although particular elements were commonly understood to fall under this umbrella term, lawyers, judges, and social workers mobilized "best interest" for starkly different goals founded on vastly different assumptions. It was a rare child welfare case in which all parties involved agreed about what factors should be considered in determining what was in the "best interest" of the child. Children were understood, from a legal standpoint, to be able to express their desires but not to assess what decisions might be in their own "best interest."[26] Furthermore, social workers and legal actors often saw the procurement of U.S. citizenship, or continued U.S. residency for a U.S. citizen child, as in the de facto "best interest" of the child, although child welfare policy officially privileged placement with relatives regardless of citizenship or country of residence. Such things as better access to schooling, support services, more "sanitary" housing conditions, superior medical services, and a vague sense of future opportunities were all cited as aspects of the privileges and luxuries that U.S. citizenship afforded.

The "best interest" principle was typically understood to incorporate a tense and precarious balance between children's, parents', and state's rights. In the case of deported and deportable parents, legal scholar Yablon-Zug provocatively argues that a U.S. citizen child's interest in remaining in the United States aligns with the state's interest in preserving meaningful relations with its citizens and outweighs the importance of the non-citizen parent's right to their child. In these cases, she suggests,

> The state's interest in citizen children far exceeds the state's interest in their non-citizen parents. Consequently, although it is well established in other contexts that fit parents have the right to the care and custody of their children, this presumption is not appropriate when considering the rights of undocumented parents. Once the parent of an American citizen child is facing deportation, the rights of the child should be viewed as superior to those of their non-citizen parent. At this point, the overriding concern must be ensuring that the child's best interests are served and, in some instances, this will require terminating the rights of fit immigrant parents. (2011:1138–39)

Thus, in some legal interpretations, the "best interests" of the child may well include the termination of parental rights for no other reason than their lack of authorization to reside in the United States.[27] As Thronson (2008) notes, the conflation of U.S. residence with "best interest" is of particular concern for U.S. citizen children with non-U.S. citizen parents. He argues that, "when family members, social workers, and courts assume that U.S. citizen children must remain in the United States, they have essentially decided that a parent forced by immigration law to leave the country can no longer care for that child" (413). Interestingly, in Thronson's portrayal of child welfare and immigration actions leading to the de facto removal of children from their non-U.S.

citizen parents, he emphasizes that the equation of U.S. residency with "best interest" is not limited to social workers or legal actors but can also be attributed to family members. In this way, the coming together of immigration and child welfare policy created a situation where parents had to choose between caring for their children or allowing their children to remain in the United States to take advantage of the "privileges" and "luxuries" of U.S. citizenship.[28]

Contemporary Forms of Child Removal

> There's also a question; the reservation is sovereign. How does the state of South Dakota drive a car onto the reservation and take away an Indian child? Indian agencies couldn't drive into Pierre, South Dakota. . . . And drive away with white children. (Neal Conan, *Talk of the Nation*, NPR 2011)

As Conan reminds us, not all children and parents are equally subject to the threat of child removal. The removal of children from the custody of white parents, particularly, but not exclusively, those who are low-income or otherwise marginalized, does happen. However, the vast majority of children targeted for removal from their parents' custody throughout U.S. history have been outside the white Christian middle-class majority. This is largely a result of the structural aspects of racism, poverty, and class categories being situated outside the realm of political debate, despite these processes positioning particular individuals as more vulnerable to being framed as neglectful or morally lacking. That is, the blame for neglectful behavior is placed squarely on the shoulders of individual parents rather than being understood as, at least in part, the result of structural inequalities that predispose racially marginalized, impoverished parents to be unable to meet the basic standards of care for their children, and that result in such parents being more likely to come under the scrutiny of police and other government officials. In this way, the social positionalities of parents whose children are removed from their custody are at once central to child welfare interventions yet outside the scope of the issues that officially inform determinations about child removal, placement, and custody. The stories recounted throughout this chapter illuminate the depoliticization of the processes through which poverty is translated into neglect and the linking of visions of the impoverished with processes of racialization. This is particularly evidenced by cases as divergent as the Arizona orphan abduction, the removal of Native American children to boarding schools, and the removal of infants from young, unwed urban mothers. This depoliticized framing assumes that impoverished individuals are responsible for the neglect of their children rather than calling into question the social, political, and economic circumstances that both position certain individuals to live impoverished lives and equate that condition of poverty with the willful "neglect" of a child.

Although few would oppose the removal of children who have been subjected to severe abuse by their parents, few would support legislating "poverty" as an official category of neglect. Poverty is not an institutionally valid reason for removal within the child welfare system, yet social workers' concerns about empty refrigerators or about leaving children unattended while their parents are at work cannot be delinked from economic circumstances. In effect, policies that advocate removal, as opposed to providing financial support or other social services to keep children in the custody of their parents, interpret "neglect" as a result of "parental pathology, rather than as in good measure a structural aspect of women's powerlessness and poverty" (Gordon 1989:113). In this way child removal operates as an "index of vulnerability" (Briggs 2012), marking out individuals who occupy a position of subordination, whether based on race, class, or gendered positionalities.

In her analysis of contemporary social workers in the Los Angeles County child welfare system, Swartz (2005) laments social workers' disdain for the biological parents whose children they have removed. She states, "Their severe lack of material resources, social support, and other serious problems were too often flippantly dismissed as moral failings, immaturity, or a lack of love for their children" (17). It was this concern that the child welfare system converted the economic hardship and structural position some parents faced into a moral failing, thereby assessing some parents as more worthy to parent than others, that Josh, the foster father introduced at the beginning of this chapter, seemed to lament. Josh wanted to step in as parent only when there was no other option. Yet his experience in the foster care system had led him to believe the system did a better job at removing children than it did of providing the social supports that would allow children to remain in their homes of their biological parents. As such, "neglect" of children was framed as the failure of individual parents, rather than the failure of the social policies and political-economic arrangements that inevitably positioned some parents as impoverished, and then translated poverty into a discourse of willful mistreatment of their children.

"Bad" Parents: Deportation, Illegality, and Parental Rights

The cases of Isabel and Miguelito, two Esperanza foster children, highlight the translation of structural inequality into individual parental failings, and, in Isabel's case, the equation of a "deportee" or "detainee" status with the status of an "unfit" parent. I draw on these cases to illuminate how structural obstacles facilitate processes whereby social workers recommend the termination of parental rights for undocumented or non-U.S. resident parents, not because they abused or neglected their children, but because their undocumented, deported, or nonresident status kept them from meeting the guidelines necessary for reunification.

Undocumented status affected the ability of parents to reunify or to maintain custody of their children in a number of ways, including financial inability to access support services such as drug rehabilitation programs or mental health or medical services, or to provide adequate childcare, food, housing, clothing, or medical attention to their children. Undocumented parents who were detained or deported were legally and physically barred from meeting the terms of the reunification process due to their inability both to access necessary support services and to "demonstrate" their commitment to reunifying with their child through attending weekly visits while their child was in foster care.[29] How did social workers, whose job it was to look out for the best interests of the children on their caseload, align the decision to terminate the parental rights of undocumented or non-U.S. resident parents with their sense of what was best for these children? How did undocumented and non-U.S. resident parents who did not abuse or willfully neglect their children become "bad" parents in the eyes of the child welfare system and the dependency courts?

Viable Placements and Cross-Border Presumptions

Parents, even those who have been detained or deported, have the legal right to participate in a reunification process. However, there were substantial obstacles to doing so.[30] Parents' ability to reunify typically hinged on their successful participation in a court-ordered reunification plan, commonly consisting of weekly visits with their children, parenting classes, and a variety of therapeutic services based on the initial reasons for the child's removal.

However, because a dependency court judge's order could not supersede that of another court—whether a criminal or an immigration court—if the reunification plan conflicted with the terms of the parent's incarceration or probation, then the parent was considered to have failed to comply with the reunification plan. Thus jails or detention centers might fail to transport inmates or detainees to their child's court hearings or allow them to participate by phone. Solitary confinement punishments might override visitation schedules with children. And although federal and state prisons typically were able to provide access to parenting classes, drug treatment programs, and other forms of counseling, detention centers almost always lacked access to these services because law makers felt such resources should not be "wasted" on a population scheduled to permanently leave the country (Wessler 2011:40; Rabin 2011:121–12). Thus a parent's detention, or in some cases, incarceration, created a situation of "noncompliance" with the reunification plan. Although these circumstances might not be the result of a parent's lack of desire to reunify, they might be interpreted as such and made equivalent with a parental stance of noncompliance. Furthermore, social workers were often unaware that similar parenting classes and drug treatment programs were available outside the United States, and some social workers I interviewed who were aware did not trust the quality of programs elsewhere. The greatest obstacle detained or deported parents faced in reunifying with their child was often the social worker's assessment that, for the host of reasons discussed above, they were not a viable placement option.[31] In this way the criminalization of undocumented immigration and concerns about the quality of social services outside the United States were translated into concerns about the "best interest" of the child.

Consider the case of three-year-old Isabel, who had been in foster care for over a year when we first met. Although I had spent a number of afternoons with Isabel and her adoptive parents, learning about her struggles in relation to some of her ongoing health issues, it was a brief note in her case file that unearthed the complexities of her case:

> Isabel's 12-month review hearing was held this morning, Monday March 30th, 2007 at 8:30 am in the Juvenile Court located at 2851 Meadow Lark Drive, San Diego 92123. The mother has been granted 6 more months of services. Rights for father will be terminated since he is currently in immigration custody, most likely he will be deported or sent to Florida (he is Cuban).[32] (social worker's case notes, March 30, 2007)

I came across this note in a case file I examined at Esperanza. Corinne had asked me to inventory the agency case files, update Esperanza's digital database, and do my best to track down any missing information in an effort to keep agency records up to date. When I found this case note in Isabel's file indicating that her father's parental rights would be terminated, purportedly because of his impending deportation, I dug through the file in search of further discussion of his role in the case and his interest in reunifying with his daughter. As I read, I learned about the domestic violence that had led to Isabel's initial removal, about her mother's mental illness, the foster parents' desire to adopt Isabel, and the mother's appeals as the case moved toward a termination of parental rights. However, there was no further mention of her father, no discussion of his role in Isabel's life prior to her removal, and no mention whether criminal activity or his citizenship status alone had landed him in immigration custody.

Isabel's mother's eventual loss of parental rights was framed in relation to her ongoing mental health issues. Her father's loss of parental rights, however, seemed to have been based on his deportation (or relocation to Florida), even though dependency law specified that parents and children had a right to attempt to reunify regardless of citizenship status or country of residence. In this case, the social worker's preference for the stability and U.S. citizenship possibilities offered through adoption by her foster parents superseded the value of reunification with one or both of her parents. What is striking here is that the murkiness of Isabel's father's legal status is irrelevant to the case. His relative absence from the file indicates that he was removed from the reunification process regardless of whether he was, in fact, deported. Isabel's case therefore represented a situation where a parent's (apparent) removal from the United States automatically eliminated that parent from being considered as a custodial option for their child. As numerous scholars have noted (Dreby 2012; Golash-Boza 2012), deportation is a gendered process, affecting far more men than women. As such, it is entangled in the production of single-mother headed households, and the attendant precariousness and economic instability that often plagues homes with only one primary provider of both childcare and household income.

The judge's approval of the social worker's recommendation to remove Isabel's father from the reunification plan did not necessitate a specific determination that he was unfit in order to eliminate him as a viable placement option. The assumption that her father would be deported from the United States made placement with him a non-option for Isabel, without need to investigate the quality of their relationship, though no law stipulates that non-U.S. resident parents should lose custody of their children on those grounds alone. The legal actors involved in this case were thus reasoning that continued U.S. residency was the de facto "best interest" option for the children on their caseload, seemingly without investigating the viability of the array of possible custody options or the strength of the relationship between parent and child. In fact, in many of the cases I examined, consideration of non-U.S. resident relatives arose only when there were no U.S. resident relatives who were viable placement options. However, no policy required that U.S. placements were mandatory or even preferable in any systematic way. Social workers were able, and some might argue that they were obligated, to pursue international joint custody, or custody with a non-U.S. resident parent, as possible custody arrangements. Miguel's case, introduced below, is one such case where the social worker investigated and ruled out a number of extended family members in Tijuana before approving his adoption by his U.S. foster family. However, this was not an option child welfare authorities tended to explore except as a last resort, as long as U.S. options remained, citing very real logistical roadblocks, bureaucratic obstacles, or simply a preference for life in the United States.

Cases like Isabel's present a story of (possible) deportation being translated into an allegedly willful absence, one where the termination of parental rights was justified by a parent's nonparticipation in a reunification process, even if that parent had not been provided with feasible means for doing so. In this way, citizenship and country of residence intervened and superseded parental rights, shaping social workers' perceptions of "good" and "bad" parents. National status was thus produced as a privileged status, in that it created the conditions of possibility for the assessment of the quality of a parent-child relationship, rather than this assessment being foreclosed by a parent's undocumented status, as in Isabel's case. This distinction is illuminated by Taylor's case, discussed in Chapter 4, where his white U.S. citizen parents were able to regain custody of their child, despite ongoing domestic violence that violated the technical terms of the reunification plan. Miguel's case, which I turn to next, was somewhat distinct, as his mother Elena was both a Tijuana resident and a U.S. citizen by birth. Elena's story highlights the equation of all Latina/o individuals with the trope of the undocumented immigrant regardless of their citizenship status, and emphasizes the way the workings of the child welfare system situated Latina/o families in a differentially precarious state.[33]

When I first met Angélica, her foster son Miguel had been with her only one month and was just taking his first tentative steps. Miguel had originally been placed with another Esperanza foster family, but that family had to stop fostering when they were displaced by the 2007 San Diego wildfires. Angélica explained that he had been moved to her home specifically because she lived closer to the United States-Mexico border than Miguel's previous foster home. The county social worker had hoped that an easier commute would make visits more consistent for his mother, Elena, who was traveling weekly from her home in Tijuana. Angélica told me how much she and her husband loved Miguel from the moment he arrived and how hard it would be when he returned home, a decision the county social worker planned to recommend at his upcoming court hearing.

Two years later, Miguelito was running up and down the stairs, shaking my hand and saying "nice to meet you!" I sat down with Angélica while Miguel played upstairs with their housekeeper, Lupe, to be filled in on what had happened with his case and how she had come to adopt Miguel. Miguel had entered the foster care system because his mother, a U.S. citizen and Tijuana resident, had given birth to him in a San Diego hospital where he and his mother, Elena, both tested positive for methamphetamines. Because of his birth in San Diego, Miguel entered the San Diego foster care system, despite his mother's residency in Mexico.[34] Angélica told me, as she did when we initially met in 2008, that Elena complied for the most part with her court-ordered reunification plan, attending a drug rehabilitation program and weekly visitations with Miguel. The county social worker was on the brink of recommending overnight visits, often the last step before reunification, when Angélica and her husband raised concerns about the safety of her home and neighborhood, after a short visit to his biological family's home. The county social worker also raised concerns about Elena's ability to meet Miguelito's developmental needs, which included speech and physical therapy related to his exposure to methamphetamines in utero. She recommended to Elena that her best chance of reunifying with Miguel was to move to San Diego where she could qualify for more support services. Elena's social worker offered her a spot in a homeless shelter for women and children, which she refused.

A few weeks later Elena was arrested at the San Ysidro border crossing when a large amount of marijuana was found in the trunk of her car. Elena spent a brief period of time in jail, and the judge terminated her parental rights soon after this event. Although the judge cited her arrest as indicative of her willingness to put Miguel at risk, Angélica told me she felt that parental rights were largely terminated because Elena's lawyer was inept and because Elena did not read or speak English and thus did not always follow court protocol, which frustrated the judge. Angélica believed Elena was not a regular participant in drug smuggling, and interpreted the event as a last ditch effort to get together the money necessary to rent a San Diego apartment in order to reclaim her child. Like Josh, the foster father introduced above, Angélica read Elena's actions as a response to structural demands, not as an indicator of parental pathology.

The initial circumstances of Miguel's removal had been clear—he had been removed due to in utero exposure to methamphetamines.[35] In response to these circumstances, Elena had largely done what the child welfare system required her to do—kicked her drug habit, attended parenting classes, and demonstrated her commitment to reunifying with her son through attending weekly visits with him. Yet Elena's social worker had felt that her home in Tijuana was not up to acceptable standards and that social services in Tijuana would not be sufficient to provide the necessary support for her and her son. In Angélica's interpretation, this was the direct cause of Elena's smuggling attempt and subsequent arrest. Angélica expressed sorrow that Elena had seen this as the only option to earn the money necessary to rent an apartment in San Diego, and believed that had this incident not occurred, Miguel would have been reunified with his biological mother. This requirement was particularly egregious due to the high cost of living in San Diego, making a suitable apartment out of reach for most families earning a minimum wage in U.S. dollars, much less pesos. Thus, although the judge interpreted Elena's arrest for drug smuggling as evidence of her continued involvement in the "drug world" and disregard for her son's well-being, it could alternatively be read as an attempt to satisfy requirements to which Elena should never have been subjected: procurement of a San Diego home and access to U.S. social services for Miguel. Here the social worker's assessment of what was in Miguel's best interest included San Diego residency and access to San Diego social services. This assessment was rooted not only in what she thought was technically best for Miguel, but in her assumption that comparable supports could not be accessed in Tijuana.

A similar example is the case of Cirila Baltazar Cruz, widely covered in the national media. Baltazar Cruz was a Chatino speaker from Oaxaca, who gave birth to her daughter Ruby in November 2008, in a hospital in Pascagoula, Mississippi. Through a series of gross mistranslations, Pascagoula social workers determined that Ruby was being abused and neglected, and removed her from the care of Baltazar Cruz. Reporters stated that the judge assigned to the case supported the belief that "the baby would have 'developmental' problems [if returned to Baltazar Cruz] because she would not communicate with the baby in English," and moved the case toward adoption by Ruby's foster parents (Flatow 2014; see also Padgett 2009). The case came to the attention of the Southern Poverty Law Center, and a year after Ruby's initial removal she was returned to her mother's custody. While Ruby's case was remarkable, particularly in the judge's interpretation of English language exposure as in the child's "best interest," it was not unique. What made this case exceptional was that Baltazar Cruz received widespread national media coverage and capable pro bono lawyers took up her case. Absent these two circumstances, it is likely she would have been deported and her parental rights terminated.

It was not just citizenship status that differentially impacted the experience of Latina/o families enmeshed in the child welfare system. Residence outside the bounds of the nation-state was suspect due to assumptions about the quality of services, supports, and neighborhoods in Tijuana, alongside institutional roadblocks that impeded, or at the least discouraged, San Diego social workers from pursuing the means necessary to adequately assess the safety and desirability of placement options across the U.S.-Mexico border. Each of these cases was based on the premise that a noncitizen, nonresident, or non-English speaking parent constituted an "abusive," "neglectful," or "unfit" parent. As such, a "best interest" reading in the context of U.S. immigration policy has the propensity to position undocumented, racially marginalized, low-income parents as more vulnerable than others to the intervention of the state, and the subsequent loss of custody of their children.

Discretionary Processes

As I have demonstrated throughout this chapter, the discretionary decision-making processes of social workers, attorneys, state dependency judges, and federal immigration judges are central to the operation of the "best interest" principle and to the processes of translation that remake conditions of poverty into "neglect." Legal scholars have highlighted the potential of discretion in mitigating the draconian impacts of immigration law, impacts illustrated by the experiences of Isabel's father and of Baltazar Cruz described in the cases above. The mitigating potential of discretion is primarily enacted through giving immigration officers and attorneys the ability to detain and prosecute or to release undocumented individuals, particularly in the climate of reduced judicial discretion following the enactment of the 1996 Illegal Immigration Reform and Immigrant Responsibility Act (IIRIRA).[36] In a context where a law is written to formally transcend racial bias, as each "best interest" determination is purportedly based on the unique needs of each individual child, racism resides primarily in this space of discretion where lawmakers rely on the differential application of the law for the pursuit of racially motivated exclusion.[37]

Discretion gives the "best interest" principle both its force and its flexibility, asserting that no law can possibly reflect the varying needs of the messy, complex lives of children and their families, but that the uniqueness of each case must be considered to make a "best interest" determination. As Zavella (2012) notes, the "best interest" principle sets a new precedent in immigration law, as it does not begin from the question whether an individual meets a set of immigration criteria based on the interests of the nation-state itself.[38] Rather, this approach centers questions about the need for protection and care that a child migrant may face. This is in contrast to the way that international adoption, as a form of migration, has historically subordinated the "best interests" of particular children to nation-state interests that manifest as conceptions of "ideal" immigrants, through admitting children from some sending nations but not others (Lovelock 2000). The possibilities of this policy are undeniable. However, my focus here is on the other side of what discretionary processes enabled; applications of "best interest" that were undergirded by discretionary decisions that enacted racist, classist and nationalist notions of what was "best" for the U.S.-resident children of undocumented immigrants.

In a dependency court hearing I attended in 2010, three children were reunited with their white, U.S. citizen mother who was homeless, jobless, and unable to regularly transport her children to school or to obtain the medication prescribed to her two older children because it was not covered by Medi-Cal.[39] The children's advocate was horrified that the children would be returned to their mother under these circumstances and that many of her support services would be terminated when her case closed. The judge explained that because there was no "threat of imminent danger," it was in the children's "best interest" to return to their mother's care and to terminate state custody.

In this case, the judge interpreted "best interest" as the retention of family integrity over the possible material benefits of the children remaining in foster placements. When juxtaposed with the cases of Isabel, Miguelito, and Baltazar Cruz, we see how these determinations each focus on the "best interest" of the children. While the judicial ruling in the case of the U.S. citizen mother clearly prioritized the maintenance of the parent-child relationship as central to the "best interests" of her children, the cross-border cases described above seemed to privilege U.S. residency, stable economic circumstances, and English-language capabilities over the initial bond between parent and child. Each case was nominally decided on the shared ground of "best interest." However, these determinations imposed radically divergent standards on the parents in each case.

I suggest that the "best interest" principle can be read in two distinct ways. First, best interest began with the premise that immigrants should not be judged by whether they meet certain entry requirements but by whether it is in their "best interest" to immigrate or, perhaps, not to be forcibly removed to the country from which they came. This is distinct from standards for asylum in that judges are given broad discretion to interpret whether or not it is "best" for a child to remain in the United States. In other words, a child could qualify for citizenship in the United States as long as the judge deemed that path best for the child, rather than the child being held to narrowly defined immigration standards, such as the necessity to demonstrate a well-founded fear of persecution, to qualify for political asylum. Yet this consideration was extended only to minor migrants whose "unprotected" status as wards of the state provided the impetus for judging their right to enter under different terms. This sort of distinction is demonstrated by the reception of unaccompanied Central American minors during 2014, discussed in Chapter 1, where minors were returned to their countries of origin without an in-depth examination of their "best interest" simply because they wound up in immigration detention rather than in the child welfare system. Had they been received as wards of the state within the child welfare system, their experiences would have been markedly different and questions of "best interest" would have come more forcefully into play. As such, Dalrymple (2006) argues that all cases involving non-U.S. citizen minors should, in an ideal world, be founded on the principle of "best interest."

Second, the "best interest" principle, while potentially aligning with international law that privileges the unity of children with their parents regardless of their country of origin or residence, can also be mobilized to support a view that posits U.S. citizenship and residence as inherently in the "best interest" of all children, regardless of the implications of this determination for their family circumstances. This interpretation was one that social workers, lawyers, and advocates faced in their attempts to argue in court that the best placement for a child was with parents or extended family residing outside U.S. borders. This was arguably the key element in Miguel's case, where concerns about Tijuana social services and neighborhood environments profoundly impacted the trajectory of his case and the custody determination that was made.

The principle of "best interest" invokes the view that in the case of a minor the safety and well-being of that child supersedes regulations about "illegal entry." This reading of the principle sidesteps immigration debates and ascribes to universal notions of child protection that nullify questions of the worthiness of individual claims. In this sense, minors were seen as both inherently blameless and inherently worthy of citizenship status, as long as they were legible as in need of "protection." Yet the judicial interpretations and decisions social workers and legal actors made that equated "best interest" with U.S. citizenship and residency risked delegitimizing legal commitments to the preservation of the family. These commitments posited that family integrity, in the absence of severe neglect or abuse, was the surest indicator that the best interests of children would be addressed. As such, this second reading of "best interest" suggests that a child's residence in the United States will lead to a better life than remaining with family outside these borders. This view implicitly places elements assumed to be superior within the United States, such as schooling, medical care, and employment, above emotional and psychological aspects of well-being, which are largely believed by child advocates to be best supported for children who remain with their biological families. In this sense, common interpretations of "best interest" appear to be driven by primarily economic, and therefore inherently classist and racialized, readings of a child's life trajectory. I suggest that although best interest opens the possibility of taking a child's circumstances into account in important ways, it also risks creating a space for judges, lawyers, and social workers to assert their own perceptions of U.S. superiority, arguing that even children's residence in a long-term foster care placement in the United States is superior to residence with their own family in another nation.

The types of families who have been subjected to the removal of their children have varied throughout U.S. history. Similarly, the categorization of particular parents as "unfit" has varied in both form and function, caught up in the political and social anxieties of particular historical moments. Although the focus of these interventions has shifted over time, the targeting of families living in poverty and those who are categorized as immigrants or racially "other" have remained constant throughout the periods I have considered here. Constant throughout these various interventions has been a framing of individual parents as immoral or deviant. Absent in these same interventions is any consideration of how social inequalities, such as systematic income disparities, get translated into individual instances of purportedly willful neglect. Throughout the history I have recounted here, the ideal family in which a child should be placed has been almost unwaveringly white, Christian, and not impoverished. This shift in focus from child protection to the twin actions of intervention and removal highlights the centrality of the child and the family as key sites for the production and reinforcement of racial, cultural, class, national, and religious hierarchies.

Instances of child removal considered in this chapter sometimes had explicit goals of assimilation or cultural genocide, such as the removal of immigrant children during the progressive era, and the removal of Native American children throughout the twentieth century and into the present day. In the context of contemporary child welfare court decisions, some scholars and legal actors argue that parental deportation may create a situation where the termination of the rights of otherwise "fit" parents is an appropriate judicial decision (Yablon-Zug 2012; see also Gilger et al. 2012; Simons 2013). In this way, differential application of the "best interest" standard aligns with historical uses of the principle whereby state actors relegate some parents outside of the bounds of citizenship and rights, while emphasizing the interest of their children in remaining in the United States as full citizens.

Contemporary instances of child removal are not part of an explicitly assimilationist project. However, I contend that a position that holds that children are better off in the care of U.S. citizen parents, the majority of whom are both white and middle class, can be productively understood in the context of the history here described. In this way, the systematic removal of children whose parents are caught up in immigration enforcement actions is rooted in a politics of citizenship that categorizes undocumented parents as irredeemably "unfit."

CHAPTER 3

Working the Gap

Four-year-old Lucas, Liliana's foster son, entered the child welfare system when his parents were caught up in a drug raid where Lucas was present. Lucas's parents were arrested; his mother was jailed and released the following week, and his father, a Mexican citizen, was briefly detained by ICE before being released across the border into Mexicali. Lucas spoke with his father a few days after his removal, using a speakerphone so that Liliana could monitor the call. Lucas struggled to speak, gulping and crying through the static buzz of the pay phone his father was calling from and begging Liliana to tell his father where he was so he could come pick him up. During our first home visit to check on Lucas's progress, Liliana told Corinne and me that she was relieved to have been able to console him with a hug and to distract him with his foster brother and the lure of the Nintendo soon after the brief call ended. Lucas had weekly visits with his mother and with a cousin who was pending approval to take over Lucas's foster care until he could be reunified with his mother. His father was no longer considered part of the reunification plan, due to his deportation. Lucas's only contact with his father was when his mother asked Liliana's permission to call him during her visits, a few tearful moments on a crackly cell phone call across the border.

In Lucas's case, obstacles to his reunification with his family arose through his father's deportation and the subsequent geographic separation of his parents. Unless Lucas's mother was willing to argue in court for her right to move with Lucas to Mexico, his father's fight for reunification services would have entailed a struggle to take custody from the mother and to prove himself, in Mexico, to be a better placement option for his son. He could not fight to share custody with Lucas's mother, since immigration policy barred his legal return to the United States after a forced deportation.[1] The impacts of immigration law had foreclosed the social worker's ability to work toward a complete family reunification.[2] Her job was to determine the best possible placement for Lucas, which in this case was Lucas's newly single mother, acting suitably repentant and recently released from jail.

Like that of Alba, introduced in Chapter 1, Lucas's case was emblematic of the circumstances that involved a family's simultaneous entanglement in both the child welfare and immigration systems. This chapter examines the trajectories of families who must contend with these two legal systems, systems that are both deeply enmeshed and starkly estranged. Much has been written about contexts in which multiple legal systems operate, commonly referred to as "legal pluralism" (Pathak and Rajan 1989; Clarke 2009; Benda-Beckmann et al. 2013; Shahar 2013). This scholarship has traditionally focused on "describing multiple moral-normative orders as plural forms of law" (Demian 2015:93)—troubling the distinctions between "state" law and "customary" law, the uneven power relationships between distinct legal systems, and the movement of the study of law beyond the confines of the courtroom (Merry 1988; Benda-Beckmann 2002). Throughout this chapter, I focus explicitly on legal systems that not only are operating in the same social space but are deeply entangled, even while social workers, legal actors, and family members view each system as distinct. As Santos (1995) states, "We live in a time of porous legality or legal porosity, multiple networks of legal orders forcing us to constant transitions and trespassings. Our legal life is constituted by an intersection of different legal orders, that is, by *interlegality*" (Butler 2009:473). The circumstances I describe below emphasize the way individuals enmeshed in both the child welfare and immigration system are "caught between," one system limiting, foreclosing, and shaping outcomes in the other in profound, unintentional, and unexpected ways.[3] In this sense, I propose an examination of legal systems that does not move from codified law out to its effects on individuals. Rather, I begin at the edges, highlighting the unintended effects of entangled legal systems, as a way to see the central project of each legal apparatus in stark relief.[4]

In the cases that follow, I examine how policies, decisions, and actions in the immigration and child welfare systems impact families that are simultaneously entangled in both systems. I consider how these systems, when they come together, position Latina/o families as vulnerable to state intervention. I examine the ways the engagement between these institutions is shaped by ongoing processes of translation across institutional categories and varied contexts. Throughout this chapter I explore the key role these institutional engagements play in demarcating between citizens and noncitizens, and between the United States and other international contexts. And finally, I suggest that because these systems both had the potential to profoundly impact people's lives, the ways they came together, and spoke past each other, produced unexpected outcomes.

The immigration and child welfare systems, although they sometimes worked in tandem, were not designed to communicate directly with one another or to collaborate. Immigration officers had the discretion to consider child welfare issues such as releasing nursing mothers or single parents, or allowing parents to arrange alternative child care before being detained, but they were not required to do so (Morton 2011a, b). One advocate told me of a mother who, on being detained, informed the immigration officer that she had three young children left at home unattended. The officer did not release her, nor did he inform child welfare authorities that the children were left alone and might need alternative care. The children eventually came to the attention of a neighbor, who notified child welfare services that they were home unattended. They entered the foster care system as children who had been abandoned. This process of translating immigration detention into child abandonment was central to the way immigration enforcement and child welfare systems came together.

Citizenship, Violence, and Human Rights

I first met Luz, executive director of Refugee Legal Aid (RLA), a pro bono immigration law firm, in March 2011. I had contacted her in the hope of learning from her agency's expertise on children's rights and obstacles to immigration. Luz, in turn, had convened a group meeting that included Katya, lead lawyer for the children's program at Refugee Legal Aid, and Sister Margaret, one of the organization's founders, with the hope of learning from me about some of the obstacles foster children faced in their attempts to qualify for immigration relief.

It is important to note that the child welfare system does not formally treat non-U.S. citizen children differently from foster children who are U.S. citizens. They receive the same access to medical care and therapeutic services, they are placed in the same county or FFA foster homes, and they are not differentiated from other children within the dependency court system.[5] There are nevertheless informal inequalities. These include a lack of available bilingual social workers, foster families, and service providers, as well as a reduced chance that these children's noncitizen parents would have the available resources to meet the reunification requirements stipulated by the county social worker assigned to their case, as was made evident in Miguel's case in the previous chapter. Additionally, there was less likelihood that these children would be placed in the care of a relative, rather than in a nonrelative foster home, due to social workers' perceptions of barriers to placing children in the care of undocumented adults. Refugee Legal Aid was primarily interested in foster children who were not U.S. citizens because they were often eligible for legal status and eventual citizenship through their position as foster children. However, these children were unlikely to be able to take advantage of that option without the intervention of an immigration lawyer, since this was not an issue social workers were equipped to pursue independently. RLA lawyers often worked with children who were refugees or victims of domestic violence, living in homeless shelters or detention centers, and they hoped to extend their practice to the children in San Diego's foster care system.[6]

Refugee Legal Aid was founded in 1997 by two Catholic nuns who were sent by their order to address humanitarian issues in the Southwestern region of the United States. The agency began its work as a division of an existing organization of pro bono lawyers in San Diego, but over time developed independent status as a nonprofit law firm. Since its founding, the organization steadily expanded to meet the growing need for legal representation of non-U.S. citizens in the region. Over time, RLA developed three programs to meet the most pressing needs of their clients, focusing respectively on asylum seekers, victims of domestic violence, and children.[7] The children's program provided legal representation for all detained children in San Diego County who required and accepted legal counsel. Detained minors most frequently included children who had traveled to the United States without a parent or guardian and were apprehended during or soon after crossing the border. However, some detained minors were also children who had been living in the United States for an extended period, most often teenagers picked up by police for some other infraction and transferred to the detention center when it was determined that they were not U.S. citizens. The RLA children's program received a list of detainees directly from the county's detention centers and conducted interviews with all minors to determine which of them might qualify for immigration relief. Luz explained that this close collaboration was facilitated by the fact that judges "hate to see clients 'pro se',"[8] meaning without legal representation. Hearings were

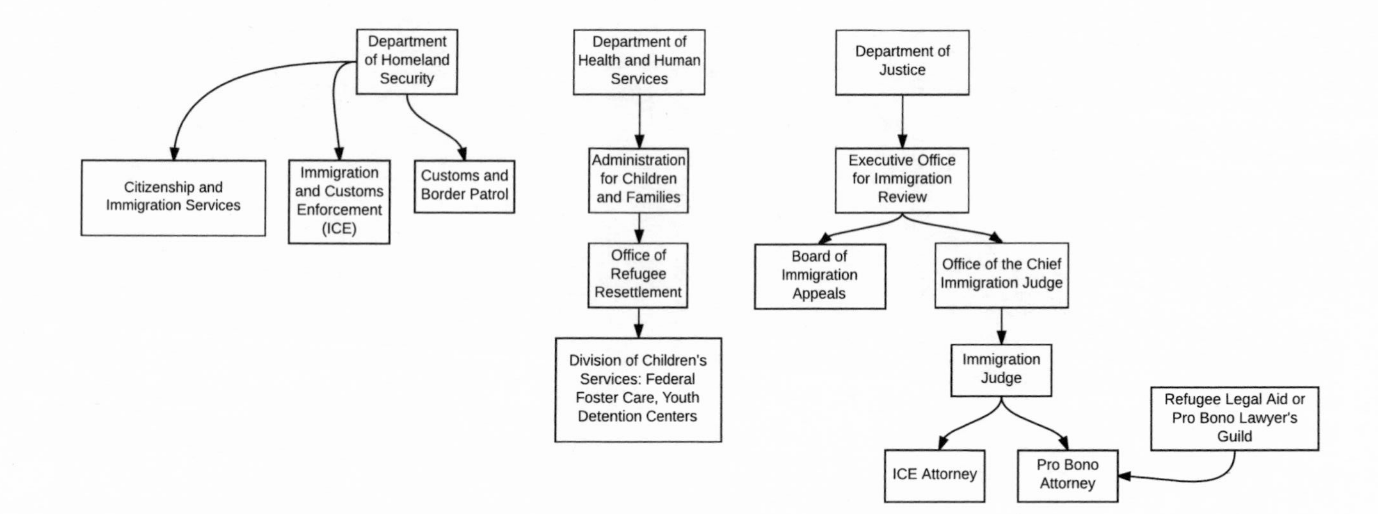

Figure 2. The immigration system.

expected by judges and lawyers to be much easier and faster if the judge could communicate directly with the lawyer, fluent in both the procedure and the legal jargon.

Children who had traveled to the United States for reasons characterized as primarily "economic" or because they wished to be reunited with family members residing in the United States would not typically receive immigration counsel in the courtroom. Children who had some claim to derivative citizenship status, who were victims of abuse in their home country, or who were victims of violent crimes during their immigration journey, would be interviewed further to investigate their potential to qualify for relief.[9] Refugee Legal Aid partnered with pro bono lawyers from private law firms in San Diego to provide immigration lawyers for these cases. Although some senior lawyers were committed participants in RLA's volunteer lawyer recruitment efforts, most lawyers who did pro bono work for RLA were junior associates who had little experience with immigration law. Many of them were drawn to this work by the opportunity to argue a case before a judge, an opportunity frequently unavailable to the newest members of a private law firm. As such, individuals applying to legalize their status benefited from the volunteer efforts of a pro bono lawyer but were subject to the skills of an attorney who was young, inexperienced, and rarely an expert in immigration law.

So as to sidestep knee-jerk, anti-immigrant responses to their work, Luz explained that RLA staff describe their aim as humanitarian rather than as pro-immigrants' rights. Luz and Katya had found that the word "immigration" often elicited negative reactions from community stakeholders and policy makers, but that a broad mission of human rights and equal access to the law garnered considerable support. In addition to providing legal counsel, RLA staff actively researched country conditions to ascertain which applicants they would most likely be able to win relief for and also advocated for changes to policy which they believed would increase equal access to legal avenues for immigration relief.

Pathways to citizenship were available to children in the foster care system through a number of avenues. Special Immigrant Juvenile Status (SIJS) was created in 1990 and expanded to its present form in 2008. Referred to as the "J-visa," it provided the most readily available path to citizenship for children who were dependents of the state or victims of abuse.[10] This was the pathway foster children who were not U.S. citizens most frequently used.[11] The Violence Against Women Act (VAWA) was created in 1990 and reauthorized most recently in 2013. Its aim was to protect victims of domestic violence. It provided a path to legal permanent residency, called the "U-Visa," for women and children who were victims of violent crimes, provided they aided in the prosecution of their assailant. The Trafficking Victims Protection Reauthorization Act was signed into law in 2006 and provided victims of human trafficking with a path to legal residency via the "T-visa." This provision, Luz noted, was significant for its availability to Mexican citizens, who have historically been ineligible for broader claims to refugee or asylum status.[12]

Although all three of these legal avenues were potentially available to children caught up in the child welfare system, I focus primarily on Special Immigrant Juvenile Status (SIJS), the most readily obtainable status for foster children. The vast majority of SIJS applications filed in San Diego County were successful. Applications that lawyers expected to be denied were those for children who could be deemed guilty of a particular set of violations, such as smuggling, trafficking, or being a member of a communist organization. However, because a denied SIJS application could potentially set a deportation order into motion, the lawyers I spoke with engaged in detailed background checks on their clients and did not file applications they could reasonably expect would be denied. Luz referred to SIJS as a "beautiful law," specifying that winning SIJS status led to a green card much faster than other avenues, such as asylum, and that the adjustment of status to U.S. citizen was relatively easy.[13] Luz was not the only lawyer who was enthusiastic about the structure of SIJS. Many lawyers felt that SIJS was woefully underutilized and, as noted in the previous chapter, some legal scholars argue that all immigration relief for detained children should be decided not on current principles for asylum or refugee status but on the same guidelines as SIJS, the only form of immigration relief that explicitly centers the "best interest" of the child.

Jurisdiction in the Border Region

A few months prior to my first meeting at Refugee Legal Aid, I attended a number of hearings at the San Diego dependency court. After a quick pass through a metal detector staffed by security personnel, the dependency courthouse opened up into a large, echoing main room. The main room was bordered by dark wooden walls sparsely adorned by a few murals local school children had painted. Families and children filled the wooden benches that lined the main room, waiting to meet with their lawyers, who poured in through the front entrance minutes before the first court session of the morning, balancing enormous stacks of papers and steaming mugs of coffee.

Dependency court had eight courtrooms. Each courtroom was presided over by an appointed judge and staffed with a handful of dependency attorneys and a single investigator.[14] Cases were assigned to a particular courtroom by county region. The number of attorneys available in any given courtroom was based on historical numbers of cases in each of the county's regions. The typical range for minors' attorneys was between one and three per room. The result of this structure was that clients would cycle in and out of the courtroom while the attorneys usually remained, chatting with each other and occasionally with the judge between hearings. Social workers, families, and other observers were not typically allowed in the courtroom between hearings, however; the lawyers not involved in the current hearing would merely shuffle between the front table and the back benches as the court moved through that day's hearings.

On the morning of the hearings I attended, I was accompanied by Stacy, a high-level administrator at the local court-appointed special advocate (CASA) organization, a woman with an enormous presence in the dependency courthouse and more than a decade of experience in child welfare. Stacy gave a quick tour of the courthouse before we settled into the benches at the back of Judge Carmichael's courtroom. As lawyers shuffled papers and the court secretary filled in the hearing schedule on a large whiteboard, Stacy explained the arrangement of the courtroom, noting where parents, lawyers, and social workers would be seated. Judge Carmichael, when she entered the courtroom in her black robes, sat high up on a raised platform flanked on one side by a large U.S. flag and on the other by a large carved seal of the state of California.

There were nine dependency hearings scheduled that morning, each lasting roughly between five and ten minutes. The fourth hearing of the morning concerned a four-year-old foster child whose parents' whereabouts were unknown. The child's maternal aunt and cousin had come to the hearing, traveling from Tijuana to express an interest in having the child placed with them. Judge Carmichael spoke briefly with them to determine whether they could help locate either parent, thanked them for attending, and scheduled an upcoming hearing to determine the child's placement. As the courtroom lawyers shuffled to prepare for the next hearing, I asked Stacy how the case would change if the child were placed with her aunt and cousin in Tijuana.

She explained that the case would not substantially change and that the San Diego County Child Welfare Agency and dependency court would maintain jurisdiction until the case was closed, even if the child resided in Mexico. On my drive from the courthouse back to Esperanza, I mulled over this information, confused about how the child would be transported to court in San Diego for regular hearings and how a U.S. social worker could regularly travel to Tijuana to visit the child, given the time constraints of social work and the hours it often took to cross back into the United States from Mexico. It was not the border crossing itself that seemed prohibitive, but the idea that this process could happen in an official capacity across the border. It did not make sense, but perhaps, I thought, I had misunderstood.

Back at Esperanza I asked Corinne about this, and she agreed it seemed unlikely, since a San Diego social worker could have no legal jurisdiction across the border. During an interview, a seasoned judge of dependency court later confirmed the lack of social workers' jurisdiction across borders. She described jurisdiction as one of the major roadblocks to a cross-border child welfare system, as it effectively prevented continuity in the care provided to a child. It also produced a situation where judges, lawyers, and social workers were hesitant to consider placements and visits across the border, even though such placements were within the bounds of the law, since they could not monitor the safety of their recommendation. Mexico's social service system, the DIF, was capable of providing parenting classes, home visits, and other such services. However, there were few formal instances of collaboration and a general lack of optimism on the part of U.S. social workers, about the quality of care and the degree of oversight provided in Mexico. Geopolitical boundaries thus determined which kinship ties were most likely to be preserved. I continued to question social workers and Tijuana orphanage staff about jurisdictional issues, posing scenarios of mothers arrested at the border, of U.S. citizens in Tijuana orphanages, of Mexican citizens in San Diego foster care, and received a wide range of responses as to the likely trajectory of these cases. This lack of consensus suggested that jurisdiction in the border region, and knowledge of the law, was murky at best.

On Jurisdiction and Detection

My conversations with social workers and foster families about cross-border jurisdiction had produced a picture that was cloudy, haphazard, and disjointed, where even the people seemingly most knowledgeable about the system, those who were enacting its policies and practices on a daily basis, could not answer basic jurisdictional questions in a clear, consistent manner. For this reason, my initial meeting with immigration lawyers at Refugee Legal Aid was surprising, as from their perspective the jurisdictional limits and legal avenues for navigating cross border cases were crystal clear. RLA lawyers like Luz and Katya understood the legal code, and what it made possible, and did not understand why bureaucratic obstacles within the child welfare system seemed so insurmountable. For these lawyers, children caught up in the child welfare system faced not the problem of unclear jurisdiction but one of detection. As Luz explained, "The biggest problem for foster kids is just identifying who need services, legal avenues exist and the pro bono force to handle the cases, though there will always be more need than available lawyers."[15] Although the San Diego County child welfare system typically had between five to seven thousand foster children, Luz noted that there were consistently fewer than forty children referred to an immigration lawyer for citizenship issues at any given time.[16] She wanted to know what I thought about the fact that of the five to seven thousand foster children in San Diego at any given moment, only forty or fewer were not U.S. citizens. I responded that I could not possibly believe this to be the case. Luz smiled and noted that everyone responded the way I had when asked. However, because the county was unable to produce any figures, since it did not collect data relevant to citizenship status, a hunch that this number was grossly inadequate was all she had to go on.[17]

Sister Margaret interrupted Luz to ask why I thought this issue of detection was such a problem. She explained that they regularly held trainings for county social workers and dependency lawyers, demonstrating how to recognize a non-U.S. citizen child in need of an immigration lawyer and the procedure for referring them to Pro Bono Lawyer's Guild (PBLG), the agency that contracted with the county to handle these cases. I told Sister Margaret that there were numerous possible reasons children in need of immigration relief were not being detected. Social workers were trained to provide the same services regardless of citizenship status to all foster children, so they might have been hesitant to reverse this behavior and mark these children as separate and in need of specific interventions. Furthermore, social workers regularly had caseloads of more than thirty children and anything that was not absolutely necessary (adjusting a child's citizenship status was not technically the responsibility of the child welfare agency) might be eliminated.

From a social worker's perspective, immigration issues were simply not part of their regular responsibilities, so it was left to activist lawyers and legal advocates, such as CASAs, to address that gap in the system.[18] And finally, a small minority of young children arrived in foster care with no documents or even a last name to identify their parents or their country of origin.

Luz asked, "is it possible that social workers legitimately don't know if children on their caseloads are United States citizens?"[19] I did not believe that this was the case. All foster children received Medi-Cal cards, and the application for this required a birth certificate or social security card. Children who did not have either of these items could be issued a California State identification card and then access their medical benefits. Due to this mandatory application process, all social workers were exposed to a clear avenue for identifying non-U.S. citizens, probably those children without a U.S. birth certificate or social security number. However, because social workers did not have a pressing need to identify non-U.S. citizens in order to do their work, they were not always attentive to these issues.

Some time later, an administrator from the San Diego Child Welfare Agency gave me a policy document that laid out a clear protocol for recognizing a non-U.S. citizen child and the reporting steps following this discovery. Although the policy expectations were clear, what was unclear was how many social workers were cognizant of this process and whether they remembered, or prioritized, the protocol in the busyness of their everyday work environment. One legal advocate explained to me, "The social workers never have time to apply for SIJS since it involves a mountain of paperwork and they have no time for such things due to having a caseload of more than thirty kids. Immigrant status isn't an issue they are required to address. But that is the benefit of a CASA who really has no limits to what they can try to advocate for, and because their focus is on the child solely, and not the parents, or the budget, or anything else."[20]

Ironically, these children were embedded in an institution that relied on an extensive documentation system. The requirements for social workers to maintain all sorts of records for each child on their caseload—developmental assessments, payment records, documentation of every trip to see a physician—were onerous. These paperwork requirements were specific to the everyday workings of the child welfare system and to the documents necessary to demonstrate the quality of care the children received while in state custody. From the perspective of child welfare administrators, documentation of citizenship was irrelevant to both these aims. Although the absence of citizenship documentation, or a mismatch between a person's documentation and lived experience, can raise all sorts of difficulties in the context of immigration, border crossing, and the quest for legal authorization, foster children were temporarily protected from the consequences of these circumstances by their embeddedness within the child welfare system.[21] County social workers knew exactly who these children were in the context of their system. The implications of citizenship status for these children's lives did not arise until each child exited the system through adoption, reunification with family, or aging out of the system at eighteen.

When I spoke a few weeks later with Stephanie, the lawyer who worked with county referrals for immigration issues at Pro Bono Lawyer's Guild, she provided an additional reason why these children might have been slipping through the cracks. Stephanie noted that foster children usually spoke English, whether they were citizens or not, and because of this, she speculated, social workers didn't think to question their citizenship status. In this way, social workers seemed to be operating with a particular attentiveness to Spanish-speaking or accented English as a necessary marker of non-U.S. citizens. Ironically, young children's ability to adapt quickly to new language environments made them less likely to receive the legal interventions needed to pursue a pathway to regularize their immigration status. Although the demand for legal services would probably always be greater than the number of pro bono immigration lawyers, from the perspective of the staff I spoke with at Refugee Legal Aid, legal assistance was sitting idle. And according to Sister Margaret, this tragedy was primarily caused by social workers who were failing to do the job young foster children could not do for themselves—identify their status as non-U.S. citizens as significant to their case and then refer them to an expert to determine whether they might be eligible for immigration relief. To the RLA lawyers I spoke with, county social workers were effectively denying access to legal aid to children in their custody, and this seemed to be nothing less than a gross act of negligence and irresponsibility. Luz exclaimed, in a conversation with me and another researcher working on similar issues in the region, "I don't care how many years of therapy these kids get, or whether they graduate from high school . . . if they are immediately deportable when they turn 18, unable to work legally, ineligible for financial aid."[22] Her sentence tapered off but the implications were clear—all the services in the world wouldn't help eighteen-year-olds navigate life in the United States without legal status, nor when they ended up deported to a country with no social support, no credentials, and no language skills.

While detection was the primary problem that the RLA lawyers I spoke with felt they faced, an additional problem was one of jurisdiction—not between nation-states, but between federal and state courts. The problem of jurisdiction stemmed from the fact that although immigration court, a federal court, was needed to make the ruling that an individual qualified for immigration relief, many of these decisions were based on establishing that the applicant was a victim of abuse. Congressional legislation, based on determinations that immigration judges were not qualified to make rulings about child welfare, specified that in order for a child to qualify for a law like SIJS, a state court, such as a dependency court or a family court, must take jurisdiction. However, the state court would only take jurisdiction of a minor if it determined that the child's circumstances required protective custody. The problem, Katya pointed out, was that state courts categorized children who were in a federal system, such as those housed in detention centers for unaccompanied minors provided by the Office of Refugee Resettlement, as taken care of. She explained, "This is a real barrier to getting state courts to take on a child. If the Federal government has this procedure set up, why should the State bother?"[23] These children were seen as safe from harm and there was no reason, from a fiscal perspective, that the state should take on the case.[24] But children who remained within the federal system would not qualify for SIJS and would languish in a state of legal limbo until they were eighteen and found themselves potentially homeless, subject to deportation, and ineligible, due to citizenship status, for legal employment or financial aid to attend a university.

One such obstacle to state jurisdiction was the child abuse hotline, a 24-hour staffed phone line that put into motion investigations into children's welfare and was the first step through which child welfare authorities might take custody of endangered children in an effort to protect them from further mistreatment. Katya explained that abused migrant children held in a San Diego detention center awaiting deportation, potentially back into the custody of their abusers, did not qualify for services via a call to the child abuse hotline. This was because, from the hotline worker's perspective, detained children were considered "safe from abuse" in the detention center. Thus, although these children might qualify for citizenship through the SIJS provision, they could not apply for this status without first being taken out of the detention center and placed in state custody. It seemed fair to say that children who were housed in a detention center or a homeless shelter were likely safe from their abusers in a short-term sense, though of course, many children experienced circumstances that might be categorized as abusive within these settings. In addition, this temporary "safety" did nothing to address the long-term precariousness of a child's situation or the potential of their return to an "unsafe" or abusive situation.[25]

When I remarked how frustrating it was that the hotline could not be called to aid these children, Katya interjected to correct me. "No, no," Katya clarified, "you can call the hotline. It's just that nothing will happen. They won't do anything about it."[26] I was baffled by Katya's assertion that a completely ineffective hotline call could be made. She made similar comments throughout our discussions, describing forms that could be filed but that would not be approved, and legal avenues that could be pursued with no hope of a positive resolution. Over a series of meetings with RLA staff I came to realize that my emphasis on the potential outcomes for children caught up in the immigration agency's detention system caused me to overlook the distinctions Katya was making between available avenues and effective ones, distinctions that were crucial from the perspective of an immigration lawyer. These moments of failure—the rejected hotline call, the form filed though its denial was certain—mattered very little in terms of the trajectory of the child on whose behalf they were processed. But they did matter a great deal, I came to understand, in terms of marking which legal avenues were technically available and which legal battles remained to be waged.

It is important to note that even for a child who was in state custody and was referred to immigration court for relief, the two systems worked separately, though in tandem. The dependency court, by recommendation of a social worker, lawyer, or advocate, could request that a child be referred to the immigration court. Dependency judges had to make this official order and could do so by recommendation or on their own initiative. At this point the dependency case was effectively put on hold in terms of planning long-term custody outcomes while the child, represented by an immigration lawyer, appealed to an immigration court for relief. Once the immigration judge made a ruling, the dependency court case could resume. Much of the training that Refugee Legal Aid and Pro Bono Lawyer's Guild did in dependency courts consisted of an appeal to dependency lawyers and judges not to terminate jurisdiction of a case until the immigration ruling had been made. This was because eligibility for relief via the SIJS provision depended on a child's status as a dependent of the court, a status lost when a dependency case was legally closed. A dependency judge might close a case, satisfied a child was no longer in "imminent danger," without realizing that this decision might simultaneously shut off an avenue to legal status and lead to the precarious future that so often plagues mixed-status families.[27] In this way, immigration lawyers appealed to dependency judges to incorporate considerations that were typically outside their purview.

Legal Entanglements

Beyond the question of state/federal jurisdiction, the child welfare system and the immigration system came together in numerous ways, producing all sorts of unexpected obstacles and circumstances. Lucas's case, discussed at the opening of this chapter, was a prime example of Wessler's (2011:53) claim that "Many child welfare departments and dependency courts treat deportation as the end of all prospects for family reunification." A social worker's recommendation to terminate reunification services for a deported parent, as in Lucas's case, was not final, nor was a judge's court order to do so, since a parent had the right to appeal this decision. However, the majority of parents did not, and could not, pursue an appeal from across the border, often due to lack of effective communication about upcoming court hearings, obstacles to participation in the court process or reunification plan, and lack of information about parental rights following a deportation. Parents who were not able to be physically present could request permission to appear at hearings by telephone, and would be provided with legal representation in the San Diego courtroom. Participation was inhibited by distance, by social workers' and judges' skepticism about the viability of Mexican social services, such as drug treatment programs or home study reports, and by a deported parent's difficulty obtaining authorization to cross the border or the financial resources to do so. For social workers, this distance, along with a lack of U.S. jurisdiction across the border, foreclosed the viability of pursuing a placement with a deported parent—this option was almost always considered only if there were no kin to place the child with in the United States. Even in such a scenario social workers might be more likely to support adoption by foster parents with whom a child has been temporarily placed, citing the affective bonds they developed as the case dragged on, as well as the educational, health, and life opportunity "benefits" for a citizen child who remains in the United States. As one dependency lawyer discussing barriers to reunification with family in Mexico explained, "A lot of problems are caused by a lack of confidence in Mexican agencies—actually any agencies outside of the U.S."[28] Lawyers and social workers alike expressed concern that children would not receive needed services and support outside of U.S. borders.

Although dependency judges were not responsible for considering immigration issues in their courtroom, they nevertheless played a significant role in these matters (see Figure 2). A judge's act of taking and maintaining jurisdiction made a non-U.S. citizen child potentially eligible for immigration relief and eventual status as a citizen. Furthermore, it was only by a dependency judge's court order that a ward of the state could be referred to an immigration court for consideration of citizenship status. Although dependency judges did not technically take a parent's citizenship status into consideration in the courtroom, many judges felt this status was impossible to ignore. As one judge described, a reunification with a parent who was "deportable" was a "very fragile reunification."[29] Some judges expressed the feeling that it was their legal duty to ignore this, while others felt that, regardless of the law, they were required to consider any information they understood to be relevant to that child's future well-being. Some judges also expressed discomfort with ordering services, such as drug rehabilitation programs, for parents they knew to be undocumented, feeling that this was not appropriate based on their state of "illegality," even as they acknowledged that it was necessary for the reunification process to proceed. In this way, the nationalist sentiments of some judges that U.S. social services should not be provided to undocumented immigrants came into conflict with the course of action they believed would lead to the best situation for the child.

Although immigration authorities had discretion to consider or to ignore child welfare issues, dependency court judges in San Diego County were, in fact, formally prohibited from considering an individual's immigration status in the courtroom and from weighing this status as a factor in custody determinations.[30] As one legal advocate explained, while describing a case of reunification between a group of siblings and their undocumented father, "Yes, it is a very tentative, very fragile reunification with a lot of instability. But the juvenile [dependency] court is not in the business of deporting people or following up on legal status."[31] The lack of official communication between child welfare authorities and immigration enforcement was crucial. Though it limited judges' engagement with the full circumstances of the children and families in their courtroom, it allowed parents to appear in dependency court without fear of being turned over to immigration officials. A situation where parents had to decide between appearing in court in an effort to regain custody of their child and avoiding exposing themselves and their families to deportation would have been untenable. However, it was quite difficult for judges to separate these issues from court proceedings. As one dependency judge explained, "Reunification is *very* tough across the border . . . just for obtaining services and the practicality of visits . . . there is no question that these issues have a huge impact on the possibility of reunification and the outcome of a case."[32] And although judges and lawyers were well versed in the requirement to ignore the immigration status of parents, foster parents, or guardians, social workers generally seemed less clear on this regulation.

When I met with Judge Marshall, who had served as a dependency court judge for more than a decade, she greeted me in her back office behind an official courtroom, where, surrounded by towering stacks of case files and outfitted in a button-up navy blue blouse, she presented a much less intimidating image than she did in her official robes. In our discussion, Judge Marshall explained that the biggest barrier she felt existed in cross-border dependency cases was jurisdiction. The fact that neither the court nor the social worker had any authority mere miles across the border from San Diego barred a multitude of reunifications that she imagined might have otherwise been possible. She explained:

> Judges and social workers technically have no jurisdiction across the border. It really is an arbitrary line across the San Diego-Tijuana metropole—it would make an enormous difference if social workers could go within so many miles [across the border]. Because this isn't the case social workers can't supervise visits. They can at the visitations room at Customs [the San Ysidro Port of Entry] but that's not a very good place for a visit and how often is it really going to happen? . . . It would be helpful if there were some formal collaborative practices statewide but since it's an issue in San Diego more than elsewhere, I don't think it's a legislative priority. Immigration is a national issue. I think it would take a national movement to promote legislative changes that might actually impact the dependency process.[33]

Although a U.S. dependency court judge had no difficulty taking jurisdiction over a Mexican citizen child in the United States, U.S. authorities had no jurisdiction over a child who was legally in their custody if that child was physically across the border. In this way, geographic location was a more pronounced obstacle and a more defining feature in these circumstances than either citizenship or legal custody. While numerous individuals I spoke with—social workers, foster parents, legal advocates—asserted that reunification was legally and technically possible across the border, no one was more direct about the challenges and obstacles faced in these circumstances than the dependency court judges with whom I spoke.

The clarity on jurisdictional issues that legal actors conveyed to me stood in stark contrast to the varied and contradictory opinions expressed by social workers, whose job was to follow agency protocol and policy, rather than to interpret legal code. Numerous social workers informed me that there were no technical barriers to placing children in the care or custody of undocumented adults, while others asserted that undocumented adults could not be certified as foster parents or that undocumented kin could not receive the financial stipend to help them provide care to a relative child in foster care. As one veteran social worker explained, "Officially, the first priority is always with family members regardless of citizenship or country of residence, but in practice, well in practice, of course, it varies widely from worker to worker."[34] Approval requirements such as home studies, fingerprinting, and background checks could in fact be carried out for undocumented individuals with the collaboration of the Mexican consulate and Desarrollo Integral de la Familia (DIF), the Mexican social service agency. However, many San Diego social workers erroneously believed that undocumented adults living in the United States could not be screened or approved at all.[35]

Indeed, although Esperanza was a foster agency devoted to working with Latina/o children and families, the agency had an institutional policy that undocumented individuals were ineligible to be foster parents, primarily because of the misperception that they could not be fingerprinted and background checked without being exposed to the threat of deportation. This issue arose when an Esperanza foster family was discovered to have an adult cousin living part-time in a shed on their property. Although child welfare policy required that any adult living on the premises where a foster child was housed must be fingerprinted, the foster family had neglected to disclose the cousin's presence lest he be subject to deportation due to his undocumented status. Upon his discovery the San Diego county licensing agency revoked the family's foster care license. However, the cousin could have been background checked with collaboration from the Mexican consulate, and without threat of deportation, had the social workers and family members involved been aware of this option.

During her time as program manager for Esperanza, Corinne explained to me that licensing an undocumented parent was unlawful and would put the foster agency at risk. Alicia, who became program manager after Corinne left the agency, similarly believed that licensing undocumented individuals as foster parents would expose them to the possibility of being deported and that it would be "irresponsible and thoughtless" of the agency to take that risk.[36] Many undocumented relatives of foster children agreed with this assessment, and hesitated to present themselves as a placement option for their relatives because of concerns about the risks involved in interacting with a government agency. When I noted separately to both Corinne and Alicia that I knew at least one undocumented family who had successfully fostered and adopted two children, this information was met with the response that the family was incredibly lucky and that the decision to take that risk had been a big mistake on the part of the agency.

Although undocumented parents were viable foster placements in accordance with dependency law, many social workers erroneously believed they were ineligible. These misconceptions came to have the force of law through dependency courtroom interactions and agency protocol. No social worker I spoke with intentionally violated dependency law. Social workers simply did their best to follow agency protocol and their own sense about what seemed best for any particular child. Because dependency court judges typically followed social workers' recommendations unless they met with opposition by the minor's or parent's attorneys, these misunderstandings could be easily translated into standard legal protocol.[37]

Judges tended to assume that social workers' actions were occurring in accordance with legal regulations and many were shocked when presented with evidence to the contrary.[38] The San Diego dependency judges I spoke with prided themselves on thoroughly reading the files for each of their cases. And though they knew social workers were constrained by time and agency budgets, they approached these workers as acting in good faith, rather than approaching them with suspicion. Judges also assumed that social workers were basing their recommendations on the same sets of standards and understandings of dependency law judges themselves possessed. And social workers assumed judges would trust social workers' expertise and their knowledge of each case in guiding their recommendations to the court. Judges might disagree with a social worker's recommendation or ask for further information from some of the individuals involved in a particular case. However, they were unlikely to question the process through which social workers constructed the recommendations articulated in their reports to the court. For example, if a social worker determined that a particular relative should not be considered as a placement option and included what seemed to be a reasonable explanation for that exclusion, a judge would be unlikely to question how the social worker came to that determination unless there was strong protest from a parent, child, or attorney involved in the case. The translation of social worker recommendations into judicial rulings was a process through which decisions based on vastly different sets of experiences, observations, and interactions came together to produce the authority of the child welfare agency. In this way, the individual decisions of social workers, immigration officers, and dependency court judges became moments where state authority was constituted and where the limits of citizenship and family rights were constructed relative to the state.

Deportation as Abandonment: Losing Parents (and Children) Across the Border

All the lawyers, judges, and social workers with whom I spoke asserted the legal right of parents to reunify with their children or to adopt their kin, regardless of their country of residence or citizenship status. Yet there was widespread agreement that there were numerous obstacles to be navigated for international or mixed status citizenship cases. Cases certainly occurred where children were adopted by U.S. families without due consideration being given to the child's undocumented or non-U.S. resident parents or extended family. Magdalena, a lawyer with more than a decade's experience representing minors for the San Diego public defender's office, met with me over lunch to discuss the obstacles she had faced in representing non-U.S. citizen clients as a public defender in dependency court. Magdalena was frank about the challenges non-U.S. citizens faced. She felt that most lawyers did not have the time or the expertise to successfully advocate for clients in these circumstances. She explained:

> Undocumented status doesn't impact a case unless a social worker or judge or lawyer is racist. Potential deportation is not deemed a "valid risk" in dependency court to bar reunification. The DIF can do a

> home evaluation of a deported parent who is "non-offending" [not responsible for abuse, neglect, or other child welfare issues] and the county worker is obligated to ask for services for the parent regardless of what country they are in. The DIF can provide therapy, rehab programs, and so on, pretty much whatever a worker needs. The law always prefers the non-offending, non-custodial parent regardless of country of residence over a foster/adoptive home but that is not always what happens.[39]

According to Magdalena, there were two tragedies that occurred with some regularity within the child welfare system. The first was a situation where parents were deported and did not know whom to contact in order to locate their children and attempt to regain custody. The second was when relatives wanted to be considered for adoption but social workers were unresponsive, failing to return phone calls or actively pursue the possibility of adoption, or when relatives were simply unable to obtain the necessary visa to cross the U.S.-Mexico border for the court hearing and were therefore deemed uninterested. These circumstances were regularly compounded by the likelihood of a non-U.S. foster child having working-class or impoverished extended family networks, circumstances that predisposed families to lack the available space, employment, and resources to present themselves as suitable options for foster placement or adoption. In these cases, Magdalena explained, the child often ended up adopted by a foster family, the court having determined either that there were no viable relative placement options, or that the parents had abandoned the child. In such cases, a social worker's report noting that relatives were unable to be located, uninterested in adopting, or ruled out because of histories of drug use, abuse, or a home determined not to have sufficient space for another child, became grounds for a judicial decision that moved toward termination of parental rights and a search for an adoptive home. Carlos, a former county social worker and native Spanish speaker, echoed a position reiterated by both lawyers and judges, explaining that there was often a certain resistance to placing children across the border or even approving cross-border visits due to the lack of U.S. jurisdiction. Although children may be in state custody, Carlos explained, if they were not returned across the border after a visit, or if they were adopted by their grandmother in Mexico who then returned them to the care of the abusive parents from whom they were initially removed, the U.S. dependency court would have no legal right to intervene.

Lawyers and advocates have widely cited the impenetrability of the Immigration and Customs Enforcement (ICE) detention center database as one of the reasons parents who were detained were at risk of having the courts categorize them as having abandoned their children.[40] This was because the database was not reliably updated, so it could not always accurately determine whether parents had been detained and, if so, where they might be located.[41] Court protocol required that, at a minimum, multiple letters must be sent to the "last known address" of any parent on record. As long as that requirement was met, a court case could proceed, even with such decisions as the termination of parental rights and the legal adoption of a child. Thus, even for social workers who imagined that an unanswered letter might indicate a detained or deported parent, the ICE database did little to facilitate their continued search for an absent parent.

Social workers were required to make a "good faith" effort to ask any known relatives for contact information or knowledge of the parents' whereabouts. If this effort proved unsuccessful, courts would determine that parents had abandoned their children, even though the parents could very likely have been detained or deported and unable to locate their child or gain any knowledge of court proceedings. For example, a San Diego County Child Welfare policy document on how to locate a parent in Mexico with the help of the Mexican consulate in San Diego instructed social workers to provide the full name of a child's parents, the date of birth and location of birth of that child, and any information about a current address, phone number, or other relatives. The document noted, "A letter of 'insufficient information' will be produced [by the consulate] if the above information is not provided. This letter could be used to show search efforts for Court purposes," suggesting that it was the effort, not the result, that might matter most to the court. County social workers legitimately made efforts to locate the parents of the foster children on their caseload. Yet the paper trail social workers created through sending multiple letters and inquiries served primarily to substantiate the claim that protocol had been followed prior to a court decision to terminate parental rights or approve an adoption.

This issue arose in numerous cases. For example, one adoptive mother explained to me that the court had been unable to locate the biological father of her adopted son during his dependency court proceedings. It turned out that he had left San Diego County for Los Angeles, and had been difficult to trace due to his undocumented status. He had appeared a few years later asking whether it was too late to fight for custody of his child. The social worker explained to him that it was, since his son had been legally adopted, but that his child could find him if he chose to when he turned eighteen.[42]

Notably, it was common that lawyers, judges, and social workers were unclear about whether a child had actually been willfully abandoned.[43] Missing parents were a common part of the dependency court process, and cross-border cases made parents particularly difficult to locate. During a hearing I attended, the judge asked an eight-year-old foster child if he knew the whereabouts of his mother. He shook his head, shyly clutching the stuffed flamingo he had chosen from the judge's shelf of toys. The judge then asked the boy's father, who was present at the court hearing. He responded through the court translator, "All I know is that she is staying with an uncle and aunt."[44] When asked if he knew their names, he responded with a single name, which sounded like "Barí." The judge smiled, thanked him, and directed the county attorney to continue to look for information.

Under these sorts of circumstances, social workers went through the motions of mailing letters to out of date addresses because they were required to do so, not because they expected these letters to produce results. The gaps and fissures in this system were not moments of breakdown but part of the routine dependency court process. In other words, the translation of a detained parent into an abandoning one, or an undocumented relative into an unsuitable placement for a child, were not aberrant exceptions but part of the everyday workings of the child welfare system. These decisions enabled the child welfare system social workers to doggedly pursue their charge to remove children from circumstances that had been deemed to be "unfit" into stable, permanent homes and families. Although a determination of willful abandonment was a weighty accusation to level at an absent parent, it was a necessary element of a system focused on moving children into permanent situations as quickly as possible.[45]

There were two exceptions to the complete severance of family ties: guardianship and long-term foster care. If the judge ordered either of these options, then parents were not awarded physical custody of their child but maintained their legal parental rights, albeit with little ability to exercise them. Long-term foster care, either with a foster family or in an institutional setting, was most commonly chosen for children who were considered "unadoptable," those who had reached their teenage years in foster care or those with severe mental health problems, medical needs, or behavioral issues.[46] A guardianship arrangement was often used when children were placed with a member of their extended family or an older sibling, someone willing to care for them in the long term, but unwilling, often because of a relationship with the biological parents, to legally assume parental rights. Courts and current legislation categorized these liminal states of long-term foster care or guardianship as the least desirable of outcomes for a child welfare case as they increased children's experiences of a drawn out state of instability and temporary care in contrast to adoption which secured a child a new, and permanent, legal family.

These policies existed in response to an overburdened child welfare system, lacking both time and sufficient funds, and eager to move children to stable homes and close their cases as quickly as possible. Prevailing notions of child development bolstered this approach through an assertion that the most damaging aspect of the life of foster children was not the abuse they may have experienced but the period of time they remained in limbo. In this liminal state, research suggested, foster children were subject to frequent changes of location and lacked a sense of stability and permanent caregivers.[47] In this way, the child welfare system was more focused on children's stable futures than on the potentially problematic circumstances of their removal and entry into the foster care system.

These policies, coupled with a child welfare system that was not able to reliably locate detainees or deportees, alongside immigration officials who were not required to consider child welfare issues, created situations where some parents with no history or evidence of abuse lost custody of their children without an opportunity to participate in the process or appeal a judge's ruling. In these cases the lack of communication between international social service agencies and the opacity of the detention and deportation system in the United States effected a translation where physical absence could become understood as a willful abandonment and in many cases led to the legal termination of parental rights. In this way, the entanglement of these two legal systems through individual child welfare cases produced the vulnerability of undocumented or non-U.S. resident Latina/o families before the law, a vulnerability that could not be mitigated by an effective lawyer or by the worthiness of a particular parent's claim to custody of the child.

Jurisdictional Limits and the "Problem" of Poverty

Although many individuals I spoke with did acknowledge, in vague terms, that there was racism and prejudice against Latinos and Mexican nationals within the foster care system, nobody admitted to experiencing a specific example of such prejudice. No social worker, lawyer, advocate, or foster parent ever articulated a feeling of having witnessed instances where an individual was attempting to terminate the parental rights of Tijuana residents or Spanish-speakers due to explicitly racist motives. However, many did note that there was structural prejudice against Mexican nationals, largely due to jurisdictional issues in the border region and to the limits of cross-border reunification.

Jaime was a CASA with years of experience working with bilingual families caught up in the child welfare system. He explained that if a family lived in San Diego, a judge could order a parent and child to be reunified along with stipulating myriad support services such as food and housing support, therapy, or subsidized child care. However, because a San Diego court's authority did not extend across the border, in order to reunify a child with a parent residing in Tijuana, the judge had to be confident that the parent could provide for the child "on their own."[48] In Jaime's view, this led to de facto termination of parental rights for parents residing in Mexico who were impoverished or who a judge assumed lacked access to necessary resources, but who would have qualified to reunify if they had been eligible for services potentially available to them if they resided in the United States. In this way, structural prejudice against Latina/o families was perpetuated regardless of the disposition of social workers who might be theoretically open to cross-border reunification.

Similar views were articulated by numerous foster parents who, with the exception of those accused of physically or sexually abusing their children, saw the biological parents of their foster or adopted children not as bad parents, but as parents confronted with a "legitimate lack of resources." Many foster parents asserted that biological parents did love their children but were beleaguered by obstacles to transportation and to balancing their work schedules with court-ordered therapy, parenting classes, rehabilitation programs, and weekly visitations. Biological parents also articulated frustration with these requirements, which they sometimes saw as secondary to more pressing requirements of negotiating food, employment, and housing concerns.

Social workers, like foster parents, frequently expressed sensitivity to the obstacles biological parents confronted. However, often in the same breath, they asserted that biological parents needed to do whatever it took to get their children back, and that if they failed to do so it was because they did not truly want to reunite their family. Many foster parents and social workers who had never experienced the removal of their own children asserted that if they found themselves in these circumstances they would certainly do whatever it took to keep from missing a visitation entirely or from arriving late to class. In this way, social workers and foster parents, although aware of the substantial obstacles biological parents faced in their daily efforts to regain custody of their children, managed to disregard this knowledge and to assess parents' actions in relation to their desire, not their capability, to meet agency requirements.

Many social workers acknowledged that biological parents were in an almost impossible predicament where they had to maintain secure employment and housing to demonstrate that they could provide a stable home for their children to return to, while also consistently participating in court-ordered programs as well as visitation schedules negotiated with foster parents. Although foster parents were encouraged to accommodate biological parents' schedules, many foster parents preferred to limit weekend and evening visitations in order to preserve their own "family" time. These limits sometimes caused biological parents to struggle to fit visitations into their busy schedules of work, therapy, and other required services. Biological parents who did not appear for visitation or who showed up late or left early were seen as lacking care and commitment to reunifying with their child. Yet these parents, many of whom lacked their own vehicles, often had to navigate multiple bus transfers, two hours or more of wait time at the border if they were traveling from Tijuana, and concern about losing their job if they canceled or modified their schedule too often. Furthermore, undocumented parents were particularly susceptible to the risk of losing their employment if they were seen as unreliable or unavailable and had little recourse if they believed they had been unfairly terminated (Gleeson 2010). Even as social workers often overlooked and devalued the obstacles biological parents faced, these same workers confronted their own obstacles to facilitating successful family reunification when they confronted the complexity of cross-border cases.

Reunification Across Borders

Social workers, particularly those who were bilingual, often articulated a sense that they had to go above and beyond their daily requirements in order to enact a successful cross-border reunification. With thirty or more cases per worker, translating into far less than one day per month per case, most social workers did not blame themselves when they were unable to put in this extra effort, nor did they expect other social workers to do so. However, their inaction often resulted in a foster child being adopted by a U.S. foster family or remaining in a residential facility rather than being reunified with their parents or placed with relatives internationally. The extra effort necessary to facilitate a cross-border reunification often involved tracking down parents' whereabouts using international liaison and consulate services, navigating the maze of immigration bureaucracy in an effort to facilitate cross-border visitations and court hearings, and requesting help from foreign social service agencies, such as the DIF in Mexico.

Like the U.S. Child Welfare System, foreign social service agencies could also provide home studies, background checks, parenting classes, or supervised visits. However, collaborative endeavors with foreign social service agencies were complex to facilitate, given disparities in agency size, focus, protocol, and practice. This collaboration was particularly difficult in a city like Tijuana, which had a population of over one million residents and, in 2010–2011, employed only eight social workers for the entire city. San Diego, by contrast, had a population of roughly 1.3 million residents during this same time period and employed over 1,500 social workers. A lack of Tijuana social workers fueled San Diego social workers' assumptions that Mexican social services were not up to necessary standards, enabling them to more easily discount the efficacy of pursuing cross-border custody options.

Carlos, the former county social worker mentioned above, described a case in which he was advocating for the adoption of a sibling group of children by their aunt in Guatemala. The court supported his recommendation over the recommendation of the attorney who represented the sibling group, who preferred the two youngest siblings to be adopted by their foster family and afforded the "luxuries" of U.S. citizenship. Carlos then had to face the difficult task of acquiring the visa necessary for the aunt to come visit the children. This visit was mandatory to allow the child welfare agency in San Diego to assess her relationship with her nieces and nephews in order to approve the adoption. Although Carlos had contacted the visa office to explain the aunt's situation, her application was denied because she did not possess the necessary funds to demonstrate to immigration authorities that she would not overstay her visa in the United States. After numerous phone calls during which he was told nothing could be done, Carlos managed to contact an official at the consulate who was able to issue a humanitarian visa and the children were eventually sent to Guatemala to live together with their aunt. Although the reunification was ultimately successful, Carlos recounted this story as a demonstration of the failure of the system to accommodate cross-border reunifications and the lengths to which a social worker had to go to make it happen. He asked, shaking his head, "what worker is going to take the time to make all the necessary phone calls and not give up in such a situation?"[49]

I have aimed here to emphasize the fragile position of parents attempting to reunify with their children while entangled in the cross-border politics of citizenship and illegality. In foregrounding this fragility, I suggest that the immigration enforcement system's inattention to child welfare issues, coupled with the child welfare system's inability or unwillingness to attend to cross-border issues, led, in many cases, to the termination of parental rights. As such, the child welfare system was one way Latina/o families were denied full citizenship and rights in the nation. However, because dependency judges were legally barred from considering a parent's citizenship in the courtroom, this inattention, which frequently had devastating results, could also create a space of possibility for parents and children to be reunified. It is these moments of possibility that I turn to below.

Creative Navigations, Legal Loopholes, Advocacy

Jaime, the court appointed special advocate introduced above, worked with children who were caught up in the foster care system, advocating for their wishes in court and attempting to guide their case toward whatever he understood to be the best outcome possible. At the time I met Jaime in 2010, he had been working as a CASA for several years, focusing on cases involving Spanish-speaking families because of his skills as a bilingual speaker and his status as a former Mexican national, which enabled him to forge relationships with Spanish-speaking parents and to more effectively navigate institutions on both sides of the border.

Jaime was a well-established businessman in the local community, with silvering hair and a neatly trimmed mustache. He greeted me with a firm handshake and an enthusiasm for my interest in cross-border child welfare issues. After giving Jaime a brief overview of my research goals and outlining my hopes for our conversation, I asked him how feasible it was in his experience for reunifications to happen across the border. Jaime was dismissive of the formal system that was supposed to facilitate communication across the border, explaining that you needed someone like him who was willing to cross the border to find a relative and able to navigate Tijuana streets to track someone down at a vague address. Without that, he claimed, parents would routinely be lost and extended family members would remain unfound.[50]

Tijuana was notorious for its lack of street signs. It was common practice, even for local residents, to use a series of landmarks rather than street names to arrive at a given destination. It took an intrepid driver to navigate Tijuana's streets, which ranged from pothole-filled narrow dirt roads to broad boulevards in the center of the city, with roundabouts of six lanes circling the city's monuments. Like many cities that had experienced a condensed period of explosive population growth, Tijuana's roadways were sprawling and dense, the antithesis of a predictable grid. This encouraged a driving style that was both aggressive and friendly, where cars might pause within an inch of each other's bumpers, but where drivers would block traffic to wave you through a left turn from the far right lane, or help push your broken-down car through the border line without complaint. The geographic distance from San Diego child welfare offices to Tijuana neighborhoods was minimal, particularly since a substantial portion of child welfare activity was located in the central or southern parts of San Diego County. However, the lengthy ordeal of border crossing and the complexity of navigating Tijuana's streets, particularly for San Diego social workers who were not Spanish speakers, was a strong deterrent to social work involvement across the border, regardless of jurisdictional obstacles.[51]

Jaime described an ongoing case in which he was currently involved in advocating on behalf of four siblings in the foster care system. The older two siblings were Mexican citizens, and the two younger siblings U.S. citizens. Their parents had both been deported to Tijuana, but the father had recently managed to return. Since the children had been removed from their parents' custody because they were left alone and not because of an abuse allegation, they were promptly returned to their father's custody once he demonstrated that he had both a vehicle and a job, which were taken as evidence of his ability to support his children. Here the lack of communication between child welfare and immigration produced a space for reunification: everyone present in the courtroom knew that the father was in the United States without authorization, yet they were able to place the children in his care because his citizenship status was deemed irrelevant to the court proceedings. The case was further complicated because the siblings' mother desperately wanted to cross the border to reunite with her family. However, Jaime felt it was strategically valuable to the children to make sure all four were U.S. citizens, so that if their father were again deported, the siblings would not risk being separated from each other along citizenship lines, the U.S. citizens remaining in foster care and the others repatriated to Mexico.

In order to gain U.S. citizenship for the two older siblings, Jaime had to argue three points necessary for gaining Special Immigrant Juvenile Status (SIJS). The first point was that the children were dependents of the court, which was satisfied by their status as foster children due to their initial "abandonment." The children remained eligible as long as their dependency case was ongoing, even after their father was able to return to the United States and resume caring for them. The second point was that it was not in their "best interest" to return to their home country. This was established by the fact that the children's father was a wage-earner in the United States and there was no relative deemed financially stable enough to accept the children in Mexico. The final point was that the children were unable to reunify with at least one of their parents. This last stipulation was the most difficult, because Jaime had to convince the children's mother not to try to cross the border, as a successful crossing would immediately nullify the children's eligibility for U.S. citizenship. Jaime's negotiations were successful, and the older siblings were awarded SIJS before their dependency case was closed. Although the label "abandoned" seems dubious when applied to these children's circumstances, Jaime was able to use SIJS guidelines to effectively pursue what he saw as the most stable outcome for this family.

Jaime was not alone in advocating such tactics.[52] Magdalena, the veteran dependency lawyer described above, described a scenario where she encouraged a deported parent to give up custody of a teenage child as a pathway to U.S. citizenship. She explained: "I convinced the parents to give up reunification services so the girl could be put in long term foster care, get her green card, and finish high school. She wanted to be with her parents but they decided this was best; she could join them as a U.S. citizen later."[53] Attorneys and advocates who took this position argued that these children could gain their U.S. citizenship and high school diplomas, after which they could return to their parents in Mexico with expanded options for the future. Although such strategies may extend family separation in the short term, advocates expressed a belief that they created stability for families in the long term and opened up possibilities for children's education and employability for the future.[54] Such strategies were notably counter to a social work approach that often focused on immediate safety and an emphasis on permanency, without thinking as much about the implications of their recommendations for the child and family over the long term. Lawyers who advocated for these kinds of practices were certainly in the minority. As many legal advocates, including RLA lawyers, pointed out, the majority of San Diego foster children who were not U.S. citizens "aged out" of the foster care system at eighteen, their immigration status having remained unaddressed by their court-appointed lawyers.

Some might argue that this kind of maneuvering could be understood as a distortion or manipulation of the intended purpose of the law. But Susan Coutin suggests in her work on Salvadorans' struggles for legal residency in Los Angeles that "negotiating the meaning of legal categories to argue that their clients fit and attempting to make clients' life narratives conform to predefined prototypes of the deserving" (2000:79) are part and parcel of the work advocates must do to work within the confines of immigration law. Coutin notes that, "in liberal democracies, law is supposed to reflect generally accepted social norms and ideas of justice," yet it is common for legal advocates to equate "U.S. immigration law to racism, xenophobia, discrimination, exploitation, injustice, and inequality" (100). In this way, lawyers and legal advocates like Jaime put what they perceived to be the "best interest" of their client as their first concern, and then considered how they might achieve that goal within the bounds of immigration law. For these lawyers the necessity to navigate limits of immigration law, where the aim was often to admit as few applicants as possible, led to creative maneuvering and efforts to push the boundaries of the accepted interpretation of the law.

Productive Gaps, Restrictive Gaps

Although the various actors present throughout this chapter—social workers, advocates, judges, and lawyers—understood themselves as a team all working toward the goals of maintaining families and protecting children, each had vastly different access to information, institutional restrictions, understandings of the process, and authority in the courtroom and in the lives of children and their families. Child welfare interventions were moments where individuals were marked out as deviating from parenting and family norms, giving the state both the right and the responsibility to intervene. Yet immigration policy marked out individuals in different ways, and made delineations about rights that often conflicted with commonly held notions of the "best interest" of the child. As I have discussed above, custody outcomes for cross-border cases too often depended on whether or not a social worker was willing to put in the extra time and effort to locate parents or extended family, arrange visits and necessary visas, and work with international agencies to obtain the necessary permissions, approvals, and paperwork. This was made strikingly clear in the case of the Guatemalan family Carlos described. Ever increasing budget shortages led to untenable case loads and reduced resources and time for social workers to confront these challenges. Ultimately, it was faster and easier to assume that detained or deported parents had abandoned their children than it was to make the effort to locate them. And even the social worker most committed to cross-border reunification faced substantial linguistic, jurisdictional, temporal, and institutional obstacles.

It was the dependency court's directive to turn a blind eye to citizenship status and to the potential fragility of reunifying a child with a "deportable" parent that in some cases enabled the reunification of families. The same gap between systems that led to the translation of a parent's deportation into a form of "abandonment," as in the case described by Jaime, led both to the ability of the children to qualify for U.S. citizenship as dependents of the court (as foster children, due to their "abandonment" through the detention and deportation of their parents) and to the creation of a space where a dependency judge could reunify that family with no compulsion to report the father's immigration status to immigration enforcement. I consider these moments in an effort to capture what Coutin calls the "'shimmering' quality of incompatible realities" (2007:6), where parents were simultaneously deportable, unauthorized "aliens," and legitimate members of a court of law with rights to representation, court-ordered services, and the ability to regain or retain custody of their children. It is this "incompatible reality," a reality that emerged through the lack of communication between the two legal systems, that both created the precarious situation of vulnerability to the removal of one's children, as in Lucas's case, and also opened a space for maneuver, a possibility to reclaim children and reunify the family on legal grounds.

Lawyers, judges, social workers, and parents harbored widely varied opinions as to what extent, and in what ways, non-U.S. citizen parents and children were treated, or should be treated, differentially within the child welfare apparatus. Formal avenues and protocols existed, as did international agreements, such as the Hague convention, that guaranteed protections for children and families regardless of their country of citizenship. The existence of these policies did not reliably translate into equitable or predictable outcomes for children and families, largely because child welfare services was not an agency where strict protocol led to standard outcomes. Rather, it was an agency where discretionary decisions made by a variety of actors gave shape to placement and removal decisions, and to ultimate custody rulings.

I approach these moments of discretion, which are the focus of the following chapter, not as abnormal departures from institutional protocol but as part and parcel of the manifestation of state authority in the lives of Latina/o families, in this case via the child welfare apparatus. It is through these uneven, discretionary decisions, rather than through the routine or systematic workings of an institutional apparatus, that the authority of the state takes shape.[55] Determinations social workers, lawyers, and judges made could permanently sever the legal relationship between parent and child, activating the state's authority to define the limits of the family. As social workers made decisions about who might be considered a viable placement option based on erroneous understandings of the law, as immigration officers used their discretion to release single parents or to detain them, as judges ruled Tijuana social support services to be inadequate for a child's care, these actions delineated boundaries between the rights of citizens and noncitizens, produced and reinforced political borders and international hierarchies of nation-states, and enacted and determined the authority of particular individuals to dissolve and constitute families in the name of the state. These actions constituted both the reach and the limit of the state—fiscally and spatially marking the terrain in which state authorities were willing and able to intervene.

CHAPTER 4

Decisions, Decisions

One thing I know is that a good heart and good intentions are not enough.

—Corinne, Esperanza Social Worker, Interview, March 10, 2011

I was driving with Corinne, the Esperanza social worker and program manager, to pick up baby Maya from daycare, and we were late as usual. Corinne was weaving through the traffic lanes at well over twice the speed limit. I was trying to surreptitiously cling to the car door while taking advantage of our driving time to ask longer questions than the office work pace usually allowed. I had been working as a part-time intern for Corinne for several months, updating her database of current foster children, transcribing her handwritten notes from weekly visits, meticulously documenting the content of each phone call with county social workers, and generally producing an enormous amount of paperwork on the health, well-being, and weekly events in the life of each Esperanza foster child. These methodically constructed documents constituted the rarely consulted archive of Esperanza cases.[1] A few months into my research, Corinne had mentioned to me in an off-hand way that no one except myself or perhaps a newly hired Esperanza social worker ever read the notes in the case files. I had initially assumed that these files formed a substantial aspect of the decision-making processes that shaped each child's case. Because Corinne had mentioned that the agency files were rarely, if ever, consulted, I wondered what material case decisions were primarily based upon.

As we drove through the city streets, I asked Corinne to describe her understanding of the basis on which county social workers made their recommendations to the court about whether a family should be reunified or whether parental rights should be terminated. Corinne put hours of effort into drafting her notes after weekly home visits, typing up handwritten observations and adding any details she remembered but had not written down. As I accompanied her on more of her home visits, I often took over this task once we were back in the office, freeing her up to take care of other agency business. Foster parents also spent time meticulously writing observations during visits with children's biological family members, and keeping a written log of all phone calls with the biological family, recording any notable discussions and the children's reactions to their family members for their case file. Social work practice is, like many other bureaucratic contexts, largely a documentary-based practice. Writing and filing papers, compiling binders and files, faxing and signing forms, were a substantial portion of Corinne's work day, in addition to answering and making phone calls and visiting foster families.

Although social workers frequently discussed the case file as a crucial cache of historical information that follows the child from worker to worker, Bowker (2005), in his discussion of what he calls "memory practices," provocatively considers the archive as a tool not for remembering, but for forgetting. He states, "The jussive nature of the archive comes down to the question of what can and cannot be remembered. The archive, by remembering all and only a certain set of facts/discoveries/observations, consistently and actively engages in the forgetting of other sets. This exclusionary principle is, I argue, the source of the archive's jussive power" (12). In this way, the structure of the archive, in this case the child welfare file, determined what kinds of information could be preserved and what kinds did not fit within the format of the file. Interactions, anecdotes, and observations that were not recorded were rendered invisible as social workers resigned from their positions or passed the case file off to a subsequent worker. The social workers' impressions about particular cases and the way they characterized the members involved were critical to the development of those cases over time. Yet these were not the kinds of details that could be explicitly recorded in the file, although they did inflect social workers' notes about their interactions with children and families and guide what was recorded and what was omitted.

The file also served as a method of action for social workers who felt that their hands were tied by institutional regulations or hierarchies. Esperanza social workers often felt powerless, due to their lack of official voice in the courtroom, to contradict the recommendations county social workers made to the judge.[2] Former Esperanza social workers, as well as the organization's founder, had been chastised by the county for a number of cases in which Esperanza administrators had instigated letter-writing campaigns to the judge involved in cases where Esperanza staff disagreed with the county social worker's recommendation. This had led to a souring of the relationship between Esperanza and the county social workers, a relationship Corinne worked carefully to rebuild. Although Corinne, and later Alicia, often disagreed with county workers' assessments of what might be best for a particular child, they held back from openly disagreeing with the worker's assessment of a case. Both Corinne and Alicia took the position that while a particular outcome might not be best for that specific child, maintaining good relationships with county social workers would enable them to benefit more children overall than fighting for one case and alienating the agency as a whole. Corinne and Alicia focused primarily on supporting Esperanza foster parents in whatever ways they could and encouraging county workers toward decisions they thought would be best for particular foster children, without pushing too forcefully. The file was a place where they could record what they saw as bad decisions or incorrect assumptions, hoping that the records might somehow, eventually, come to light.

As social workers inherited cases, the file seemed to stand mostly as a record of past work completed and as a site for practical details, such as contact information for lawyers or therapists. Missing information was rarely detected, and if it was, social worker turnover made it almost impossible to recover. Workers did not routinely scour the files in an effort to discover and reinterpret a history. They did not often reassess decisions about what parent or relative it was best to pursue reunification with or revisit placement options that had been ruled out by a previous social worker. Rather, they turned to the task at hand—finalizing the adoption, terminating parental rights, or finding a long-term placement. The uncertainty of previous decisions and possibility of other interpretations were foreclosed by the materiality of the file.

The file is built as time goes on, but rarely reconsidered or reworked through investigation, except, perhaps, by a researcher like myself. Matthew Hull, in his discussion of the role of the file in an Islamabad planning agency, argues that, "The physical perdurance of files beyond the circumstances of their creation situates them within a horizon of uncertainty" (2003:290). For Hull, these files have lives that extend beyond their initial construction, as they can be reinterpreted as policies change over time and as the files move through the hands of different bureaucrats. In this way, files are constructed in response to the agency's needs at a particular moment in time, but the future volatility of the information contained therein cannot be predicted at the time of their construction. Yet child welfare agency files are rarely contested sites where new meanings are constructed. The files do record contestations, but the story they tell is not often given new life through reinterpretation or a new reading.

Esperanza social workers viewed the construction of the file in two distinct ways—as a hedge against future problems and as a potential source of danger for the agency. Corinne filled the Esperanza files as carefully and thoroughly as possible, explaining that during a Community Care Licensing (CCL) audit a file had the power to demonstrate that all regulations had been met—foster parents were adequately trained and licensed, children were routinely visited, and any significant concerns or medical issues had been properly recorded and reported. CCL was the organization that licensed all foster family agencies as well as the county child welfare office and the county's two emergency children's shelters. It was charged with ensuring that proper procedure was being followed at Esperanza in terms of frequency of home visitations, renewal of foster parents' licensure, and other such details. CCL looked into agency practices when conducting the yearly audit, a process that could result in fines, admonishments about any problems in agency procedure or incomplete agency files, or even, in extreme cases, revoking a foster family agency's license.[3]

This chapter considers how the effects of government interventions into families are constituted through daily interactions among biological parents, foster parents, children, and social workers. I attend to the way impoverished, undocumented, and racially marginalized parents are particularly vulnerable to the translation of their circumstances into the category of "unfit" parent. I begin by examining competing forms of expertise, asking how particular individuals are positioned as possessing adequate knowledge to make the decisions that affect the trajectory of a child's case. I then explore how the impacts of child removal manifest through the individual decisions and actions of social workers, biological parents, and foster parents, constructing boundaries of citizenship, worthiness, and national belonging. I consider the shaky, partial, and fragmented nature of the ground on which expertise and authority are claimed. I ask, whose knowledge is institutionally supported and who is authorized to determine what may be the best outcome for a particular child?

Corinne described herself as more meticulous than former Esperanza social workers, carefully recording the date and content of every phone call or interaction with foster parents, lawyers, county social workers, or other individuals involved in a case. Corinne was also infamous among Esperanza foster parents for harassing them until they completed their CPR certification or took the necessary continuing education credits to maintain their foster care license. Because auditing the files happened only once a year, the assessments were too infrequent to effectively protect the interests of a child by catching violations of safety regulations or visitation schedules. For this reason Esperanza social workers approached the files primarily as protection for the foster family agency. A carefully constructed file ensured that the agency would receive CCL approval to continue to operate.

On the other hand, files could potentially provide evidence of the wrongdoing of social workers or foster parents. Any accusation of abuse or misconduct against foster parents would lead to an investigator from CCL conducting a thorough reading of the files for both foster children and foster parents.[4] Social workers did, from time to time, purposely leave out some information about their visits or interactions with foster children and parents, particularly things foster parents said in impassioned moments that social workers feared might reflect negatively on the foster parents and the agency itself, or become fodder for a future investigation.[5] For example, one foster mother, frustrated by threatening phone calls she had received from the biological parent of her foster child, threatened to retaliate with physical violence. The social worker, believing the foster parent was just blowing off steam, said "I didn't hear that!" and changed the subject, neglecting to note the conversation in her home visit notes. Concerns about future investigations could not but have informed social workers' self-censorship as they wrote documents for the file.[6]

The holes and omissions present in the files were glaring for a reader who did a complete reading of a file in one sitting, with frequent gaps in the dates of case notes or cryptic notes about the outcome of a decision whose precipitating details were never discussed. The files that seemed to tell the richest and most complex stories were those concerning cases that involved contentious disagreement between the foster and biological parents or between the Esperanza social worker and any of the other players involved: foster parent, biological parent, or county social worker. In these cases all communications, including emails and phone conversations, were printed and documented carefully. Corinne lamented the fact that there was not time to make the case notes and files as detailed as she would like. She felt that most of the crucial information, the details that really gave a sense of the families and the children involved in a particular case, were in her head, or the heads of former social workers, and never made it onto a page or into a file at all. For Corinne this failure was most acute in instances of social worker turnover, a frequent occurrence at Esperanza and a broad trend in child welfare and social work more generally. In these moments, the institutional memory of the agency was shattered, and Corinne encouraged my development of the agency's database as a hedge against her future departure. In some ways my project to update the database was a scavenger hunt, sorting through partial information and scribbled notes like clues to the larger picture and sequence of events that made up a particular case.

I had assumed that the Esperanza case files were involved in county social worker's recommendations and court decisions, partly because foster family agencies, Esperanza included, billed themselves as providing detailed case information to the county social workers, thereby saving them time and allowing all the decision-makers involved—lawyers, judges, social workers, supervisors—to be better informed about a particular child and his or her case. Corinne confirmed she would send regular updates to the county social worker assigned to the case of each Esperanza child, usually by phone but sometimes via email. Although she offered them full access to her case notes, no social worker had ever taken her up on this offer.

Corinne described her relationship with county social workers as a partnership when speaking to Esperanza foster parents, but it was clear in her conversations with me that she saw herself as subordinate. Her relationship with county social workers was one of supporting or assisting, rather than advising or collaborating. Once it became clear that the county social workers who made the official recommendations about custody and placement decisions to the court did not read these notes in the file, I began to wonder what it was that formed the basis of those decisions. To be clear, county social workers took their own case notes; Esperanza's notes and files were supplementary to county practices. And county social workers did see agencies like Esperanza as resources for children on their caseloads. One county social worker I spoke with over the phone was astounded to learn that Esperanza foster parents were paid a lower rate than county foster parents, since she saw Esperanza services as specialized, and therefore, more costly. Yet FFA staff expressed concerns that county social workers were so pressed for time that they were not really able to appreciate or fully utilize what FFAs offered. As one FFA director of recruitment explained,

> Typically, let's say a child is removed, let me grab a situation that is not uncommon. Let's say there is a drug bust and two children are removed from that home and one of them is a one-year-old. The regional county worker is called. If the child is removed in North County then the North County worker will be called. The worker needs to find placement quickly, maybe in the next three hours. 'I need a home for this child who just was added to my caseload.' So the worker is not deciding which of the kids in her caseload would most benefit from [the FFA] but rather, where can I best place this child *now*?[7]

Yet the lack of information sharing seemed to me to undercut the degree to which an FFA's provision of more involved oversight and more frequent visits, touted by both FFAs and the county agency as a positive benefit for foster children with particular needs, actually impacted the trajectory of each case.

Corinne explained that from her perspective, county social workers based their case recommendations on their visits with the children (about one per month), their interactions with biological parents, which often included monthly check-ins and communications with therapists, drug counselors, or other service providers, their intuition or "gut feeling" about a case, and trends in agency policy. As the director of recruitment introduced above explained,

> Trends wax and wane, and depend mostly on the approach Child Protective Services is taking to removing abused and neglected children from their birth families. Recently fewer children are being removed as efforts have ramped up to provide support for families, allowing children to remain in their homes. Therefore the cases we do get are becoming more and more severe and less and less likely to reunify successfully. More than 50% of the kiddos we place now ultimately become available for adoption due to permanent termination of parental rights. We are seeing more severe physical abuse as well.[8]

In this sense, agency inclinations toward more aggressive removal practices or more conservative family preservation practices shaped individual social worker decisions and the sorts of cases that came into the system in the first place. County social workers were, on the one hand, constrained by institutional protocol and policies, and on the other hand, somewhat free to interpret their observations as they saw fit. In large part this was because the oversight of county social workers happened via written reports and regular meetings with their supervisors. Because county supervisors did not regularly visit or speak directly with the individuals involved in the case, unless a serious problem arose, reported material was largely filtered through the perspective of the county social worker assigned to the case.[9] This kind of discretionary decision-making enabled social workers to shape their decisions in relation to their gut feelings about parents, what Corinne described as whether they "liked" the biological and foster parents.[10] Of course, Corinne acknowledged, it wasn't that simple. County protocol, assessments by therapists or drug rehabilitation counselors, agency requirements for a steady parental income or safe housing all shaped and constrained social worker's decisions. However, the degree to which social workers connected with or related to parents certainly filtered into their assessments of parents' abilities to provide safe, loving homes for their children. For Corinne, this lack of oversight into social worker's decision-making was problematic, since it allowed "bad" decisions to go unchecked. These decisions then became the basis for the county social worker's court report, which typically formed the starting place for lawyers' negotiations and judges' rulings. County social workers could not legally fabricate or overlook whether biological parents were doing what they were court ordered to do, but they could grant extensions, overlook or emphasize small missteps, and make recommendations that might or might not have been well-founded but which the judge would nevertheless be likely to listen to. Importantly, social workers were not just recommending case outcomes but also determining the standards parents needed to meet for reunification, assessing the bond between parent and child, and making predictions about the future safety of the children they were working with.

I asked Corinne how intuition, or "gut feelings," about prospective foster parents informed her own work. She explained that when foster parents were going through the application process, she would often get a feeling about them, that something just wasn't right. She admitted she'd had a feeling of unease about one of Esperanza's current foster parents, whom she eventually came to like quite a lot. When she learned that their marital history was, in fact, quite complex, she felt more at ease, since this information explained her initial feeling that "something was just off." Yet Deanna, an Esperanza intern and student in a local Master's in Social Work program, told me after a foster parent recruitment session, "Talking to so many people, I get a sense for people, I pick up on little cues. But I get surprised a lot by who follows through and who doesn't, I guess you can never really tell."[11] Corinne admitted she could not refuse to certify a foster family based on a "feeling," but, she said, there was often some technicality that could bar those parents from qualifying. If that failed, she explained, she could certify them but avoid placing a child in their home. This was a tactic she used with Estela and Hernán, a foster family who lived in a trailer home that, as I describe below, Corinne was not sure qualified as a suitable place for a foster child.

Intuition, or gut feeling, was one element of what constituted a social worker's decision-making process, particularly in the absence of adequate knowledge about a particular case. They were, in this sense, visceral indices of bureaucratic ideology.[12] Alicia and I once had a disagreement about this issue after she spoke with a divorced father who was interested in being a foster parent. Alicia had a hunch, based on the way he had discussed his divorce, that this father may have cheated on his former wife. She did not think she should place foster children with him, "because of his values."[13] I pointed out that others might make the same judgment about the same-sex couples Alicia regularly placed foster children with. Alicia conceded the point, asserting that no one should be disqualified from being a foster parent unless the social worker had a "justifiable gut feeling." Alicia and I dissolved into laughter at this nonsensical idea, since a gut feeling must by definition be based on intuition, not concrete, justifiable evidence.

Although the dispute Alicia and I had ended in laughter, the intuition of social workers served as a filter through which they processed the always rushed and partial details of each case. Though institutional policies dictated what could and could not be grounds for disqualifying a foster parent from fostering, or for making decisions about whether parents would regain custody of their children, both county and FFA social workers often felt there were rarely clear guidelines about how any particular case should proceed. It was through the institutional processes of writing reports, weekly case notes, and making recommendations to the court that discretionary decisions became solidified into key elements of child welfare practice and agency protocol.

Social workers described their sense about each particular case as manifestations of their expertise and experiential knowledge. Corinne, in struggling with the daily anxiety and pressures of feeling responsible for the lives of the children on her caseload, described trusting her own intuition as a way to mitigate the uncertainty of not knowing which decisions would serve a child best. These feelings also shaped interactions between social workers and parents, which had material consequences for how each case might proceed. A social worker who "just knew" that a mother was a good mother might be more inclined to overlook a missed appointment or a single failed drug test if there were other signs of progress that could be emphasized in the social worker's narrative of the reunification process. On the other hand, these same missteps could be emphasized in the construction of a narrative that enabled a strong case for termination of the parental rights of a parent about whom the social worker "just didn't have a good feeling."

Judges officially made all legal decisions on the circumstances impacting child welfare cases, down to the minutiae of approving a haircut or, as one judge recounted to me, authorizing a sleepover between a foster child and her friend. However, because judges regularly had more than 500 cases under their supervision at any given time, they relied heavily on the recommendations of social workers and legal advocates "on the ground."[14] As I suggest throughout this chapter, this authority structure facilitated conditions that enabled the translation of a social worker's assessment of a parent into legal evidence and eventually, judicial rulings.

Corinne's opinion, one that was shared by the many Foster Family Agency (FFA) social workers and foster parents I spoke with, was that those individuals who spent the most time with a particular child were best positioned to know what was in that child's "best interest." In this sense, expertise was crafted not through knowledge of the child welfare system or legal authority in dependency court, but through daily, sustained interactions with foster children. The foster parents and FFA workers who visited the children weekly spent significantly more time with the children than the other adults involved in a child welfare case. However, because they lacked a legal voice in court, their opinions carried less weight than those of the county social workers, who typically visited children on their caseload for less than one hour per month, but who also had the authority and training of their Master's in Social Work degrees, ongoing contact with the biological parents and service providers involved in each case, and sometimes, years of experience in child welfare. Importantly, the biological parents who, in many cases, knew their children most thoroughly and had, except in the case of very young children, spent the most time with them, did have a legal voice in court. However, as I discuss below, by virtue of parents' entanglement with the child welfare system, social workers, lawyers, and judges often viewed biological parents as less than ideal parents, and these views undermined parents' ability to speak authoritatively about their children. Although constrained by institutional protocol, county social workers were empowered and required to make discretionary determinations based on the limited time they spent with children and their families. However, foster parents and FFA workers felt that the county social workers discounted the importance of their opinion, disregarding the fact that they spent the most time with the children and might thus be best positioned to assess the unique needs of a particular child.

Competing Forms of Expertise

The position of county social workers as agents of government imbued with the authority to enter any home and take a child into custody was central to producing child welfare as a space of knowledge, power, and expertise.[15] Through quotidian processes of writing and filing reports, transporting children, and authorizing their removal and placement, social workers inhabited an enforceable authority not based on their individual actions or knowledge but on their status as "social worker." This is not to say that biological and foster parents were not engaged in producing and shaping the actions and outcomes of the child welfare system. Indeed, social workers, biological parents, and foster parents often felt that other members of these respective categories exerted an inordinate amount of power and autonomy within the system, though these assertions were, of course, complex and contested. As I discuss below, the manifestation of the child welfare apparatus was not only a coercive, unidirectional system, but also a collaborative process that came into being through ongoing interactions among differently positioned actors. Rather, the authority of the social worker as an expert enabled them to set the terms of much of the terrain, defining the contours of "fit" and "unfit" parenting and determining to whom, and how, those categories applied.[16]

Carr (2010b:18) suggests that expertise is "always ideological because it is implicated in semi-stable hierarchies of value that authorize particular ways of seeing and speaking as expert." County social workers' assessments, and the official court reports where these assessments became formal recommendations, were backed by the force of their institutional authority, which was encapsulated in their official status as social workers acting in the name of the county agency. The formalized protocol of the child welfare agency, the force of dependency law and judicial authority, and the social workers' position as experts in child protection and child welfare policy authorized their assessment of a case and their determination about what might be best for any particular child. In contrast, the expertise and the degree of emotional intimacy biological and foster parents developed through the numerous hours they spent with their children were not commonly recognized as an authoritative perspective in the eyes of child welfare social workers or the dependency court. As Herzfeld (1992) notes in his ethnography of Greek bureaucrats, discretionary decision-making plays a central role in the enactment of an institutional apparatus. Social workers, with their capacity to literally make and unmake families, embody a form of state law with an inordinate amount of power, where the consequences of discretionary decisions are tremendous.

Social theorists (Mitchell 2002; Latour and Woolgar 1986) emphasize the processes through which terrain is marked out as the realm of the "expert." As Mitchell argues in relation to the concept of "economy," and Latour and Woolgar argue in relation to laboratory science, this notion of expertise, authority, and empirical truth was produced through processes of demarcating specific terrain as distinct from the "social." Social workers' institutional and legal expertise was based in bureaucratic protocol and practices that enabled a narrow view of family circumstances focused on individual behaviors rather than structural conditions. In her discussion of contemporary child welfare social workers Swartz (2005) notes that social workers often judged biological parents on the moral grounds of "good" and "bad" parenting, overlooking the knowledge they had of the financial and social constraints that limited parents' ability to meet the agency's standards and requirements.[17] As I discuss in further detail below, these interpretations disproportionately impacted racially marginalized, low-income, and non-U.S. citizen families, those most at risk of being affected by conflations of the consequences of poverty and racial prejudice with "bad" parenting. As such, the maintenance of social work "expertise" was predicated on a gaze that was narrowly focused on the requirements and expectations of the agency, a gaze that sometimes required social workers to ignore, or at the least to repackage and reinterpret, the messy particularities of everyday life.

FFA social workers often saw themselves as having superior knowledge of the case based on their weekly visits and their expertise as social workers. Their expertise was based on a sense of both depth and authority, on their knowledge of each particular child, and on their training in child development and child welfare policy. County social workers clearly saw themselves as the central authority in each case, based on their role as government agents, their social work licensure, and their interactions not just with the foster family and child but also with biological parents, service providers, and the judge. However, the foster parents often saw themselves as the most knowledgeable individuals involved in the case, based on their time spent interacting with their foster children. In addition to spending every day parenting the child in question, they also often served as the "supervisor" for weekly visits with the child's biological parents. County or FFA social workers, or staff at supervision facilities, sometimes supervised visits. However, due to social workers' institutional time constraints, the majority of visits were supervised by foster parents who were asked to observe, take notes, and assess the interactions between parent and child. This circumstance, while common, was particularly troubling in cases where foster parents were hoping to adopt their foster child at the same time that biological parents were fighting to regain custody. These supervision practices meant that foster parents were not only likely to be in tune with how their foster children were doing in terms of physical health, schooling, and other factors, they were also likely to be the adult who most often observed interactions among biological parents, extended family, and children, and therefore had a broad understanding in contrast to social workers' and legal actors more narrow "expertise."[18]

County social workers generally had more detailed knowledge about biological parents' progress in relation to their reunification plan, treatment program, or other ongoing programs, yet foster parents often forged a relationship with biological parents that might reveal information the county social worker involved in the case was not privy to. Foster parents, however, lacked the institutional position to translate their assessment into a form of recognized and valued knowledge. These competing forms of expertise—based on knowledge of a particular child, child welfare policy, or legal authority—constituted the complex terrain in which social workers made decisions that profoundly impacted the trajectory of children's and families' lives.

Corinne drew on the authority of her experiences in her role as a foster family agency social worker to take a critical view of county social workers' decision-making processes. Corinne and other FFA social workers I worked with argued that because they were members of small agencies focused on intervention into a troubled system, they were well equipped to engage with a degree of compassion and understanding beyond what county social workers were capable of, and thus to actualize a particular expertise in knowing what outcome would be best. The primary indicator of this distinction, according to Corinne, was that she regularly had fewer than fifteen children on her caseload, while county social workers often had thirty or more.[19] This enabled her to visit each child for a solid hour per week and to be in regular phone contact as unexpected issues arose. Corinne based her status as an expert on the depth with which she got to know each child, a position county social workers countered with the assertion that they had "seen it all before," meaning that they had seen the same circumstances—domestic violence, drug addiction, homelessness—and knew how a case would proceed without needing to know the particularities of each family. Yet as one dependency lawyer explained to me, even the same routine circumstances manifested uniquely in each family's particular circumstance: "The thing about dependency law, which is why I love it, there is lots of room for interpretation, lots of gray area, make our argument, make an appeal, have it looked at by the appellate court, that's what's exciting about this area of the law. So many individuals, the issue may be the same, domestic violence, abuse, but when you get down to the individual family there are lots of issues that make each case unique."[20]

Corinne felt strongly that county social workers often made decisions without considering all available information on a case, due to lack of time, and without, in her view, always having the children as their foremost concern. Corinne acknowledged that county social workers did have inordinate loads—not only numerous foster children but also obligations to work with biological parents, service providers, foster parents, and county lawyers. FFA social workers were responsible only for the foster children and the foster parents they certified. Importantly, of the three FFA social workers I worked with most closely, only one, Alicia, was actually a licensed social worker.[21] And none of them had children. Their lack of official social work licenses undermined their expertise in the eyes of county social workers and administrators, and their lack of children and life experience, due to their relative youth, sometimes undermined their authority in the eyes of the biological and foster parents with whom they interacted.

At a meeting of San Diego FFA staff members that I attended, this tension between FFA social workers and the county agency was clear. The facilitator of the meeting raised the problem of "premature reunification," a term he used to describe foster children returning home before home circumstances had significantly changed. He said, "The County turns a blind ear, a deaf ear to our concerns. We're stuck in the middle, trying to resist reunification when the families aren't ready, asking therapists to write letters. But in the end we have to comply without questioning the county's decision." Another meeting attendee responded, "A lot of kids go home right before the holidays, even though parents don't seem ready for the kids." The meeting facilitator then shared a story about a foster youth who was placed with her mother's boyfriend after her mother's death, and subsequently abused by him. "There were a bunch of red flags but the county didn't listen. When the county makes up their mind, it's going to happen." Another FFA social worker responded, "People should be held accountable for that, it's almost criminal . . . when you have five professionals, all of whom spend more direct time with the child, saying 'don't do it,' it's not just a mistake."[22] Though the details of these particular cases were not clear, the tension between the FFA social workers and the county agency was severe.

Further, the relationship between FFAs and the county was somewhat nebulous. The county child welfare agency was organized into geographic regions, and each region contained units that specialized in different phases of the foster care process—investigation units, placement units, court intervention units, continuing services units, and adoption units. Each month, Corinne faxed to each regional office a form stating the number of "current placements" and the number of "empty beds" Esperanza had. As Corinne explained this task to me I noted that this seemed to be her only formalized mode of communication with the county agency. She agreed, joking that because she'd never met most of these people, and because there was never a response to the monthly faxes, it was possible that none of these people even existed. She explained, "I don't know what they do, if they pass on the list of vacancies or not. When a worker calls for a possible placement they don't seem to know if I have an opening, they just call and ask."[23] It wasn't clear to Corinne why she would get requests for placements at some times and not at others, or why she would have Esperanza foster parents with vacancies for months at a time when she knew there were county workers out there, scrambling to find placements for children on their caseload. From Corinne's perspective it all came down to personal relationships between her and county workers she had worked with in the past.

As Corinne spoke to me about the gaps in her knowledge and her lack of a complete picture about how decisions were being made, I recalled a conversation I had with a county social worker about an infant, Rosie, who had recently been placed at Esperanza. Rosie had been with her Esperanza foster parents, whom the county social worker seemed to like very much, from the second day of her life. I had visited this foster family a number of times. Although they had not had a foster child placed with them in a number of years, they participated in annual home inspections to keep their license current in the hopes they would soon receive a foster child. The father, Hernán, was boisterous and energetic, often gesticulating with his hands to emphasize whatever he was saying. His wife, Estela, was a soft-spoken woman, shy but quick to smile, and though she was bilingual, she was much more comfortable in her native Spanish than she was in English. They had three biological children—a twelve-year-old son, a seven-year-old daughter, and a twenty-two-month-old toddler with a headful of curls and a glowing, chubby-cheeked smile. Although their small three-bedroom trailer was packed to the brim with a living room full of toys and walls lined with photos of their children, they were absolutely committed to being foster parents. They regularly expressed their disbelief at their friends and family who didn't support their decision to foster or understand why they might choose to "open their home" to someone else's child. They seemed ecstatic when Alicia, the Esperanza social worker who replaced Corinne, placed the newborn Rosie with them.

I accompanied Alicia to her first home visit with Rosie and her foster mother, Estela. Estela led us through her narrow kitchen and into her living room. Rosie was tiny, about six pounds, and covered with a thin layer of fine dark hair. She had been born a few weeks early and tested positive for crystal meth, which was what prompted her entry into child welfare custody. I sat next to Rosie, who was swaddled and sleeping on the couch, while Estela's toddler daughter ran back and forth from her mother to me, alternating between enthusiastically shouting "bebé!" and "surprise!" while offering me a pretend cup of tea. While I sipped my pretend tea and watched Rosie sleep, Estela spoke to Alicia and me about the case. Estela said that Rosie was sleeping well, contrary to what her doctor had expected. Since her nails were too small for Estela to comfortably cut, she had slipped socks over her tiny fists to keep her from scratching her skin. Estela's own children had each been between eight and nine pounds at birth, so they hadn't had any suitable baby clothes when they took Rosie home from the hospital, which she had left wearing only a tiny T-shirt and a diaper. Estela told us that Rosie's mother had fled the hospital without leaving any contact information. According to the county social worker assigned to the case, Rosie's father was a Mexican citizen, undocumented and in federal prison for domestic violence involving her mother. Estela said her whole family loved Rosie and were surprised by how well she was doing, given her drug exposure. Estela was considering breastfeeding her, since she was still breastfeeding her youngest daughter and the doctor had said it would be good for Rosie's detox process and help her to gain some much-needed weight. Yvette, the county social worker on the case, had encouraged Estela to take her time before making such a commitment to Rosie, as parting with an infant while breastfeeding would be a difficult task. Alicia seconded Yvette's recommendation to be cautious at this early stage about getting too attached.

When I spoke with Yvette later that week, she explained that although Rosie's mother had abandoned her at the hospital, they had now located her and the "alleged" father, currently serving out his prison sentence.[24] Yvette bemoaned the fact that even though both parents expressed no interest in gaining custody of their infant daughter, the case would proceed more slowly since they had to be offered services and given a chance to refuse them before parental rights could be terminated. She explained that even if Rosie's mother abandoned her for six months, if she then showed up and wanted reunification services, she could have them. If that occurred, then the case would be that much more delayed.[25] She explained that cases went much faster and easier "when we cannot find the parents; unfortunately, in this case, we did find them." Yvette wrapped up our conversation saying that she felt that the foster family treated the baby "as their own" and that she hoped it "goes that way" (meaning an adoption by the foster family), "but it is only my hope at this point."[26]

I understood why Yvette might not be motivated to pursue reunification services with Rosie's biological parents. And I appreciated Yvette's willingness to value Estela and Hernán's expertise as Rosie's de facto parents, based on the intimacy of their caretaking role. Yet I was struck by how much the trajectory of any given case was based on information that seemed to me thin and partial. Yvette had spent a limited amount of time with these foster parents: just a short visit or two and a few phone calls, in addition to the information Alicia had provided her about the foster family and their fostering history. Yet Yvette clearly hoped the foster parents would be able to adopt this child. And it was hard to imagine this would not shape her assessment of Rosie's biological parents, and the assumptions she had already made about Rosie's mother's motives for fleeing the hospital, should they have opted to pursue regaining custody of their daughter, which they had a legal right to do.

The problem of gaps in knowledge, and of a partial view of the operations of the child welfare system was not limited to particular individuals within the system but was endemic to child welfare as a whole. As foster father Trevor explained, "It is a real crapshoot as to whether the CSW has adequate info or not. I don't blame the worker but they're pushed by the agency to make a recommendation prematurely."[27] Corinne regularly lamented a similar lack of knowledge, relying on Esperanza foster parents to get the name of a child's social worker, the results of developmental assessment evaluations, or updates on court hearings and decisions. This information should technically have been available to her via the county agency but was not, primarily due to the difficulty she had in getting hold of county social workers, to faxes or emails that went unanswered, and the reality that communicating with an FFA was an extra step for county workers in their already busy day.

One CASA advocate I spoke with similarly noted the lack of information children's attorneys often had, describing a case where an attorney asked whether anyone had seen a child's parents, not knowing that they were both incarcerated. And Lucas's foster mother Liliana lamented her frustration that she was not promptly informed by Lucas's county social worker about upcoming changes to his custody arrangement: "I'm the last to know and I should be the first to know because it is my responsibility to prepare Lucas for the transition, whatever that may be."[28] Thus foster parents, county and FFA social workers, and attorneys were all variously positioned in such a way that they lacked crucial knowledge that might impact their actions and decisions. Importantly, these instances were raised not as examples of particularly incompetent individuals, but as routine elements of the quotidian nature of partial knowledge and rushed decision-making.

As I noted above, the former Esperanza social worker, Corinne, had been unsure about placing a foster child with Estela and Hernán, feeling that their trailer did not have enough room for a foster child in addition to their three biological children. Corinne had grown up in a family of substantial wealth, moving from a coastal town in Mexico to La Jolla, an affluent area of San Diego, during her teenage years. I imagined that her own class background shaped her feelings about Hernán and Estela's home, and her comfort level with placing a child in what she saw as a "trailer park." Alicia, the social worker who replaced Corinne at Esperanza, grew up in Chula Vista, a largely working-class San Diego area closer to the Mexican border. She disagreed with Corinne's assessment of Hernán and Estela's home, and placed Rosie with them. For one social worker this foster family's home had not been up to standard, whereas for another it was an ideal adoptive home. The discrepancy in these opinions was based not on particular child welfare regulations but on the emphasis of different social workers in terms of what they were looking for in a good placement, or what aspects mattered most to them.[29]

When discussing this case, Alicia, the Esperanza social worker for Rosie, also told me that "the mother didn't want the child."[30] When I asked if Rosie's mother had actually said she "didn't want her child," Alicia acknowledged that she hadn't, but asserted that she had demonstrated this by not showing up or calling to ask for reunification services. The slippage between not showing up and not wanting your child was particularly problematic in light of obstacles posed by such circumstances as drug addiction, detention and deportation, lack of transportation, or homelessness. These circumstances could impede a parent who lacked resources for making a phone call or who could not adequately express interest in a manner that was intelligible to a social worker. In these cases, the absence of a parent was the only information available to the social worker, particularly for a mother who had not previously been involved with the child welfare system. Thus the structural elements of the system that required social workers to move children into stable family situations if they could not stabilize a child's family seemed to encourage the view that providing services to reunify families was primarily a slow, troublesome detour to the project of placing a child in an adoptive home.

"What are we doing this for anyway?"

Taylor was sitting at the kitchen table in a white tank top, enthusiastically eating macaroni and cheese from the local Weinerschnitzel. Waving his spoon in the air, he exclaimed to Corinne and me that he was having a "Rainbow day!" We looked at his foster mother Anna for translation and she explained that Taylor was having a rainbow day, as opposed to a stormy, cloudy, rainy, or sunny day, which meant his behavior had been excellent. He was eating his macaroni and cheese reward because he had been pushed by another child at school and had told a teacher instead of pushing back.

Taylor had come to Anna as an animated five-year-old, brought into the foster system because of domestic violence between his two young parents. He was prone to fighting when angry, bed-wetting, and the more benign mischief making of any spirited child his age. Taylor was one of the few white children who were placed at Esperanza. He had been moved from a previous foster home due to some physical altercations with a younger foster sibling, although throughout his time at Anna's he had been reliably patient and gentle with the three other young foster children who had been in the home at various times during his stay. Anna was a no-nonsense mother, full of laughter and playfulness but not shy about setting firm guidelines and high expectations. Anna and Josie were both Latina. They had both been raised in large families and Anna in particular loved to be surrounded by kids in her home. According to Corinne, Krissy, Taylor's county social worker, who described Taylor's biological family home as "out in the boonies" and a place where "they let the kids run naked and wild," felt he was settling in well to Anna and Josie's urban, bilingual home, with rules about eating at the table, doing homework, and not jumping on the couch.[31] Anna had been working with Taylor, his teachers, and a therapist to address his more problematic behaviors. She set clear guidelines in her home and in Taylor's school, where she worked in the cafeteria. She provided rewards when he reached small goals, and when his behavior got out of control she employed a time out strategy to which he had not been regularly exposed before. Anna and her partner Josie felt they had been making significant progress, though there were frequent setbacks after each of Taylor's unsupervised, weekend-long visits with his biological parents, who did not employ the same strategies or house rules. A significant blow to this progress occurred when Taylor came home and told Anna that his mother had explained that Anna was "just the babysitter."[32] After this incident, Anna continued to work with Taylor but became more frustrated as she reported to Krissy the various issues with Taylor's behavior that arose after his visits with his biological parents. Anna grew increasingly frustrated with the situation the more she felt her concerns continued to go unaddressed.

The situation came to a head when Taylor came home from a visit and reported that he had again spent the day with both his parents. This was a violation of their reunification plan because parents who have a case involving domestic violence, whether children have been implicated in that violence or not, were often not allowed to visit with their child together.[33] Such parents were often forbidden from speaking or having any relationship at all. The requirement for partners who experience domestic violence to separate in order for one of them, usually the mother, to regain custody of their children posed a substantial obstacle to many parents caught up in the foster care system. Once parents were forbidden from relying on or communicating with their former partner, they often found themselves in need of procuring new housing, employment, childcare options, and a social support network. Many were not financially equipped to be able to live alone. Furthermore, regardless of a history of abuse or domestic violence, many couples were unprepared, unwilling, or unable to sever their relationship in the short timeline required by child welfare policy.[34] Parents had the right to address their domestic violence issues and attempt to regain custody of their child together, but a separation was the easiest and quickest way to regain custody.

The directive to sever relationships involving domestic violence, while often rigorously enforced throughout the duration of the case, commonly resulted in couples coming back together once one of them had regained custody of their child. However, interaction between two parents in front of their child in a domestic violence case could be, and often was, grounds for termination of parental rights. In court this was categorized as a "failure to protect," since domestic violence between parents, even though a child may not be physically harmed, was understood to constitute emotional and psychological abuse. As Anna noted to me during a visit with Taylor, this sort of requirement often led to parents being forced to choose between their child and their partner.

Taylor came home from his visit happy but exhausted and spent the next hour vomiting up the candy he had eaten during the visit. Anna reported this situation and the fact that his parents had seen him together to the county social worker, Krissy. Anna was dismayed when Krissy did not respond and visits with his parents continued in the same manner.[35] When Taylor's lawyer called Anna to get her perspective on Taylor's well-being before his first six-month hearing, Anna told him all her frustrations with the case, with Taylor's parents, and with what she saw as the social worker's lack of action.[36] The lawyer relayed this information to the judge in court, who scolded Krissy, for not doing her job. Krissy called Corinne, irate, demanding that these sorts of issues were supposed to be handled separately, not raised in court. Krissy asserted that this court incident would never have happened had the lawyer not been young and inexperienced. She expressed feeling that her authority had been undermined. Corinne called a mediation meeting between Krissy and the foster parents to resolve this issue, but she privately felt Krissy had little grounds for complaint and was merely upset that the judge had publicly scolded her for not doing her job.[37]

The meeting between Corinne, Krissy, and foster parents Anna and Josie went well in terms of repairing working relationships, but left Corinne and the foster parents feeling dejected. Corinne explained:

> Krissy emphasized that this is a DV [Domestic Violence] case, not one about Taylor's welfare, and while she saw the foster mothers' concerns as legitimate, they reflect a high parenting standard which the county is not equipped to aim for. She said that DV cases tend to be quick—the parents separate, one gets a restraining order, they work out a custody agreement, and the child is returned. She told us it ultimately didn't really matter if the parents are together when they shouldn't be, since the county will have no control over that and it'll be the reality of Taylor's life. Anna and Josie, obviously, were upset by this low standard of care but there weren't any explosions or anything so I think things will go okay from here on out.[38]

Krissy's position that the county does not look for good parenting, but rather works toward the "bare minimum"—no threat of imminent danger, is a standard, I note below, that was differentially applied. Krissy felt confident that Taylor would return to his parents, who would not have resolved their lack of parenting skills or their domestic violence issue. Although Krissy appreciated that Anna was working diligently to improve Taylor's behavior, she saw these concerns as tangential to the protective goal of foster care.

For Krissy, Taylor's behavior was an issue that did not substantially affect the trajectory of the case. This was largely because she had decided, based on her own assessment of the case and experience as a social worker, that the main issue to be resolved was the explosive incidents of domestic violence between the parents, rather than the behavioral issues Taylor displayed, issues that may well have been the result of his exposure to parental violence.

Ultimately, Krissy may have determined that a return to Taylor's biological family would do less damage in the long term than remaining in institutional care. This was a commonly held position. As a CASA administrator explained to me:

> We're starting to feel more and more that kids just don't age out well no matter what services they are provided with, maybe kids just can't be raised by a system. So we want to expand our early intervention, getting involved in cases before they become problem cases but also working with younger children. The aim here is to increase reunifications and adoptions and to hopefully shrink the pool of kids who grow up in state care. Because the statistics on kids who age out are abysmal . . . teen pregnancy, incarceration, homelessness. If you have "staff" as your parents, rather than an adult who cares for you, and is responsible for you, it just seems like all the services in the world can't make a difference.[39]

Krissy also stated, during the meeting, that Taylor would likely reenter the foster care system at some point. After hearing this, Corinne and Anna wondered aloud why they were doing anything at all. They also wondered whether removing him in the first place would ultimately be more damaging than his exposure to domestic violence, given that it would disrupt his family without resolving any problems. After this meeting Taylor's behavior problems escalated as his visits with his parents increased. However, because there had been no other documented issues of domestic violence, the case proceeded to move toward the reunification of Taylor with his mother. Anna almost asked for him to be removed when he spit in her face during a disagreement. Taylor's therapist intervened, arguing that his placement with Anna was doing Taylor a world of good, and Anna temporarily relented. Ultimately, Anna did ask for his removal from her home a few months later. Her decision was precipitated by an incident where Taylor's mother filed an abuse allegation against Anna after finding a bruise near the base of his neck.[40]

Although Krissy's portrayal of the minimum county standards for reunification was accurate, the implementation of this policy varied widely from one social worker to another. As social workers routinely handed off cases as each case progressed, as often as every six months, a new worker might change visitation guidelines or the terms of the reunification plan.

For instance, the county social worker, Tom, who took over Taylor's case after Krissy, required Taylor's biological parents to have supervised visits with Taylor, rather than the unsupervised visits Krissy had approved. This was a step away from the parents' progress toward regaining custody of Taylor and was evidence of Tom's assessment of how the case ought to proceed. These changes were based not on a difference in parental behavior but on the individual style and preference of the social worker and his interpretation of child welfare policy and what constituted a legitimate threat of "imminent danger." These decisions were also informed by budgetary constraints, dominant trends, and styles in social workers' regional offices, the preferences and expectations of their direct supervisor, agency emphasis on the often competing goals of family preservation and child protection, and the realities of compassion fatigue and social worker burnout.[41]

Under Tom's supervision, Taylor was returned to his mother's custody, a decision accelerated by Anna's request for his removal following the allegation of abuse. Tom preferred to rush Taylor's return than for him to experience another move to a new foster home, whereas another county social worker might have recommended that Taylor move to another foster home until his mother had technically met all requirements laid out in her reunification plan. The discretionary decisions of the social worker assigned to a case at any given moment determined the frequency of visitation, the specific requirements for reunification, and the likelihood that parents would regain custody of their children. Taylor's case raised questions about the whole enterprise of fostering, the purported goal of which was temporary removal of a child for protection while parents resolved the issues that had put their children in harm's way in the first place. But Taylor's case seemed to Corinne, Anna, and Josie to be an exercise in futility, an empty gesture toward intervention, which in fact did nothing to alter the situation or protect Taylor for the future.

As Scherz (2011) notes, social workers must navigate the tension between risking the destructive act of removing children from a family in an effort to protect them from future harm and risking the injury or death of a child who should, in retrospect, have been removed but was not. Even though such cases are very rare, the potential for lawsuit and media backlash over the death of a child who has been brought to the attention of child welfare services was a far more problematic outcome for the child welfare agency and the individual social workers involved in a case than the outrage of an individual family who experienced the removal of their child without good cause. This was especially the case for under-resourced or undocumented families who had little recourse to protest a removal that they saw as unjustified. The imbalance of these potential outcomes tipped the scales toward removal, rather than family maintenance, as the safer option for the social worker and the agency as a whole.[42] As one county social worker noted, of the three aspects she saw as the central goals for foster children—safety, well being, and permanence—she felt that "all the focus is on the first goal, the others are sort of seen as extra credit."[43] Although protecting children from harm was certainly central to social workers' decision-making processes, the tension between a family's rights and the agency's liability left little room for consideration of children's rights or children's own desires to remain in or leave their family's home.

This defensive stance was exemplified by Corinne's assessment of the case of Maya, introduced at the beginning of this chapter. Corinne and I supervised visits between Maya and her father, Patrick, at Esperanza offices. Corinne had made this arrangement after a conflict erupted between Patrick and Maya's foster mother during a visit with Maya in a public park, which ended with Patrick yelling and swearing at Maya's foster mother while she threatened to call the police. Maya's foster mother continued to supervise separate visits with Maya's biological mother, which had been proceeding smoothly. Maya had been removed from her parents' care due to domestic violence between her parents. Patrick, who worked as a bouncer for concerts and other events at one of San Diego's largest event venues, was gentle and tender with Maya during visits, singing to her, rocking her to sleep, rubbing Vaseline into her scalp, and spending every moment of his allotted time with Maya fully focused on their interactions.

For these reasons, I was astounded when Corinne told me that, in her opinion, the county social worker would never reunify Maya with Patrick. Corinne asserted that Patrick had demonstrated himself to be belligerent and explosive, through interactions with Maya's mother as well as her foster mother and the county social worker involved in Maya's case. "He's violent and aggressive," Corinne said. "But he's so sweet with his daughter," I responded, "isn't that what's supposed to matter?" "What's going to happen when she grows up?" Corrine asked, "She's cute now, but how's he going to respond the first time she says 'no'?"[44] As such, Corinne presented the severance of legal ties between Patrick and Maya as a foregone conclusion because social workers would not risk being responsible for exposing a child to the possibility of future domestic abuse.

Although the agency's policies seemed to position the removal of a child as the safest option for a social worker, as it removed the feeling of responsibility if a reunification or the initial decision not to remove a child resulted in future harm, not all social workers felt this was the best approach. I met Ruby, a veteran county social worker, at a training she held for social workers and community partners, such as therapists and counselors. Ruby dedicated the latter half of her career to educating social workers about how to make "good" decisions. As Ruby discussed social workers' decision-making processes and the institutional barriers to making thoughtful decisions, she was frank about the mistakes she felt that she had made in the past. She felt haunted by the damage she had done to children by removing them.

Ruby told us the story of one of her first cases, triggered by the birth of an infant who was exposed to drugs in utero. Ruby went to investigate the conditions of the infant's three older siblings, two girls and one young boy, who were in their father's care. The father was an ex-military man, who, enraged by Ruby's investigation into his parenting, intimidated Ruby to the point where she fled her first visit to his home in fear for her physical safety. His son had told Ruby some concerning details about the way he was disciplined by his father (he was made to stand against a wall and hold his arms up at shoulder height, an exhausting punishment for a seven-year-old boy), so Ruby returned with a police escort and removed all three children. The two girls and the infant were soon reunified with their mother. However, because the boy had a different mother from his (half) sisters, and foster cases were typically organized in relation to the biological mother rather than the father, his case was managed separately. With his own mother residing in another state, he bounced from foster home to foster home, getting in increasing amounts of trouble, and eventually moving through a series of institutional group homes before aging out of foster care at eighteen.[45] Ruby noted that following her initial decision the child welfare system "institutionalized him, pathologized him, and sent him on his way."[46] She explained that she ultimately felt she had caused this child more harm than his biological family had, in spite of what may have amounted to physical abuse. Ruby did not feel that her intuitive concerns about particular families had been wrong. Rather, she felt she had not adequately weighed her concerns against the perils of life within the foster system.

The main argument of Ruby's workshop was that heavy caseloads and limited time were serious obstacles for all social workers and care providers, but that these were not sufficient justifications for sloppy or rushed decisions.

She walked participants through what she saw as the four major pitfalls for social workers—burnout, cultural insensitivity, authoritarian attitude, and inexperience. Each of these categories, according to Ruby, created a situation where the social worker could not really listen or build the trust necessary to gather the information necessary to inform a "good" decision. Ruby explained, "I've been doing a lot of consulting lately, and part of the work is focused on thinking about what your 'product' is. It is hard to know what child welfare has for a product but after thinking about it awhile, I determined that the product is 'accurate decisions' and that more accurate decisions leads to better outcomes for kids."[47] She continued, "When kids are unnecessarily exposed to more trauma, that is not okay. When kids go to adoption and they didn't need to, that's not okay." Her trademark motto was "move slow to move fast," emphasizing the importance of careful investigation rather than the safety and ease of a quick removal in the name of child protection. As biological parents were racing the clock to avoid termination of their parental rights, social workers were racing the clock to move children back into their natal families or into permanent adoptive homes, to avoid children being raised by "the system." Thus Ruby's call to "move slow to move fast" did not fall on deaf ears, but it fell on overtired and overburdened workers and agencies, individuals who could see the wisdom in Ruby's words but struggled to find the space and time to translate those words into actions.

Institutional Roadblocks

Regardless of Corinne and Anna's disappointment in Krissy, social workers did face substantial obstacles to providing parents with support services to improve their family situation. As Magdalena, a dependency lawyer, explained to me, "It is not necessarily about a problematic CSW. They may disagree with the recommendations they are obligated to deliver based on county policy."[48] This was a central issue in the dependency case described in Chapter 2, where three children were reunited with their mother who was homeless, jobless, and unable to regularly transport her children to school or obtain the medication prescribed to her two older children because it was not covered by Medi-Cal. The judge urged the mother to "hang on" to her social worker's phone number and to call if she felt herself "drowning, sinking," or otherwise slipping back into trouble, but the agency could not really do much to support her without a serious threat to the children's safety.

Furthermore, the mother found out at the court hearing that her social worker was retiring. What was supposed to be a safety net for her ended up as an anonymous mass of regulations and rulings, coupled by an ever-changing cast of social workers and shifting expectations.

A substantial portion of the obstacles to support services were due to the financing structures of child welfare services, which provided far more funding for children once they were removed from their families than for services to prevent the initial need to remove a child or a return to foster care.[49] Thus, because of budgetary constraints, social workers were limited in the resources they could provide to families attempting to avoid the removal of their children. In this way, state support was not fully available until a child was a dependent of the state.[50] These financial constraints contradicted, and seriously limited, social workers' ability to effectively pursue family maintenance in a way that did not first involve the removal of a child into foster care. For example, Esperanza partnered with an organization to provide free childcare to foster children placed with Esperanza foster families—this same service was not available to families at risk of losing custody of their children because they were left home alone without supervision when their parents went to work due to the family's inability to afford daycare. Such a financial situation was frequently interpreted by the child welfare agency as indicative of neglect. This financial imbalance, structured into budgetary constraints, situated the child welfare agency in a responsive stance toward child protection rather than a preventive stance focused on proactive support and family maintenance prior to instances of abuse or neglect. In this way, budget constraints and fear of taking responsibility for leaving children in dangerous circumstances came together, privileging removal rather than maintaining parental custody as the easiest way for a social worker to improve a child's circumstances and ameliorate problematic conditions. Similarly, social workers often felt they were returning children to an untenable situation, due to the lack of continued services they were able to provide, and that it was only a matter of time until those children, like Taylor, would reenter the system.

In numerous cases I was involved with throughout the course of my research, county social workers seemed to be acting in a way that appeared to Corinne, to foster families, and often to myself as completely counter to common sense and to the "best interest" of the child. In many cases, these were situations where the goal of family maintenance sometimes outweighed concerns about returning a child to a family home under less than ideal conditions. At the same time, these decisions, seen by the child-focused FFA social workers as troubling, were in line with, and often spurred by, agency protocol. Jayden's story was a case in point. Jayden was a short, stocky two-year-old with a husky voice and a thick head of black hair. She had been placed as an infant with a county certified foster family, having been removed due to domestic violence between her parents, for which her father, a Oaxacan migrant farmworker, was temporarily incarcerated. The county social worker initially pursued reunification with her father, having ruled out her mother as a custody option due to mental health concerns. Jayden's social worker later decided to recommend termination of her father's parental rights because he continued to interact with Jayden's mother in violation of his probation. Jayden's county foster family wished to adopt her and the county social worker decided to move the case in that direction. However, shortly after this decision was made, Jayden's foster father was transferred out of state for work. Foster children cannot be transferred out of state, or even out of the county in which they were removed, without a drawn-out procedure involving a specific court process. This is due to the requirement that children remain close to the family they may be reunified with but also due to funding and custodial responsibilities for foster children being regulated on a county level. Esperanza was contacted to see if it had a foster family that could provide a temporary home in San Diego for Jayden, since out-of-state adoptions were notoriously lengthy.

Geographic obstacles, whether they are county, state, or international borders, pose significant problems for child welfare cases. This is due, in part, to differing policy and legal guidelines since child welfare is primarily legislated at county and state levels. However, these difficulties are exacerbated by child welfare authorities' hesitation, at both the county and state levels, to take on the financial and legal responsibility that comes with taking custody of a child from another region. As one dependency lawyer explained:

> I wanted to mention one more thing, Naomi, it's a conflict in the law and one that I think requires legislative change. Children are virtually never moved outside of the county once they are a court dependent—this facilitates the reunification plan and visits with parents, services and all that stuff. But the law demands that the county look for a concurrent home for the child, one that could become an adoptive placement if reunification fails. A lot of times there are kin that want the child, a grandparent or an aunt, who live out of the

> county and who check out as a good placement. However, it can take upwards of two years with court hearings and appeals before parental rights are terminated. During this time the child is developing bonded relationships with their foster parents and by the time adoption is an option county counsel is likely to argue that the child is deeply bonded with their foster parents and that it is therefore in their best interest to remain with them and be adopted, rather than to move to the home of their kin. It is frequent that county counsel will recommend this and it's a compelling argument, but one that fails to consider the importance of extended family relationships for the child.[51]

In this sense, the legal and financial constraints are not only significant, but are also based on the premise that keeping children in the county in which they were removed facilitates the family reunification process and provides consistency in schooling, support services, and local relationships.

Esperanza foster parents Edith and Arturo agreed to the placement. They were an older couple with grown children of their own, committed to fostering, not in the hopes of adopting but with an interest in helping "Hispanic" children. Prior to Jayden, they had fostered two young brothers for more than a year until the boys were placed together in an adoptive home. Days before Jayden's transfer to Edith and Arturo's home, her county foster mother decided to stay behind when the rest of the family moved, hoping to avoid a prolonged separation from her soon to be adopted daughter and expecting that things would move more quickly in court if she remained in-state. As the court case dragged on month after month, Jayden's county foster mother decided that she finally had no choice but to move out of state to be with her husband and other children. Jayden, then two years old, was placed with Edith and Arturo and had weekly phone calls with her former foster mother, holding the phone to her ear while kissing a picture of her, clutched tightly in her hand.

Even as the court date continued to be pushed back, everyone expected the case eventually to proceed as planned—Jayden had a loving adoptive family, ready to make their relationship permanent. Alicia and I were walking to lunch when she filled me in on the latest developments of Jayden's case. Alicia had received a phone call from the county social worker, "would Edith and Arturo be interested in adopting Jayden?" Alicia was astounded, asking what had happened to her former foster family. The social worker explained that Jayden would have a lapse in medical coverage during the process of the out-of-state transfer and for that reason the adoption out of state would not be approved. I stopped on the sidewalk, too horrified to move: "Whaaat??!?" "Yep," Alicia said with a shrug, "and now they are reconsidering the father, because they don't have any other good options at this point."[52]

The concern about a lapse in Jayden's medical insurance was based on the child welfare agency's responsibility to ensure that each foster child had consistent access to medical care.[53] It was also an instance of the difficulties that arose from a child welfare system organized differently from state to state. Foster care funds were built from complex funding streams that integrated county, state, and federal monies. States were reimbursed through matching funds for a variety of child welfare related expenses based on the number of children in their care, and most states were hesitant to take on a dependent already in another state's system. Because Jayden was covered by California's Medi-Cal program, a lapse in coverage would occur as she left California, and then waited to qualify for medical coverage in her new state of residence. Yet it seemed impossible that the system would privilege a technical concern like the complexity of medical insurance across state lines over the possibility of Jayden being permanently adopted by a family that wanted to adopt her and had cared for her from the age of four months.

The transfer of medical insurance for a foster child moving across state lines was complex, but it was certainly not an insurmountable obstacle. An Interstate Compact on Adoption and Medical Assistance existed to facilitate this process, and though all states were not members, all states were responsible for issuing a Medicaid card to any eligible child who moved into their state. This process was often delayed by miscommunications between state agencies and by variance in paperwork and processing protocol. Some states reported a lapse in coverage of up to six months. There was also nothing precluding a family from covering a foster or adoptive child under their own private insurance, although there were, of course, financial constraints to doing so. It was possible that the county social worker involved in this case was unaware of these policies. Importantly, I interpreted this possibility based not in a lack of caring, but in an overwhelming bureaucratic system and a severe shortage of time. It might also have been the case that the county social worker, unbeknown to Alicia, was using a concern about medical coverage as an excuse for changing her recommendation about how she thought the case should proceed based on other factors.

Furthermore, child welfare policy asserted that termination of parental rights was a serious decision, made only as a last resort. A reconsideration of Jayden's father as a custody option because of a technical difficulty with medical insurance suggested that a viable placement was an arbitrary decision where the aim was not a good placement but merely the best option available. Her father had ostensibly been ruled out as a long-term custody option because of his continued involvement with Jayden's mother, who had lost her own parental rights due to mental health concerns. Jayden's father had been convicted on domestic violence charges and had served a short prison sentence before being paroled. The social worker had initially judged the domestic violence to have been wrapped in Jayden's mother's mental instability, and felt that Jayden's father would be a stable placement on his own. Although his continued interactions with Jayden's mother were not violent, they were violations of the terms of his parole, ones that he purportedly lied about, eroding the social worker's trust in him. These violations, although only tangentially related to his potential to be a safe, loving parent to Jayden, translated her father into the category of a noncompliant parole violator in a manner that framed him as potentially unstable and volatile.

The fact that a lapse in medical coverage reintroduced Jayden's father as a potential placement option called into question whether the recommendation to terminate his parental rights should have happened in the first place. Or perhaps it gave the social worker an opening to reconsider her recommendation in that regard. Or the risk of placing Jayden with her father, where social worker oversight would continue for awhile, felt less risky when balanced with the bureaucratic obstacles to the adoption process across state lines. Institutional policies that demarcated the child welfare system's responsibilities and obligations, such as those that guided transferring health coverage across state lines, could not adequately predict the complex nuances of each child's and family's case and particular needs. These policies shaped and constrained social workers' abilities to address the complex needs of each family and each case, and often, though not always, privileged avenues that led to child removal and termination of parental rights over reunification. It was in these ways that county social workers sometimes appeared to foster families and FFA social workers as unfeeling bureaucrats, basing decisions on technicalities rather than sound judgments, while they struggled with the pressure to make weighty decisions while navigating the limits of the institution.

Navigating Uncertainty, Predicting the Future

The cases discussed above, while varying widely in their circumstances, had one common thread. In each case, whether the child was reunified or adopted, the parents and Esperanza social workers I spoke with felt that the case outcome had been produced by a series of decisions made by a county social worker who possessed limited knowledge about the case and the child, and who largely discounted the perspective of the foster and biological parents as uninformed. This dynamic was illuminated by Taylor's case, where the foster parents' efforts in working to improve Taylor's behavioral difficulties were largely discounted by his county social worker as irrelevant to his well-being, and thus to the trajectory of his case. At varying moments throughout a case, social workers made decisions based on their assessment of the parents they interacted with and the limitations of their authority, their time, and their available resources. This was particularly evident in Miguel's case, recounted in Chapter 2, where the limits of the social worker's jurisdiction to cross the border inhibited her ability to assess the quality of Elena's neighborhood. Biological parents, particularly those who were legally vulnerable through their undocumented status, had limited ability to impact the trajectory of a case where their own understanding of what was in their child's best interest differed from that of the county social worker. It was in this way, for example, that Patrick's attentive parenting was deemed less important than the volatile temper he displayed interacting with the adults he saw as standing between him and his daughter, Maya. Foster parents and FFA social workers, without a legal voice in court, and without recognition of their own claims to expertise and authority in relation to the particular children in their care, were limited in their ability to impact the trajectory of a case in which they were involved. The structure of the child welfare system, and the way that it positioned social workers as "experts," translated social workers' discretionary decisions—decisions inevitably shaped by assumptions based on class, race, citizenship, and nationality—into forceful legal recommendations.

Social workers' status as professional, licensed social workers and as agents of state authority legitimized decisions that were often based on their own individual proclivities. Institutional processes such as filing court reports and case notes transformed individual, seemingly arbitrary decisions into regularized and reasoned positions authorized by child welfare policy. Even despite social workers' best intentions, these decisions effectively excluded foster and biological parents' knowledge and relationships with their own children. These sorts of transformations played a central role in Jayden's case, where obstacles to interstate adoption and medical insurance seemed to override a placement decision that might otherwise be seen as in Jayden's "best interest," and shifted her father's likelihood of retaining his parental rights. Ultimately, social workers' decisions preserved some families while dismantling others, making delineations between safe homes, and "worthy" and "unworthy" parents.

Critics of child welfare policy, like Ruby, the veteran social worker and facilitator of a training session I attended for social service providers, were concerned not only with the rules and regulations, but with the quotidian interpretations that informed the manner in which these policies were enacted. The latitude social workers had to make determinations about parental "fit-ness" enabled social workers to make decisions another worker on the same case might not have made, as in the case of licensing Estela and Hernán to take in a foster child, or the decisions about Taylor's parental visitations that were made by county social workers Krissy and Tom. However, the positioning of these decisions within the boundaries and institutional categories of the child welfare system created the sense that these decisions were not personal ones but were instead determined by the limits of institutional policies. These sorts of limits were exemplified by the court case described above, where social workers and judicial authorities felt unable to extend medical and social support services to a family that clearly needed them, because there was no technical threat of "imminent danger."

Further, a social worker's status as "expert" in the realm of child welfare enabled them to rely on their discretion as an important tool of their trade, one that they trusted and described as a part of what made them good social workers, while appearing to simply enact institutional policy. It was in this sense that "gut-feelings" became a site, similar to the use of "best interest" in the court setting, that enabled assumptions and interpretations based on race, class, citizenship, or nationality to be solidified into law. As such, although social workers were key critics of the problems and limitations of the child welfare system itself, their daily decision-making practices produced the seemingly arbitrary enactment of these policies and allowed an array of concerns that were not supposed to be considered at all to emerge in child welfare cases in the form of legal categories—"best interest," "imminent danger"—and formal recommendations to the court.

As Ruby articulated, child welfare was in many ways an organization shot through with tensions and contradictions, unsure how to navigate the tension between family preservation and child protection. Was child welfare supposed to be a preventative agency or a responsive one? Was the foremost goal the pursuit of the best circumstance for a child or the minimum requirements for return to parental custody? The possible answers to these questions would produce vastly different decisions and responses in the everyday practices of social workers. These questions helped me to make sense of the vastly different case outcomes I described above, where cases followed unexpected trajectories, as in Jayden's case, or where requirements changed profoundly after the case had been proceeding steadily toward reunification for quite some time, as in Miguel's case. The same agency that would not recommend a placement with an undocumented relative because that relative might be deported in the future would recommend leaving an infant in the care of a mother who had her parental rights terminated for her three older children due to physical abuse and persistent drug use because she had not yet abused that particular child. In the former instance, the agency was acting in a preventive capacity, emphasizing the protection of a child from the future emotional harm of having a primary caregiver deported. In the latter, the focus was on family preservation, keeping the mother-child relationship intact until a report of actual abuse necessitated the agency's response. Without a clear directive about how to resolve these innumerable tensions—between preventive and responsive modes, and between the goals of child protection and family preservation—individual social workers were tasked with making decisions that produced decisive, permanent outcomes for the lives of children and their families caught up in the foster care system.

CHAPTER 5

Intimacies

Liliana had been waiting for a foster child for a few months. Earlier in the year, she had been called about the possible placement of a five-year-old foster child who was the same age as her own son, Bailey. The foster child was so malnourished he was the height and weight of an average three-year-old. Liliana had been prepared for the worst and had talked frequently with her husband about how best to help their own young son be thoughtful and kind to a child who may have faced challenges and experiences of which Bailey had never conceived. However, that placement had fallen through, as a relative had stepped up to take custody of the boy before the foster placement moved forward.

Liliana and her husband finally got a call for another foster placement, a four-year-old named Lucas who had been picked up by the police when they conducted a drug raid and arrested both his parents. They expected to receive a child who fit their imagined version of "neglect." When I spoke with Liliana about meeting Lucas for the first time, she laughed as she recounted her experience. She had been told only that she was picking up a four-year-old Mexican child who had entered foster care in the aftermath of a drug raid. When she met Lucas, she was confronted by a stocky, shy boy with blonde hair and blue eyes. He was almost a head taller than her own son and didn't seem to speak a word of Spanish. Becoming serious, she recounted their first evening together: Lucas's shyness, his unfamiliarity with their food, and his voracious appetite. She had given him a shower after their first dinner together, and described holding the shower nozzle to rinse him off, allowing him to scrub his own body in the hopes he would feel more comfortable that way. Liliana described seeing his pale pink feet and the smooth half moons of his nails, "Somebody was taking very good care of this child," she told me, shaking her head.[1] Like Emma's foster father, Josh, Liliana was confronted with the complexities of caring for other people's children, and with the meaning Liliana read into Lucas's carefully trimmed fingernails—that someone clearly loved and missed him. Although foster parents like Liliana typically expected their foster children to be clearly mistreated, this was often not the case. As foster parents formed intimate ties with their foster children, they confronted the traces of parental love, and of the intimate ties that often existed between biological parent and child. What an abused or neglected child looked like to biological parents, to foster parents, and to social workers, differed dramatically. The negotiations, translations, and misunderstandings that occurred in this field of intimacy are the subject of this chapter.

The intimacies of parent-child relationships take shape under the gaze of child welfare authorities—a gaze that brings intimate parent-child interactions into the public sphere.[2] When children are removed from their parent's care, it is often, though not always, due to highly visible interactions which have caught the attention of neighbors, teachers, law enforcement, or medical authorities. These circumstances—malnourishment, loud screaming or physical altercations between parents, drug use, or leaving children unattended, are the grounds for a child's initial entry into the child welfare system, often through removal from a parent's physical custody and subsequent placement in a foster home. Once removed, however, state scrutiny of biological parents takes a much finer-grained approach, assessing during weekly parent-child visitations such things as vocal tone, parents' attention and patience for their children, styles of play, discipline, and affection. More detailed concerns may be raised about nutrition, cleanliness in the home, a parent's romantic partner, or neighborhood safety. These concerns become the basis upon which reunification and custody determinations may be made.

Foster parents were also scrutinized in detail, both during the initial training and licensure process, and throughout their time caring for a foster child. They were trained on child development, nutrition, sleeping patterns, and nonphysical disciplinary methods. Their licensing process typically included hours of parenting classes on these topics, interviews with social workers, background checks, financial assessment, questions about job security, and a mental health assessment conducted by a psychologist. They were sometimes visited by social workers without notice, and they were expected to keep detailed records of financial expenditures and medical visits, aspects of daily parenting practices that otherwise occur without paperwork or formal scrutiny. I consider intimate relations between parents and children as constituted through emotional connection, and daily bodily care such as nursing, bathing, and rocking a child to sleep. It is not these actions and interactions in and of themselves that make them intimate. Rather, it is the context that delineates a zone of interaction typically reserved for family members, or within particularly sanctioned relations. These interactions are not normally performed with other people's children, outside kin relations or the paid work of a nanny or babysitter. In this way, the state both authorizes and expects foster parents to develop physical and emotional ties that transgress the social boundaries that normally guide interactions between adults and children who are not biologically or legally related.

Throughout this chapter I consider how biological and foster parents enmeshed in the child welfare system experienced the authoritative intervention of the state in an intimate, everyday manner that was distinct from the experience of other U.S. citizens and residents. As Sarat (1990:344) notes in his work with welfare recipients, "Law is immediate and powerful because being on welfare means having a significant part of one's life organized by a regime of legal rules invoked by officials to claim jurisdiction over choices and decisions which those not on welfare would regard as personal and private." In this sense, he argues, "law is not a distant abstraction; it is a weblike enclosure in which they are 'caught'" (345). Although I do not argue that foster parents and biological parents experienced the force of state authority in the same way, or to the same degree, I do suggest that the fragility of their family relationships and the experience, and impact, of the regulatory gaze of child welfare authorities, may be more resonant than seems at first to be apparent. Biological and foster parents often shared circumstances of race, class, citizenship, and language ability that increased their vulnerability and impacted their family stability. Both biological and foster parents experienced disruptions in the continuity of their relationships with children, the scrutiny of otherwise private parent-child interactions, and a lack of control over the children they cared for. Social workers acting in the name of the state were required to make decisions to remove and place children, sometimes abruptly and without notice, in ways that profoundly impacted and interrupted relationships between biological parents, foster parents, and children. In the cases that follow, I consider what it means to both foster and biological parents to be enclosed within the space of the child welfare system, and how this enclosure impacts their daily lives and shapes their intimate interactions with their children, marking out ideas about where, and with whom, their children belong.

Professional Distance

Corinne liked to include a picture of each Esperanza foster child in the front of the case file. She often took these pictures during a first home visit. We never talked about it directly, but my sense was that she felt that it humanized the file, and reminded anyone reading through the paperwork that ideally the file referred to a child, rather than reducing that child to a set of incidents and legal interventions. This strategy resisted the reductive language of child welfare that routinely referred to children as "cases," as in "I've got ten cases on my load right now," and referred to homes as "beds," as in "how many available beds does your agency have right now?"

One day, as I was looking for some information in the archived files, I came across Andy's file. His picture, taken when he was about four months old, showed him smiling and lying on his back, each of his infant legs in a tiny plaster cast. Andy had landed in foster care through a violent boyfriend of his mother's, who had, from what the doctors who treated him deduced, picked Andy up and twisted his small body, bruising him, fracturing his ribs, and breaking numerous bones. Although I knew this story, as I looked at Andy's picture my foremost thought was that he was a cute, smiley baby. I felt none of the horror, the revulsion, that seemed to me to be the normal reaction to seeing an image of an infant with broken legs coupled with the knowledge that the injury was not accidental. I had become inured.

Social workers were regularly exposed to trauma and horror; they saw the effects of sexual, physical, and emotional abuse. They learned about interactions that amounted to torture. They witnessed and sometimes participated in actions and decisions that destroyed families and permanently severed relationships. They protected others from pain and they caused pain. This daily exposure left many social workers feeling hardened; they regularly described and discussed abuse without really, viscerally, thinking about what they were describing. Others left the profession, unable to handle their exposure to traumatic events day after day.

Many foster and biological parents with whom I spoke felt that they could not remove themselves emotionally in this way or use strategies to distance themselves from the pain that often surrounded the experiences of their children. Biological parents acutely felt the pain of separation from their children and anxiety about their well-being. Foster parents soothed anxious and scared children, rocked them when they couldn't sleep, comforted them when they missed their mother or father, and sometimes carried them screaming and crying to, or from, a visit with a biological parent with whom that child had a relationship that was fraught with difficult emotions. As such, they lived the child welfare system intimately, and everyday, unbuffered by bureaucratic protocol, developmental language, and professional distance.

Although the majority of foster parents that I got to know through Esperanza developed what appeared to me to be intimate, caring relationships with their foster children, this was, of course, not always the case. Media reports of abuse in foster homes and social worker perspectives on foster parents who are "doing it for the money" (see Wozniak 2002 for a critique of this view), highlight concerns about blending intimate care with a financial arrangement. In the context of Esperanza, the monthly payments foster parents received were insufficient for covering the monthly basics of diapers, formula, and clothing for an infant—this largely eliminated concerns that foster parents were involved for the financial benefit, as most spent their own money to provide for the children in their care.

However, Esperanza social workers did sometimes express concerns about the quality of care extended to foster children by Esperanza foster parents as well as concerns that foster parents might be more focused on adopting a child than supporting the process of reunification of that child with their biological parents. Field notes from my first month at Esperanza documented Corinne's concerns about Esperanza foster parents who had "returned" foster children for a variety of reasons: pregnancy of a foster mother, illness in the family, displacements due to San Diego wildfires, or simply feeling overwhelmed by the demands of biological parents and county social workers. Other Esperanza parents, prior to the beginning of my own research and to Corinne's presence at the agency, were decertified for reasons that were documented as having a "dirty" home or having foster children sleep on the floor rather than in their own bed as agency policy required. These circumstances called into question the intentions of foster parents in a way that paralleled the stories of biological parents abandoning or neglecting their child, but did not often carry the same weight of moral accusation.

This distinction was encapsulated in Corinne's discussion with me about a foster child, Marco, who was in the process of being adopted by his Esperanza foster mother. His biological mother had abandoned Marco twice; the first abandonment had precipitated his entry into foster care, the second had happened after a successful reunification. Marco's foster mother, Janelle, had committed to Marco long-term, though his biological mother continued to appeal the termination of her parental rights. Additionally, Marco's turbulent early childhood experiences had manifested as a number of serious behavioral issues—he was sometimes asked to leave schools and summer camps due to his disruptive behavior, though his ongoing therapy seemed to help. As Corinne updated me on the adoption process she said that although things were moving forward, she would "totally understand if [Janelle] reconsidered."[3] In this sense, while Marco's mother's abandonment was seen as unacceptable and grounds for termination of her parental rights, should Janelle decide not to go through with the adoption, her "abandonment" would not be framed as "abandonment" at all, and would be seen as a measured, and understandable decision, at least according to Corinne.

Foster and biological parents took on a variety of strategies to survive their entanglement in the foster care system as best as they could, and to maintain both their dignity and their relationship with the children that they cared for. For foster parents this involved advocating for their foster child within agency constraints while negotiating for their own consideration as a potential adoptive home if a permanent relationship with that child was their long-term goal. For biological parents, this meant doing whatever they could to maintain or regain custody of their children, an approach that often took the form of deference to the authority of the state.

Deferring to the Authorities

Jennifer Reich, in her book *Fixing Families: Parents, Power, and the Child Welfare System* (2005), argues that deference to the authority of the state is one of the key variables that determines whether or not biological parents are likely to reunify with their children.[4] This deference takes multiple forms from accepting guilt, complying with court-ordered services, and demonstrating a willingness to change. As Reich argues, many parents confront difficulties and ultimately lose custody of their children when they are not willing to defer to the county agency's terms and categories. Carr (2010a:103) describes a similar set of circumstances in the context of drug treatment programs, where a client's disagreement with a therapist's version of the story constitutes "denial," a reaction service providers view as both a barrier to treatment and a symptom of addiction itself. Carr outlines a strategy she refers to as "flipping the script," where "Script flippers learned to inhabit the identity of a recovering addict and strategically replicated clinically and culturally prescribed ways of speaking from that position" (2010a:182). Although the script flippers Carr described must take on the language and disposition therapists require of an addict, Reich's research suggests that it is decidedly more difficult for parents to assume the role of a "child abuser," if they do not think this label describes their relationship to their child.

Biological parents who do not agree with the accusations of abuse asserted by the county may successfully complete all mandated services but continue to appear to be in "denial" and thus deemed at risk to become repeat offenders. Esmeralda, a veteran teacher of parenting classes, both to biological parents who had their children removed and to foster parents pursuing a county fostering license, told me a story of an overweight man who took his infant daughter to a hospital where he reported he had tripped and fallen on top of her while she was playing in a soft-walled playpen. Esmeralda felt strongly that the harm had been accidental. However, the hospital staff flagged the child for possessing potentially nonaccidental injuries. She was subsequently placed in foster care. Hospitals look for evidence, such as bruises at various stages of healing, to indicate abuse over time rather than a single accidental incident. However, determinations of nonaccidental injury are far from certain, except in cases where a perpetrator admits guilt or where a child is old enough to communicate experiences that can be corroborated by physical evidence.

The case of this overweight father, Esmeralda reported, was moving toward adoption because the child's parents, while complying with all court-ordered services including therapy and Esmeralda's parenting classes, were never able to accept the county's version of events. Although many of these circumstances were extremely difficult to prove, child welfare cases only rarely involved a full-blown trial. Biological parents were often willing to agree to the accusations (or a modified version) enough to allow the court to take jurisdiction. A judge I spoke with about the infrequency of trials in child welfare told me that parents would often say, "I didn't kick him, I hit him!"—protesting about the details but ultimately willing to accept the broader allegations of the child welfare agency. She went on to assert that cases that do go to trial are the ones that "really need to," the "whodunit" cases where no one involved feels sure who may have actually harmed the child. These cases often involve separated parents, each of whom holds the other accountable for the mistreatment, or circumstances where a child has truly been harmed by a third party, such as a relative or babysitter, unbeknown to the parents. What many parents might not have realized is that once they have agreed to the county's version of events, whether it involved accusations of abuse, abandonment, or neglect, this framing became the basis by which parents must prove themselves worthy to reclaim custody of their child. In this sense, an attempt by a biological parent to demonstrate that they did not in fact abuse a child was likely to be translated by the social worker into a form of "denial"; what was needed for the social worker to confidently recommend reunification was acceptance of responsibility for the alleged abuse and a demonstration, through deference, therapy, parenting classes, or other avenues authorized by the social worker that such an act would not reoccur.

I had initially expected that parents with a higher socioeconomic status would be better positioned to argue back against the county's version of events.[5] A dependency court hearing I attended contradicted this assumption. The case concerned a five-year-old girl who had been brought to the hospital with internal bleeding, purportedly from falling down bleachers at a soccer game. Before the court hearing began, the county social worker on the case mentioned to me that the case was particularly "bizarre." She explained that these parents were educated and well-off, and that the child's mother, father, and stepfather involved in the case had hired their own lawyers and were contesting the allegation of abuse. She explained:

> This one is a totally bizarre case. The little girl was brought into the hospital with serious injuries and put on a hospital hold because they [the injuries] looked like they were non-accidental. The parents said she had fallen on the bleachers at a soccer game. All the parties seemed like great parents, one [of the dads] works at [a bank], the other is a school coach . . . . The investigation was inconclusive about the infliction of the injuries, so we recommended parenting classes for both dads, since we weren't sure who did it.[6]

The social worker, relying on the assessment of the medical staff who had examined the child, didn't question the allegation of abuse, but was surprised that one of these three seemingly "great parents" had harmed this little girl. Although these parents were held accountable for the mistreatment of their daughter, the social worker's expression of surprise suggests that social positionality indelibly informs the degree to which particular parents are legible as warranting investigation, not withstanding the severity of an instance of visible harm.

In this case, the county held an investigation that was inconclusive in determining who had perpetrated the abuse. After the investigation, the county social worker required parenting classes for both the child's father and stepfather, assuming one of them to be the perpetrator. Rather than taking the classes to satisfy the child welfare agency's assessment of their case, these parents were demanding a trial so they could contest the truth of the allegations leveled against them. This was, on the one hand, a practical matter, as the family wished to avoid weekly parenting classes and monthly home visits. On the other hand, it was largely symbolic, as the daughter still resided with her mother and stepfather and her daily life had not been significantly altered by the agency's involvement. The fact of the daughter's continued residence with her mother and stepfather indicated that the social worker had determined that this child, though previously injured, was not at risk of future harm. This was, perhaps, the clearest indication of the class privilege this family possessed, as it indicated their standing in the eyes of the county social worker, regardless of her suspicions.

Despite the inconclusive county investigation, the social worker did not seem to doubt the accuracy of the abuse allegation or consider that she had perhaps misinterpreted the circumstances of the case. Instead she relied on the concerns of the medical officials, shored up by the simple presence of the family within the child welfare system, and assumed the investigation had simply not managed to find evidence of the story she already knew to be true. It was this sense of the county's ultimate authority that led so many parents simply to do what the county required of them, rather than fight for recognition of their own narrative of the events that had led to their involvement in the child welfare system.[7]

In addition to deferring to the county's authority and version of events, biological parents must comply with a sometimes seemingly impossible set of requirements. Parents must often attend hours of parenting classes, anger management or drug treatment programs, counseling services, and weekly visits with their children. Parenting classes and the parenting advice biological parents received from county social workers, and foster parents, were frequently a source of frustration. This was because they typically advocated a particular view of parenting, such as the use of time-outs as a primary disciplinary method, which didn't always align with the approach biological parents were most comfortable with. I was able to attend a training session for foster parents, taught by Esmeralda, who also taught these classes to biological parents in the child welfare system. She emphasized patience, a calm tone of voice, positive reinforcement, and the use of selective ignoring and limited choices as strategies to redirect children from "unsafe or undesired behaviors." She explained to the parents, "We never want to parent like our parents and then we do—we all tend to imitate what we know unless we learn, and practice, another way. . . . Discipline is to teach and provide a structure for kids, not to punish."[8] As Tough (2008) notes in the context of Harlem-based parenting classes, young, low-income parents of color frequently experienced these classes as a sort of cultural imperialism where white, middle-class parenting strategies were presented as the irrefutable ideal.[9] As such, biological parents were required to defer not only to a set of weighty time commitments but to a particular style of interacting with their children that was sanctioned by those in a position to recommend and approve the reunification of their family.

These dynamics were highlighted by interactions I observed between eight-month-old Zaidy, her biological mother, and Esperanza social workers. Zaidy's mother, Julie, visited Zaidy each week at Esperanza's office, where the head Esperanza social worker at the time, Linda, sat on a stool in the doorway, or stood behind the one-way window installed along one side of the playroom, taking detailed notes. The use of Esperanza as a visiting area was a service offered to county social workers to relieve them of the responsibility of coordinating visits, and it also provided Esperanza social workers more of an opportunity to observe the interactions between parent and child, and to support their own assessment of how the case was proceeding. I was only a few months into my research at the time, still getting to know the Esperanza social workers and getting a sense of their daily tasks. Linda had invited me to observe through the window so that I would be able to see and hear without being in the way.

Julie sat cross-legged on the floor with Zaidy sitting in her lap. She sprayed and combed her hair, while Zaidy cheerfully banged two wooden blocks together. Linda commented to me that the foster parents were always annoyed that after meticulously doing Zaidy's braids, her mother always undid them during visits. When Zaidy began to fuss, Julie pulled out a bag of popcorn, and they took turns feeding each other, Julie making exaggerated biting gestures and saying "num, num, num" to make Zaidy giggle. A few minutes later, Julie propped Zaidy up in a plastic child's chair and looked at her, with her hands still on her shoulders, asking "Can you sit in a chair or will you fall, fall out, huh?" Zaidy seemed stable enough so Julie got out her phone and snapped a few pictures, cooing "Zaaaidy" to get her attention. "Zaaaidy, do you know your name?" she asked. These questions struck me as unsettling but I couldn't quite put my finger on why. And then I realized: Julie was Zaidy's mother and she didn't know if her daughter could sit up yet or if she responded to her own name. These were the consequences of seeing her infant daughter for an hour only twice a week. Another Esperanza staff member came over to stand with Linda and me. Linda looked back and said to her in a low voice "She [Julie] is doing *so* much better."[10]

Linda explained to me in a low whisper that during earlier visitations, Julie had been observed kissing her daughter's vagina after changing her diaper, and telling her how beautiful she was. Linda had responded by barring Julie from changing her daughter's diaper during visits until she addressed her "sexual abuse" issues with her therapist. Notably, Zaidy had been removed from her parents' custody for a host of issues, domestic violence, suspicion of neglect, parental drug use, and possible prenatal exposure to alcohol. Sexual abuse was not a documented concern in relation to Zaidy's removal, nor was addressing this concern grounds for her reunification according to the county agency. However, through weekly observations, this had emerged as a problem according to Linda, and an issue to which Julie needed to comply to gain the support of Esperanza in her goal to regain custody of her daughter. Notably, such an issue would be unlikely to be raised as an issue prior to a child's entry into the foster care system, as it was only through the detailed scrutiny of supervised visitations that such parental behavior would be observed.

As noted in the previous chapter, Esperanza social workers were relatively unable to shift the trajectory of the case in opposition to a county social worker's recommendation. Nevertheless, biological parents experienced Esperanza as a site of powerful surveillance. Julie was likely unaware of the uneven dynamics of authority between Esperanza and the county agency. However, her focus was on gathering as many allies as she could to support the return of Zaidy to her custody, and making sure as many people as possible saw her as a good mother. "All I have is patience," she said to Linda at the end of the visit. "It is not gonna be forever, long as I stay on top of my stuff."[11] In this way, parents were subject to the scrutiny of a host of institutional authorities at a level of detail they had rarely experienced prior to the removal of their child.

Most biological parents had to comply with a broad array of requirements while maintaining or obtaining a full-time job to demonstrate their ability to provide their children with food and shelter, often while using public transportation to travel between their job and their appointments.[12] For parents, this often created a situation where they felt that they were being asked to do more than time would allow, and when they failed to arrive on time for an appointment they were seen as not being committed to reunifying with their child. This was an issue that had impacted Miguelito's case, recounted in Chapter 2, and precipitated his move to Angélica's home, closer to the Tijuana border crossing, in an effort to facilitate his mother's transportation obligations. Foster parents were frequently frustrated with biological parents' inability to comply with expectations and to reliably maintain scheduled appointments. At the same time, they were largely sympathetic with the challenges biological parents faced and the difficulties that accompanied being a parent under state scrutiny.

Cora, a foster mother and fierce advocate for young mothers trying to reunify with their children, explained her frustration at social workers' unreasonable expectations:

> So the social worker asks [the biological mother] "If you're working and the baby has a fever, what are you going to do?" And she says, "Call the babysitter to give her Tylenol." What she [the social worker] wanted to hear was that she would leave her job, drop it, and go get her baby. What I felt that she was doing was making her choose between her job and her baby. Sometimes the questions are not fair.[13]

In such circumstances, foster parents and biological parents aligned as tentative allies, both primarily concerned with their children's wellbeing, and both feeling as though social workers were laying out unreasonable expectations for what day to day parenting should look like.

Conforming to State Expectations: Parenting for "a little while or a lifetime"

Just as biological parents must allow agents of the child welfare system to set the terms that guide the possibility of their reunification with their children, foster parents articulated a similar sentiment, whereby they felt that they were shaped or "trained" by county social workers to behave in particular ways. As Corinne explained to me during a drive home from visiting foster parents Octavio and Jenny, who were frustrated with the lack of notice about upcoming court hearings for their foster children, in the eyes of the law and the county child welfare system, "foster parents are really the ones with no rights at all. The children have rights, the bio parents have *all* the rights, but the county doesn't really seem to care about the foster parents."[14] This distinction reflected one of the key differences between foster family agencies, who saw both the foster child and the foster families as their "clients," and the county child welfare social workers, whose official clients were the biological parents and their children—the foster parents were appreciated and valued as service providers for those families in need.

Esperanza foster mother Anna, introduced in Chapter 4, had worked tirelessly on the behavioral issues her foster son Taylor was dealing with, including his angry, physical outbursts at school, bedwetting, and playful and energetic misbehavior that involved things like jumping on the lunch table and singing. Anna was dismayed to find that her efforts were largely devalued and overlooked by Krissy, the county social worker. Rather than being responded to as a foster mother doing everything she could to better the circumstances of her foster son, she was seen by Krissy as demanding, meddlesome, and noncompliant. Anna told me that after her experience, and Taylor's eventual removal, she was "doing things differently . . . not pushing so much." "Look, Naomi," she explained, "They're not my kids, they're not my kids."[15] From her perspective she had put everything she had into helping Taylor to develop healthy habits, to succeed in school, and to deal with experiences of anger in more productive ways. In return, rather than being rewarded for her hard work by being respected as Taylor's (temporary) mother, Krissy had scolded Anna for overstepping her bounds as a foster mother by venting her frustrations to Taylor's lawyer, and Taylor's mother had accused Anna of physical abuse. Angélica, Miguelito's foster mother, felt similarly that the county system required foster parents to defer to the county's authority without question and did not reward parents who tried to advocate for their foster children beyond limited boundaries.

In many ways, the expectations for foster parents were largely unachievable. They were expected to provide food, housing, and transportation for children—taking them to school, doctor's appointments, therapy, and weekly visitations with biological family members. They were in this sense paid around-the-clock childcare providers. Except that they weren't actually paid for their labor. Rather, the monthly stipend was supposed to be for things children needed—diapers, soccer cleats, a car seat. Foster parents were in fact expected to invest some of their own funds in the care of their foster children—the monthly stipend was expected to offset, not cover these costs. Social workers also expected foster parents to love children and to treat them "as their own," while at the same time being willing, and happy, to relinquish them at any moment back to their biological parents' care or to an adoptive home. When children left a foster home, foster parents were not officially privileged to receive any information about their whereabouts or health. Any further contact or updates on that child's well-being were provided by the child's permanent legal family and were often discouraged by social workers in the name of facilitating the process of settling into a new home. This structure, in a sense, expected foster parents to fully commit and fully love, while remaining detached. This sentiment was aptly captured in the recruitment slogan the San Diego Child Welfare system began to promote toward the end of 2010, "Become a Foster Parent. Nurture a child for a little while . . . or for a life time."

The majority of the Esperanza foster parents whom I got to know entered the child welfare system motivated and inspired to change the lives of children. Over time, they were encouraged through their interactions with county social workers not to "make waves" or to push to meet goals, such as those Anna had for her foster son's behavior. Though foster parents saw these goals as central to a child's well-being, county social workers sometimes saw them as peripheral, nonessential issues. Social workers were primarily focused on issues they saw as placing the child in "imminent danger" of exposure to abuse, neglect, or abandonment. Imminent danger often involved things like patterns of violence, parental drug use, lack of medical care, or, as recounted in Chapter 3, deportability. Parents' focus on schooling, nutrition, or the emotional well-being of their children were sometimes seen as peripheral concerns, issues that foster (and often biological) parents took seriously but county social workers and legal actors frequently saw as beyond the scope of their duties. As one Foster Family Agency staff member explained: "The attitude of court is that you have to prove that you are not capable of reunification. The attitude of [our agency] is that you have to prove that you *can*."[16] In this sense, foster parents and FFA social workers were often focused on a different set of concerns, concerns county social workers and legal actors sometimes saw as exceeding the reach of their authority or prioritizing child protection over the goal of family maintenance to an inappropriate degree.

This distinction sometimes manifested in a surprising disjointedness between the services provided to foster parents and to biological parents. There was a lack of continuity in terms of parenting expectations and support for foster children. This issue arose for Anna and Josie's foster daughter Danaira, a two-year-old who was placed in their home along with her baby brother, Isaiah. Danaira and Isaiah were the youngest of five siblings, all of whom had been removed for domestic abuse concerns. During a visit, Corinne asked Josie if Danaira and Isaiah's mom "loved her kids." Josie responded noncommittally saying, "Well, doesn't everyone love their kids?" Anna interjected, saying, "no, she loves her kids, but she can't handle them."[17] Anna described Danaira's biological mother as loving but overwhelmed, and ill-equipped to care for five young children on her own.

When Danaira arrived in Anna and Josie's care she displayed what social workers diagnosed as attachment disorder—she called all adults "mama" and "dada," would run off across a parking lot or go with anyone who seemed friendly. She did not respond to being told not to do something (such as running out into the road or reaching for a hot pan) by ceasing the behavior. Anna and Danaira met weekly with a therapist, who helped them work on these issues together. After a few months Danaira called Anna and Josie, "mama" and "Jojo," and differentiated them from other adult women, although Anna explained she had not made such progress with adult men, as there were none in Anna's home. Danaira had also responded well to a time-out strategy and had learned to sign when she was hungry or thirsty, rather than crying until Anna or Josie figured out what she needed.

Anna told me with baffled amazement that similar therapy was not being provided to Danaira's biological mother. Her case plan focused around addressing concerns about generalized neglect, basic parenting skills, and the goal of establishing a long-term separation from her physically abusive husband. Anna told me, for example, that Danaira's mother would ask her during a visit if she was hungry, and if Danaira kept playing, her mother simply wouldn't feed her, rather than recognizing a two-year-old's relative inability to assess whether it is time to stop playing and eat. She also regularly returned from a visit with a dirty diaper that Josie described with a wrinkled nose as "not fresh." Anna and Josie didn't think the mother was intentionally neglectful, but that she was simply too overwhelmed to do what she needed to do to take care of her kids. This lack of coordination meant that visits were chaotic for Danaira, with no consistency between the parenting she received from her foster and biological mothers. Anna could only shake her head at what this would mean for the kids if and when they returned to their mother's full-time care.

Like Anna, other Esperanza foster parents felt their role as advocates were not recognized or encouraged by county social workers. Angélica, introduced in Chapter 2, and her husband had a self-described success story. Raised in San Ysidro in poverty, pregnant at a young age, they managed to put her husband through college and start their own successful business. When I visited them, they had just moved into a newly built home with lofted ceilings, granite counter tops, and couches piled with decorative throw pillows. Their sons, both in their early twenties, attended prestigious universities. Angélica, referring to their comfortable financial circumstances, expressed amusement that because her foster son received Medi-Cal health coverage she had been "put in the system" and thus would get a phone call every month from a Medi-Cal caseworker, asking her to confirm that she had adequate food and shelter and that her "basic needs were being met."[18] Angélica told me that the first time she felt taken aback and a bit baffled by this phone call, but had come to see it as a somewhat amusing monthly ritual. Because the Medi-Cal system was separate from the child welfare system, the caseworker who called did not realize Angélica had been entered into their database not because of her own circumstances, but because of Miguel's status as a foster child. Laughter aside, Angélica felt that the Medi-Cal system made its recipients feel like "second class citizens."[19] She described the Medi-Cal offices she had attended with her foster son, Miguel, as "depressing and ugly," and often staffed with overworked and rude personnel.[20] She noted that she frequently had to go to an office quite far from her home in order to find doctors who would accept Medi-Cal, and that while this was merely a hassle for her with a part-time job and a private vehicle, she could imagine it to be a substantial obstacle to obtaining care for families where parents were employed full-time and had access only to public transportation. Frustrated with the quality of care, Angélica eventually asked her older sons' former pediatrician to see Miguel. He did so but Angélica admitted she was not sure he was actually getting paid for providing Miguel's care.

Cora, the Esperanza foster mother introduced above, had been similarly incensed by the treatment of her foster child when she tried to get medical services through his Medi-Cal card:

> Our little Henry, he is just my angel. He was ten days old . . . . Taken at birth and born in withdrawal. He had hip dysplasia. Seven days in the hospital, three in intensive care, four looking for placement . . . I noticed that he hung his neck kind of strange. A few days later he had an appointment for his hip dysplasia, and received a harness. At that appointment he was diagnosed with torticollis.[21] Then we had physical therapy. My frustration, if you want to know what frustration was, they said three to four weeks for assessment, then we put in the referral to Medi-Cal for six weeks. That's just 'cause the system is overwhelmed, well these kids are really treated at the bottom. I took him to my pediatrician; we have insurance, and they saw him right away. Then I ended up taking him to a clinic for a vaccine. I got there at 11:30; I was the first one. I didn't get in until 2:30. The care that these kids receive! If I would have walked in with my flashy insurance card they would have treated him. I think that's across the board, I don't think it's Hispanic; it's white, black, everybody.[22]

Although for Cora these issues were not about racialized positionalities but about the singular position of "foster child," these patterns of treatment were certainly embedded in broader structures of inequality based on race, class, citizenship status, and language use. Despite social worker expectations that foster mothers treat their children "as their own," interactions with institutional authorities at every turn seemed to remind foster mothers like Cora that she could not reframe Henry as her child, as institutions stubbornly held him in place as a foster child, and a ward of the state. For these mothers, the foster care system was not providing their children with the care they needed. But at the same time, they were often chastised by social workers for deviating from standard protocol or they ended up feeling taken advantage of if they extended themselves beyond what was expected of them.

These Esperanza foster parents expressed feeling that they received little recognition of their efforts or acknowledgement of their role as the full-time caregiver in their foster child's life. When I asked Angélica if she and her family would foster again, she said they would adopt, but not foster, as it was just too hard. I asked her to pinpoint exactly what it was that made it feel so difficult and she said, "As foster parents we were never part of the decision making process, although we were providing full-time care to [Miguel]."[23] Angélica felt that they had been Miguel's parents on a day-to-day basis and had been seen as such by Miguel and by their own community of friends and family. Yet from a legal perspective they had no authority to make choices for Miguel's life or even to make recommendations about what they thought would be best for him. It was this experience of parenting Miguelito without being recognized as his parent, and without the security of being able to rely on his continued presence, that Angélica felt was too much for her to go through again. And as many of the foster parents I spoke with also articulated, she did not feel that the county child welfare system did an adequate job in its role as legal parent for foster children. She felt that the county used a "cookie-cutter approach" for each case, one that was ultimately unable to respond to an individual child's needs or to utilize the insights, resources, and expertise of their full-time caregivers. Trevor, Josh's partner and Emma's foster father, made a similar assertion, emphatically explaining, "each case is so individual and they just try to shove everything into one bucket—it just doesn't work!"[24]

Despite foster parents' disillusionment with the state's ability to provide foster children with what foster parents saw as loving, compassionate, and adequate care, foster parents understood that their own expertise as parents went unrecognized. They also understood that this expertise did not translate into an ability to impact the trajectory of their foster child's case or to negotiate the maintenance of a relationship with their foster child in contradiction to social workers' recommendations. The easiest solution to this problem was to maintain a degree of emotional distance from foster children, but foster parents often did not feel capable of taking this approach. The vast majority of the foster parents I knew felt that they immediately bonded with their foster children, though some foster parents, particularly those with young biological children at home, expressed feeling discomfited by the difference in affection and connection they felt to the children in their care. As Anna responded when I asked what it was like to pick up a child from an agency, rather than give birth, she shrugged, saying "You take them home, feed them, and they're yours. The only difference," she laughed, "is no nine months and no pain!"[25] This immediate bond promoted compliance with child welfare regulations based on the very real fear that a child could be removed quickly, on short notice, by the county agency.

This sort of quick, unexpected removal happened to Jenny and Octavio, Esperanza's youngest foster parents who were caring for two-year-old white twins, Carter and Sadie. Carter and Sadie had been removed from their single mother's custody after a neighbor found them on a street corner, wandering alone. The neighbor took the kids home in her own car, where she reportedly found the twins' mother on the phone and unconcerned with the children's whereabouts. This event, Corinne later told me, led to the mother's twenty-first CPS referral, and to the removal of the twins from her care.[26] The twins' mother was jailed for three weeks on a charge of "willful cruelty to children." After her release she entered treatment related to some psychological concerns. Her county social worker was hopeful reunification would be an attainable goal. The twins had four half-siblings each living with their respective biological fathers, but Sadie and Carter's father was unknown to the county social worker and uninvolved in the children's lives. The twins had been placed with Octavio and Jenny in early June, and when I first visited them in September they seemed to be well settled into a relationship Corinne referred to as "deeply bonded."

When I first met Octavio and Jenny I was surprised by their relative youth. They were in their early twenties and one of the very few foster parents at Esperanza who had not previously had biological children. Jenny answered the door in a thin tank-top and jeans, and Octavio smiled shyly from the kitchen, with his buzzed head and low-slung surf-style shorts, where he ran around the kitchen table chasing a giggling Carter who was pedaling a small plastic tricycle. Jenny filled Corinne and me in on how the kids were doing—Carter was eating better, both were finally going to sleep without difficulty, and weekly visits with their mother had improved. Jenny explained that Carter and his mother now ended their visits with "smiles rather than tears" and that Sadie seemed happier to see her mother but not sad when they said goodbye. As Corinne jotted her weekly notes, Sadie sat on my lap, drawing lines and dots on her own legal pad, a careful mimic of the social work note-taking process. Carter, frustrated that Octavio had focused on the conversation and stopped chasing him, took his tricycle out to the patio where he pedaled in furious circles hollering "follow me, daddy, follow me!"[27] The visit ended with Jenny asking nervously about what might happen at the upcoming court date. Corinne didn't know any details, but didn't expect too much to change, as this was an early court date, only three months after the initial removal of the twins. As we waved goodbye, Jenny mentioned that she was going to try to enroll the twins in a tumbling class to give them a chance to make some friends and get out some of their wiggles. Eight days later, I was helping Corinne close the Esperanza files for Sadie and Carter—they had been returned, unexpectedly, to their grandmother's care.

Sadie and Carter had an elderly grandmother; she walked with a cane and Corinne was dubious she was a good fit for two rambunctious young twins. When Corinne received a vague email from the twins' county social worker after the court hearing, discussing a visit to their maternal grandmother, she had to write back to ask for clarification about what sounded like an overnight visit, so she could talk with Octavio and Jenny about the process. The county social worker responded explaining that the judge had approved her recommendation to move the children to their grandmother's full-time care pending the reunification process with their biological mother, as a sort of interim step. She wanted the process to happen by 2 p.m. the next day. Jenny and Octavio were stunned and saddened, but there was nothing they could do. The most concerning aspect of the move, from Corinne's perspective, was that the twins' grandmother wasn't particularly friendly toward Jenny and Octavio, and was uninterested in maintaining any contact to ease the transition. The twins' mother did have a good relationship with Octavio and Jenny, and when she regained custody a few months later, she had them over for a visit the very next day.

The sorts of experiences Jenny and Octavio had—the unexpected dissolution of what felt to them like a family—was an extraordinary experience of state control they subjected themselves to willingly in order to serve as foster parents. The intimate relationship that they developed through daily care of Carter and Sadie, a relationship that was in some senses both expected and demanded by the county social worker, was abruptly terminated, and their connection was no longer sanctioned by the state. From the county social worker's perspective, this move facilitated the soonest possible reentry of the twins into their natal family, and thus satisfied the dual agency goals of child protection and family preservation. In this case, Carter and Sadie's biological mother saw Jenny and Octavio's role in her children's lives differently from the way the county social worker did, and she pursued her own relationship with them once she had her children back in her care.

The closing of cases, and the movement of children from one custody arrangement to another, were often moments where tensions between social workers, foster parents, and biological parents became accentuated as each felt that permanent, impactful decisions were being made that would shape the children involved profoundly. One such case involved the movement of Lucas, Liliana's foster son introduced at the beginning of this chapter, into the care of another set of Esperanza foster parents, Edith and Arturo, and eventually to his biological cousin's home. Liliana and her husband were planning to care for Lucas until his biological cousin was approved to take over his care, an interim step until he could be reunified with his mother, following successful completion of a drug treatment program and parenting classes. Liliana's family, who were from Michoacán, had planned a weeklong vacation in Mexico, and could not bring Lucas because he did not have a passport. They were hoping the county would approve Lucas's cousin for placement prior to their vacation, but as their trip neared and the approval had not been granted, largely due to paperwork delays, Esperanza social worker Corinne began arranging for Lucas to be placed temporarily with Esperanza foster parents, Edith and Arturo. This arrangement, called respite care, happened often when foster families had travel plans that could not incorporate a foster child, or a medical emergency where they needed a few days without a foster child to care for.

Just before the trip, Liliana called Corinne and told her her husband's family in Mexico had a temporary emergency and that she had sent them a significant financial loan. Liliana had placed Lucas in a private preschool program along with her son Bailey, which cost $800 per month. She didn't feel she could continue to pay the high tuition, but did not want to "differentiate between the two boys"[28] by placing Lucas in the subsidized daycare for foster children available in San Diego County. Lucas was then moved permanently to Edith and Arturo's care, pending approval of the cousin. However, during his first week with Edith and Arturo, they discovered that Lucas's new daycare center was the same one attended by their previous foster children, two boys they had fostered for more than a year. The young boys' transition to their adoptive home had been difficult, and Edith felt it would be too upsetting for the boys to see her when she dropped off Lucas each day. They needed him to be moved.

From the foster parents' perspective, they were making measured decisions based on what they saw as best for all parties involved—but in each case seeming to prioritize children other than Lucas. Corinne expressed frustration at these decisions but also at the county social worker who had not been able to approve Lucas's cousin fast enough to avoid these multiple moves for Lucas. When the placement with Edith and Arturo fell through, the county worker managed to rush the approval process for Lucas's cousin and move him to her care. Although I was unable to speak with the county worker involved in the case, Corinne communicated his frustration with foster parents not taking seriously their commitment to a child, and for failing to consider, from his perspective, the negative impact of multiple moves on Lucas's experience in foster care. Corinne was similarly frustrated, as the commitment to "one home for one child" was central to Esperanza's mission as a foster family agency, and interactions like this had the potential to erode the goodwill between Esperanza and the county social workers who placed children with the agency. And indeed, Corinne, and later Alicia, received resistance from county social workers when trying to place future foster children with these two particular families, as they were concerned that the families might not be fully committed to fostering a child for as long as circumstances required.

Constructing the Home, Policing Space

Although many foster parents felt that the county child welfare services were inadequate in assessing and providing for the specific emotional needs of their foster children, the agency was overwhelmingly effective, from foster parents' perspectives, in regulating their physical space.[29] Their homes were carefully scrutinized for their ability to meet agency standards. Each child must have a separate bedroom, unless two children of the same gender are close in age. There were regulations about safety barriers around a pool and about which house cleaning substances must be in locked cabinets. In many cases, foster parents were required to make substantial changes to a home in which they had safely raised numerous biological children.[30]

Shortly after Sadie and Carter left, Octavio's parents moved into their spare bedroom along with two of Octavio's younger brothers, due to financial difficulties. Octavio and Jenny desperately wanted to return to fostering a child, so Corinne suggested they could still qualify for an infant, who could technically reside in their own bedroom until age two, thereby circumventing the loss of their spare bedroom. However, when Corinne went to reinspect their home, an annual process for maintaining foster parent licensure, she realized that Octavio's parents were sharing a bed with their two sons. Corinne did not think this was a technical violation of the child welfare policy, since these children were not foster children. However, child welfare policy stipulated that a biological child could not be forced to give up his or her own bedroom to meet space requirements for the foster child in the home. Corinne told me this was a tricky situation, since the children had not given up anything. Yet she did not want to risk a situation of noncompliance, which might reflect poorly on Esperanza as an agency, or even result in a financial penalty if the licensing agency, CCL, did not approve of the arrangement. This situation was particularly uncomfortable for Corinne, a Mexican national, who understood that co-sleeping, while generally frowned on in the U.S. context after infancy, was not an unusual housing arrangement for Mexican families, particularly those who were working-class. Corinne negotiated a solution with Octavio and Jenny—they would add another bed to the spare bedroom. The children did not have to sleep in it, but the house would officially conform to child welfare standards.

Although Corinne felt that the policing of the intimacy of Jenny and Octavio's sleeping arrangements was an uncomfortable intrusion, this was not an unusual circumstance. Rosie, Hernán and Estela's foster daughter who was introduced in the previous chapter, was only able to enter their care because of changes they made to their own and their children's sleeping arrangements under the guidance of Alicia, the Esperanza social worker who replaced Corinne. Further, Corinne had avoided placing foster children in Hernán and Estela's home precisely because she did not feel the space of their trailer home was suitable for an additional child. Foster parents, many of whom had grown up sharing rooms and beds with siblings, felt that there was a dubious connection between the space of a home and the safety and happiness of a "good" childhood. And Corinne's ambivalence suggested that she had similar misgivings, despite her role as the enforcer of these regulations. Social workers felt the responsibility for the care of the children placed under their supervision, though, as Esperanza foster parents frequently noted, they weren't the ones providing and caring for the children on a daily basis.

During a meeting Alicia and I attended with a unit of county social workers in central San Diego, the social workers were visibly relieved as Alicia described the training foster parents received through Esperanza in terms of giving medication to children and their willingness to participate in Team Decision Making meetings and other aspects of the child welfare process. Their relief demonstrated the stress they felt in placing children in what they could only hope were "good" homes, and tempered foster parents' perception of county social workers as callous individuals who just want to get through their workday. As Corinne explained when talking about the thinness of information she received prior to placing a child with Esperanza foster parents, "the county doesn't give much info 'cause they just want to make the placement."[31] So many of the intimate details of parenting were out of the reach of social workers' gaze and control, but things like the space of the home, financial reports, and medical logs were squarely within their purview. It was through these avenues that social workers did their best to supervise foster parenting, both reasserting their authority as primary decision-makers and authorizers of the contours of foster children's lives, and assuring themselves they were knowledgeable enough about each foster family's circumstances to predict and prevent further mistreatment of the children.

Suspicion (the Long Reach of the State)

Esperanza foster parents and the biological parents of their foster children, despite their shared attributes of being primarily working-class, bilingual, Latina/o families, occupied distinct positions within the child welfare system. Their actions and abilities were viewed differently by the social workers with whom they interacted, and while both often felt undervalued and underserved by child welfare authorities and other legal actors, they were subject to different constraints. However, because they occupied similar social positionalities of race, class, language use, and sometimes citizenship status, the potential for slippage from the status of foster parent, lovingly caring for another family's child, to biological parent at risk of losing custody, was always present. This specter of removal shaped the case of Esperanza foster parents Antonio and Clara, who, after fostering eight different foster children at Esperanza over a period of three years, became foster parents on short notice for Clara's sister's children, a niece and two nephews. They thus moved to the uneasy middle ground of "kinship care," working as foster parents for members of their own extended family. This shift unsettled their role as exemplary foster parents who were simply "giving back" to their community. In this way, they straddled the line between intervening in, and belonging to, a family the state had defined as in need of intervention.

The shift from "caring" foster family to a family under the scrutiny of the state was brought into stark relief through the case of the Escobars. Flor and Nestor Escobar lived down the street from Antonio and Clara, who, as veteran foster parents, had taken the Escobars under their wing, giving them advice as they received their first foster placement of two young sisters, Carmelita and Juanita, two years old and five months old. The Escobars had their own biological children, two young sons, aged eight and ten. Flor did not work, and was able to be home with the girls during the day while her husband was at work and her sons were in school. The county social worker involved in the case had initially hoped to place the sisters with one of their grandmothers, but on investigation had learned that both grandmothers had prior CPS history for allegations of domestic violence, and that the sisters' young parents, twenty at the time of the sisters' removal, had both spent time as foster children themselves. Carmelita, at two, was a feisty toddler, with a propensity to holler "no!" to throw food gleefully from her highchair tray, and to follow up these behaviors with a charming, dimpled, smile. Juanita, her five-month-old sister, was a mellow baby, round and happy, and, according to Flor, "a good sleeper."[32] When Corinne and I made our first home visit to check on Flor and the girls, one of Flor's friends had stopped by on her lunch break to hold the baby. Flor explained that the kids were so cute her friends had been stopping by to admire them all week.

Flor's friend soon left and Corinne took the opportunity to ask how things were really going. Flor shook her head and began to cry. Carmelita was difficult and Flor didn't know what to do. Since her arrival, she had been making herself throw up, scratching her throat and the roof of her mouth, and often refusing to eat. Flor said she had cut Carmelita's nails "bien cortita" and that had helped—she hadn't thrown up in three days. But, Flor explained, she had moved on to reaching into her diaper during naptime and scratching herself on her "parte íntima" and occasionally smearing her feces on the crib. Flor had tried everything she could think of: constantly watching Carmelita, putting gloves on her hands, and holding her hand while she walked so that she would not fall, but she continued to injure herself in a variety of ways. Nestor was terrified someone would accuse them of abusing Carmelita, given her numerous bruises, scrapes, sores, and scabs. Corinne was concerned that these behaviors were manifesting in a child so young, but reassured Flor it sounded like she was doing everything she could. Corinne reminded Flor that many of these behaviors might simply be "attention seeking" and Flor should do her best to ignore them, heaping praise and cuddles on Carmelita for positive behaviors. In the meantime, Corinne promised to look into asking Carmelita's county social worker to authorize her to attend some therapy. Flor reiterated that they did not want to give up caring for the girls and Corinne thanked her, but reminded her she needed to take care of herself and her family as well.

Three weeks later, when Corinne arrived at the Escobars' for a routine visit, Nestor and Flor were there with the children. Carmelita was covered with bruises and her lips were scabbed from where she had bitten herself repeatedly. Nestor explained that they had just returned from a disastrous visit with Carmelita and Juanita's biological mother, who had been upset at her daughter's injuries. Corinne promised to follow up with the county social worker. The next day, the children's biological mother accused the Escobars of abusing the girls, filing an official complaint. They all went together to the hospital, accompanied by the county social worker. There it was determined that Carmelita had an unusual skin condition that caused her to bruise easily. The hospital staff did not suspect abuse but could not rule it out entirely. They took photographs and other evidence, which they sent to a special lab charged with determining whether injuries were likely accidental or intentional. The county social worker asked the girls' mother if she would be comfortable with them remaining with the Escobars in the meantime. She was not, and so the children were sent to Abrams Children's Home, San Diego County's temporary shelter. Flor, Nestor, and their sons were devastated, having grown quite attached to the girls. Although they hoped to have Carmelita and Juanita back once they had been cleared of the abuse allegation, the county social worker told Corinne she would not approve that placement again, as she didn't think the foster family would be able to continue to have positive interactions with Carmelita and Juanita's biological parents regardless of the outcome of the abuse allegation. In this way the severance of the foster family was abrupt, unexpected, and complete.

The Escobars were shaken by the experience and unsure whether they would foster again in the future. Corinne was similarly devastated. Not only had she lost a foster placement and shepherded one of her foster families through a traumatic first fostering experience, but she had potentially damaged a relationship with a county social worker simply by linking Esperanza to a difficult, time-consuming set of circumstances, whether they were anyone's fault or not. To make matters worse, Corinne was bound by her status as a mandated reporter to place a call to the child abuse hotline—the Escobars had been officially accused of abuse and had two children of their own. Corinne felt professionally bound to make the phone call, though she told me privately that she did not believe it was really the right thing to do. She made the phone call to the child abuse hotline, followed by an even more difficult phone call to Flor, explaining what she had done. The Escobars immediately asked that their foster care license be canceled, and they suffered the humiliation and trauma of their boys being pulled out of their elementary school classrooms and questioned about their treatment in their home.

Allegations of abuse are frequent in foster care, so frequent that a discussion of how to handle the circumstances of alleged abuse are part of the formal licensing training that prospective foster parents undergo. Foster parents are trained to document every minor scrape, bruise, and injury. Esperanza foster parents kept a detailed medical log of any medicines they administered to their foster children, and were required to get pediatrician approval even for such medications as children's Tylenol. Esperanza foster parents frequently texted and emailed pictures of scraped knees and scabbed elbows, along with a brief description of how the injury occurred to Esperanza social workers for placement in their child's file.

Social workers explained during foster parent trainings that while abuse does happen in foster homes, these allegations are often a manifestation of the biological parent's sense of helplessness and lack of control over the life and care of their own children. They cannot make many decisions about their child's placement, but they know that a serious allegation of abuse will probably cause their child to be moved from their current foster home. This occurred in Taylor's case when Anna and Josie were accused by Taylor's mother based on a bruise at the base of his neck. An abuse allegation was also the reason Emma had been moved from her first county foster home to her Esperanza placement with Trevor and Josh, her eventual adoptive parents. Many foster parents took this vulnerability in stride, trying to focus on the sympathy they felt for biological parents, and the suffering those parents experienced due to worry and lack of control of their child's care. Foster mother Cora responded to biological parents' feeling of vulnerability by making concrete efforts to give biological parents all the authority and respect she could. She explained that she would ask them small questions about their child—whether she should dress them in red or blue or whether they like books about trucks or animals—mundane decision-making moments that could serve as reminders that she respected their authority and their knowledge about their own child.

These moments of accusation highlighted the encompassing control of state authorities, and the way that foster parents were not immune from the scrutiny and intervention regularly wielded against biological parents. Ironically, biological parents enacted a dimension of this scrutiny when they wielded such accusations as a disruptive tactic that returned to them at least a modicum of control. In this way, biological parents could reassert their own authority by scrutinizing the parenting practices of state-authorized foster parents, and, in a roundabout way perhaps, critique the parenting decisions enacted by the child welfare authorities. These interactions illuminated not only the vulnerability of parents and families to the abrupt dissolution of families but to the fragility of the relationship between parent (both biological and foster) and child.

Fragility

Clara and Antonio, the Escobars' "mentor" foster parents, had been fed up with their foster placement—not because of the kids, whom they adored, but because of the children's grandmother, who they felt was verbally abusive toward both themselves and their older foster child, Mikey, during visits. Clara and Antonio had grown up in Tecate, just east of San Diego on the Mexico side of the border, and had been childhood sweethearts. They enjoyed having a house full of children and had fostered six children prior to eight-year-old Mikey and two-year-old Miriam. Their own children, except for one teenager, were grown and living elsewhere. They had worked with families whose situations involved serious physical abuse and ongoing drug use and they did not see themselves as a couple that would shy away from a challenge. The county social worker assigned to the case, Margo, had decided to recommend termination of parental rights because Mikey and Miriam's mother had repeatedly failed to quit her drug habit. The extended family, including the grandmother, had been ruled out as viable options for the children because of histories of abusive behavior or relationships Margo felt were "too close" to the children's mother and grandmother. But Margo told Corinne and me that she refused to make "legal orphans" and therefore would not recommend terminating parental rights until she found an adoptive home.[33] Margo was close with Mikey, she regularly referred to him as "guy," as in "How's it going, guy?" and she would affectionately put a hand on his shoulder or tousle his hair. Because she often supervised weekly visits with Mikey and Miriam and their mother and grandmother, she had gotten to know the family more closely than those county social workers who were only able to see children once a month. As another former county social worker explained to me, choosing an adoptive home is like "playing god," since you are choosing a permanent family for a child. This often motivated social workers to get to know the children heading for adoption as well as they could, so they could feel confident that they were making a good, informed decision.

Unfortunately, finding an adoptive home, particularly with a sibling pair that included an eight-year-old, was not a quick process. The majority of adoptive parents waiting to adopt a child had a strong preference for children under age three. This meant that not only did Mikey and Miriam continue to deepen their relationship with Clara and Antonio, a relationship that was likely to end once an adoptive home was found, but they also continued to interact with their biological mother and grandmother. And although Margo felt committed to her decision to terminate parental rights, Mikey and Miriam's biological family continued to assume the children would eventually return to their care, making the extension of these relationships at least potentially more damaging in the long run for everyone involved.

After seven months, Clara and Antonio finally decided they had had enough dealing with the children's grandmother. They told Margo that if she would not remove her from the weekly visits then the children would have to be moved. Margo said that she understood their concerns but felt that since the children's grandmother had practically raised them in their mother's absence she had a right to continue to visit them until parental rights were officially terminated. Margo also agreed to accelerate her search for an adoptive home for the children. Because the tension between Clara, Antonio, and the children's grandmother was so severe, Margo and Corinne took turns supervising the weekly visits, so that the foster parents and biological family would not have to interact. Corinne and I spent an awkward afternoon in a sunny neighborhood park, with Corinne trying to observe the family's interactions while we both remained as unobtrusive as possible.

An Afternoon at the Park

Melissa, Mikey and Miriam's mother, was on the phone when we arrived. Mikey yelled "Mom! Grandma!" as he got out of the car, while Corinne took Miriam out of the car seat from which she was reaching out toward Melissa, saying "Mama!" (which she also said regularly to Clara). Melissa pinched her phone between her ear and her shoulder and took Miriam from Corinne. Continuing her phone conversation, Melissa sat with Miriam at a picnic table, feeding her tiny bites of Pop Tart, one by one. Corinne and I made eye contact with each other, conveying our discomfort about the continuing phone call. Holding a child while talking on the phone is without question a frequent parenting practice and certainly not one that generally raises concerns about parental capabilities. It was only in the context of a one-hour supervised visit that this behavior became something of note, and a reflection—albeit a potentially erroneous one—on a parent's care for her children.

Mikey took off enthusiastically for the playground while his grandmother chatted with us for a few minutes. The focus of our conversation was the children's grandmother's nasty looking black eye; her skin was mottled purple and yellow, which she told us she got when she woke up in the night and tripped and fell against a bureau. She showed us, as evidence of her tale, the wristband from the hospital where she went to make sure that she was okay. It was difficult in the context of the child welfare system for Corinne and me not to wonder whether her elaborate explanation might be serving as a cover for an instance of domestic violence. Melissa got off the phone at this point and, for a while, she and her mother stood with Miriam, pushing her on the swings. Mikey was by himself on the far swing, his face turned toward his mother and grandmother. After a while Melissa went to push Mikey. Quietly, so that Melissa couldn't hear, Corinne remarked to me that she should be pushing Mikey from the back since he is older and pumps his legs; she was pushing him from the front so he kind of ran into her and could not go very high.

We tried to give the family some distance, but it was difficult to do so since Corinne had to be able to both hear and see them at all times. We sat on the edge of the playground railing for a while, watching them by looking up through the diamond patterned back of a green metal bench. After a while, Melissa and Mikey sat at the picnic table to work on his homework, while Miriam's grandmother pushed her on the swing. Miriam squealed with happiness as her grandmother pushed her knees, counting "one, two, three!" Melissa ignored the math homework spread out on the picnic table and grabbed Mikey in a hug. He cuddled into her, and they dissolved into tickles and laughter. They eventually turned to the homework and Melissa helped Mikey work through the problems by holding up her hands for him to count out the numbers.

After Mikey's homework was finished, they returned to the playground. The children's grandmother stood next to Miriam while Melissa stood facing her daughter, holding her hands as she climbed on the jungle gym. Mikey walked along the wooden rail of the playground, carefully balancing, and then sat down on the edge, slowly falling backward into the wood chips. He glanced back to see if anyone was watching but nobody turned his way. A few moments later we got a strong whiff of marijuana from across the park. Corinne exclaimed "Assholes, there are so many kids here!" and then it was time to go.[34] Although the family members were unaware, Corinne and I knew that this would likely be one of the last few visits, one of the last few times Melissa and her mother would ever see these kids.

Departures

A month later, we were at the home of foster parents Clara and Antonio, meeting with the county social worker, Margo, and her intern, Abby, who planned to meet weekly with Mikey to help facilitate the adoption process. Clara and Corinne tried to convey the urgency of the timeline for Clara's family—the stress of the case just felt like too much for them. Margo reassured Clara and Corinne that she would find an adoptive home for the children as soon as possible. In the meantime, her intern, Abby, would meet with Mikey once a week, to talk with him about his feelings on adoption using a coloring book about adoptive families as a starting place.

After several delays, Margo called to say that she had found an adoptive placement and would pick the children up the next day to transfer them there. Margo's plan was to settle them into this new home before recommending that the court terminate parental rights and approve the adoption. Corinne, Deanna, an Esperanza social work intern, and I arrived on the day of the transfer, bringing the children some gifts they missed receiving because they had not attended the Esperanza holiday party. When we arrived Mikey was visibly nervous, pacing and pulling at the front of his shirt. He greeted Corinne when we arrived and asked, "Where am I going?" She told him that Margo would tell him when she arrived. A few moments later Mikey turned to me and asked, "Am I going with you?" I smiled and shook my head no, trying to distract him from his anxiety by checking out the new stickers and matchbox cars he had unwrapped.

Margo arrived and stood in the doorway with her sunglasses on. With Mikey out of earshot she explained that the children were going to Abrams Children's Home, rather than to their new adoptive family.[35] Margo responded to our expressions of horror and sadness by saying only, "it's a long story" and "the placement worker was being a pain in the butt!" Clara quickly packed a diaper bag for Miriam and helped Mikey put his backpack on. Margo told Clara that she would pick up the rest of their things when they moved to their new home, hopefully within the week. Mikey stood in the kitchen, his hands tucked under his backpack straps. He looked over at his sister, obliviously sitting in a chair while I wiggled new hello kitty socks over her chubby feet, and asked, "Is *she* staying?" Margo responded, "No, guy."[36] When Mikey asked her where they were going she said only that she'd tell him in the car. We all walked them out to Margo's waiting vehicle where Mikey got in the back and Clara strapped Miriam into her car seat. The car backed up slowly. Corinne, Deanna, and I waved and smiled until we couldn't see Mikey's hand anymore, while Clara turned her face into Antonio's chest and cried silently, wiping tears off her cheeks. Once the car was gone Antonio walked briskly down the driveway, a bottle of windshield wiper fluid in hand. Perhaps, I thought, work was the easiest way for him to deal with the sadness of the day. Clara smiled through her tears, told Corinne that she would be okay, and hurried inside.

The children spent two weeks at Abrams Children's Home. It was there that Miriam celebrated her second birthday, and it was there that she experienced what was perhaps the first trauma of her life she would remember—she was not old enough to understand what was happening except that she was no longer with Clara and Antonio. Furthermore, although Mikey and Miriam had spent their days together in Clara's home, they would almost certainly be separated at Abrams. Abrams made exceptions to keep siblings housed together, but this was usually possible only for siblings who were of the same gender or relatively close in age.

Although Corinne understood that Margo had a large caseload and many children to be concerned with, she felt that this trauma could have been avoided—that it was Margo's fault. Corinne believed Margo had not been concerned with finding the children an adoptive home until pushed to do so. This was primarily because the foster home with Clara and Antonio seemed to be a good, stable placement for them, which allowed Margo to deal with other, more pressing cases. This was, arguably, a good decision for Margo's caseload as a whole. But because Margo did not rush to find an adoptive home, she also did not rush to terminate parental rights, since she did not want to create "legal orphans." Although Margo felt very strongly about this issue, her decision was not determined by child welfare policy, but was instead a matter of her discretion. Other county social workers recommended termination of parental rights at whatever point they felt the parents should no longer be considered a placement option. This decision might occur sometimes as many as six months before a permanency plan, such as an adoptive home or guardianship arrangement, was established. This was the procedure in Emma's case, recounted in Chapter 2, where she spent more than six months in Trevor and Josh's care as a "legal orphan" before her adoption was completed. The hesitation to delay this decision led Margo to prolong the children's visits and exposure to their biological mother and grandmother, as visits typically continue until a dependency judge terminates parental rights. Corinne saw this as a needless process once Margo had determined that parental rights should be terminated, particularly since Margo planned, for the children's well-being, to encourage their eventual adoptive home to maintain no contact with Mikey and Miriam's biological family. In this way, the crisis of separation they experienced seemed to Corinne to be the result of an arbitrary position Margo took.

Had the foster parents voiced their concerns about the grandmother earlier or more forcefully, perhaps their frustration would not have reached an insurmountable level. Had Margo responded more decisively to their concerns about the grandmother's behavior, the foster parents might have chosen to extend their care of the children until an adoptive home was ready and authorized to accept them. As such, Mikey and Miriam went from having two families—Clara and Antonio, and Melissa and their grandmother, to having none active in their daily life. The intimate bonds the children formed with Clara and Antonio were severed on relatively short notice and without advance warning, though this severance had been at the foster parents' request. Similarly, once parental rights were terminated it would be unlikely for the children to interact with their mother, grandmother, or other extended family again, unless Mikey or Miriam chose to find them once they turned eighteen. Clara's tears suggested that the trauma of the severance of this fragile relationship was felt not just by the children but by the foster parents, who were positioned as both parents losing a child and as not-quite-parents saying goodbye to children that were never truly theirs. The specifics of how Melissa and her own mother experienced this severance is something that I never learned.

Throughout this chapter I have worked to resist the process of distancing that is partly enacted through the language of the child welfare bureaucracy: the "placement," the "case," the "bed." Through a focus on intimate relations I have tried to get at the visceral, daily experiences of caring for other people's children, the pain involved in having other people care for your own children, and the impact of losing the authority over what are normally seen as intimate, private aspects of individuals' lives. The language of "removal," the "termination of parental rights," and even "fostering," is in some ways sanitizing language. It is easier to say that removing a child from a home protected them from abuse than it is to describe the scene—children crying and reaching for their parents, angry yelling, tense police officers, the drive to the shelter, the medical inspection, the waiting room, the paperwork, falling asleep the first night in a strange bed, your belongings hastily shoved into a black plastic trash bag or simply left behind.

Social workers, lawyers, and judges worked to distance themselves from the visceral, intimate details of the child welfare system through their language, their professionalism, and their enormous caseloads. Yet biological and foster parents had access to few of these protective mechanisms. They have typically cared for their children on the most intimate levels—bathing them, sleeping with them, holding them, and nursing them. They saw firsthand the depths of children's pain, joy, and confusion and they held themselves responsible for that child's safety, happiness, and sorrow. In this way, the intimacies of family life were caught up in the machinations of the child welfare bureaucracy. Biological parents and foster parents had tremendous authority over the short-term experiences of their child in different ways, shaping daily interactions during foster care or during parental visitations, constructing what time with mom and dad feels like and what their child's early memories will be of the tastes, smells, and sounds of "home." And yet foster and biological parents were caught within the grip of state authority and could exercise none of the decision-making power that typically accompanies the intimate, daily care of children. In this sense they were suspended between the categories of parent and nonparent, expected to be able to both love and leave their children at a moment's notice.

Conclusion

During the summer of 2011, the San Diego County office of child welfare completed a contract process for all foster family agencies. This process, which enlisted these agencies as formal contractors with the county, was the culmination of an effort to regularize the relationship between the county agency and private, nonprofit foster family agencies. In July, Alicia, as program manager for Esperanza, received word that Esperanza had not been approved as a contractor for the county. Alicia and I were at the dollar store when the call came, buying sand toys for the Esperanza beach picnic she was hosting the following afternoon. Alicia joked, cynically, that we were shopping for the "Goodbye Esperanza Picnic," and the mood was strained for the rest of the afternoon. Alicia had been unemployed for over a year before her hire at Esperanza, and this news did not bode well for her job future.

The denial of Esperanza's bid to contract with the county was due not to a weakness in its application or the agency's past performance as an FFA, but to the fact that Esperanza had failed to obtain the proper license prior to submitting the application. Esperanza effectively went into a suspension mode. The agency was given a grace period in which the children still on the caseload—Emma, Jayden, Rosie, Isaiah, and Danaira—had to be moved into other situations. Alicia also had the unhappy task of contacting prospective foster parents and letting them know that Esperanza's activities were currently suspended and that they could wait it out or go to another agency.

At the Esperanza picnic, part of a new effort to bring foster families together, the foster parents sat together eating pasta salad and potato chips while their children played with the sand toys we had bought the day before. I dug in the sand with Emma and Danaira and then sat holding baby Rosie, swaddled and sleeping in the sunshine, so that her foster mother, Estela, could eat. As I rocked Rosie and watched the other children play, I thought about the phone calls and visits each of them would be paid by Alicia over the next few weeks as she struggled to move forward with the temporary shut down of the agency.

Alicia worked with Esperanza's current foster families to figure out how best to handle the situation. Emma's foster parents, Josh and Trevor, were moving toward the end of the adoption process with her, so they worked with their county social worker to expedite the process and circumvent the problems Esperanza was facing. Isaiah and Danaira's foster parents, Anna and Josie, hadn't clicked as well with Alicia as they had with Corinne, and decided to become foster parents for the county instead, after being reassured by the county social worker on their case that their two foster children could remain in their care. Rosie's foster parents transferred to the county as well, not because they were disgruntled with Esperanza, but because it was the fastest way to expedite the process of adopting Rosie. Jayden's county social worker, given limited options, decided to approve her adoption out-of-state by her former foster family and Jayden's Esperanza foster parents Edith and Arturo helped facilitate that process. Alicia pursued the reapplication process, hoping to reopen the agency. Before she could complete the process, however, the umbrella organization that funded Esperanza fell into financial difficulties, laid off a number of employees, and eliminated their less financially solvent programs. Esperanza, with only five foster children prior to suspension and showing no growth in the foreseeable future, was permanently shut down.

With the loss of Esperanza, San Diego County was without an agency focused specifically on the need for bilingual foster families, social workers, and service providers. The other foster family agency in the county that specialized in providing foster and adoptive homes to young children had informed me prior to this crisis at Esperanza that they were not equipped to certify any parents who were not fluent and literate in English, since they did not have bilingual staff to work with them. The shutdown of the only agency dedicated to working with Spanish-speaking families caught up in the child welfare system in San Diego County seemed to me unconscionable given the high percentage of these families in the county. This absence was another example of the ways in which Latina/o families, particularly those who were without documentation, were differently positioned within the child welfare system, not through the intent of any particular individual or agency, but through the extraordinary legal, social, and institutional obstacles they faced. Such circumstances shape the boundaries of belonging in the contemporary

United States, creating the conditions of possibility in which decisions about family formation in the region are made.

Despite the substantial, and growing, Latina/o population in the United States, U.S. political rhetoric continues to draw on metaphors of "closing the gates," "stemming the tide" and "building walls," images that evoke a simplistic image of a geopolitical border than can be neatly drawn between an "us" and a "them." Much of this rhetoric relies on an implicit politics of worthiness through which determinations are made about what sorts of migrants have rights to citizenship in the United States. Pathways to immigration relief, such as Special Immigrant Juvenile Status, demarcate particular children as worthy not only of state protection but also of a pathway to U.S. citizenship. These children are positioned against the specter of the able-bodied, adult, economic migrant who crosses the border to steal jobs from "real" citizens, a figure that enlivens the anti-immigrant rhetoric rife in our nation. As I argue in Chapter 2, children are seen as potentially "salvageable" and worthy of rescue from unsuitable communities and families. In this way, race, class, and citizenship distinctions position particular families as objects of state interventions. This is particularly clear in the context of the child welfare system, where racially marginalized and undocumented families are more likely to experience state intervention, interventions that fuel the ongoing production of race, citizenship, and the boundaries of belonging.

At the center of these removal practices is the principle of "best interest," a framework motivated by children's rights to care and protection. "Best interest" is, at the same time, representative of a political discourse that naturalizes a particular perspective about what sets of circumstances are best for all children. This perspective might equate best interest with access to U.S. medical care or schooling, life with an affluent family, or sharing the same citizenship as your siblings, as in Jaime's case, detailed in Chapter 3. As I have laid out in the pages above, this framework is shot through with ethnocentric and xenophobic views about the unquestioned superiority of life and social service provisions in the United States. Principles like "best interest," enacted through provisions like SIJS, are discretionary frameworks through which ideas about belonging and worthiness take shape via social workers' and legal actors' ongoing interpretations of the law.

Individuals within the child welfare system possess vastly different sorts of knowledge, knowledge that is unevenly distributed, authorized, and valued. Judges "know" about the children on their caseload through such things as case files, social worker court reports, and testimony. County social workers "know" about the children on their caseload through visits, interactions with parents, reports from service providers, and their training in the fields of child development and child welfare. They "know" through their home visit notes, through their experiences with other children and other parents, and through social worker conversations about notorious cases and descriptions of the best and worst parents. These ways of knowing, I have argued, are produced through, and productive of, power asymmetries embedded in taken for granted ideas about what positionalities based on race, class, and citizenship categories indicate about parenting norms and ideals. Foster parents, adoptive parents, and biological parents "know" too, but their knowing is not typically validated in the space of the courtroom, nor does it often figure into social workers' determinations about how a case should proceed. There are many ways of knowing that are not valorized in this context, and children's knowledge of their own desires, as well as parents' knowledge about parenting and about their own specific children, are two forms of knowledge that are relegated to the realm of illegitimacy within this system. These forms of knowledge rarely factor into the official actions that shape the trajectory of a child and family through the child welfare system.

These ways of knowing are constructed through stories, through case files and court reports, through political discourse around categories of race, class, gender, and citizenship status, and through "enactments of expertise" (Carr 2010b). As institutional actors navigate the ambivalence and tensions of uneasy decision making, they rely on everyday interactions, material documents, and narratives through which they make sense of their own decisions and work to position them as inevitable outcomes of institutional constraints. As Alicia described Rosie's mother's lack of interest in parenting her, or Margo predicted a life of future abuse and drug use if she did not terminate the parental rights of Miriam and Mikey's mother, these social workers told stories about the past, present, and future that filled in the gaps in their knowledge so as to retrospectively validate decisions about which they were unsure. Documents, such as case notes and court reports, grounded discretionary decisions in formalized paperwork. In this way, agency files filled with partial glimpses of social workers' observations became reliable evidence of a seemingly measured decision-making process that shaped each child's pathway through the child welfare system. Social workers' and legal actors' appeals to the limits of the system and the law, such as the ability of the court to provide support services to a child who was not in imminent danger, highlighted very real constraints they faced in the limits of their authority and the available resources for family support. Yet these appeals also obscured and qualified the broad latitude these actors had in their enactment of agency policy and dependency law. As I have argued above, institutional arrangements and daily practices facilitate the translation of social workers' and legal actors' discretionary judgments and intuition into the abstract and authoritative realm of "expertise."

Terms such as "best interest" or "fit parents" are multi-accentual nodes that enable disparate actors to engage with each other despite the necessity of working within the particular categories and constraints of the institutions in which they are embedded. These categories allow different actors to communicate across registers and ways of knowing. The translation of the messy lives of families into social work categories such as "good" or "bad" parent is at the core of how the child welfare system is constituted in the lives of children and their families. As I discuss in Chapter 2, the translation of poverty into neglect, and of deportation into abandonment, serve as moments when the intersection of child welfare and immigration enforcement come together in unintended ways. As social workers struggle to make sense of the families who become objects of their interventions, they struggle with the ambivalence at the core of these discretionary processes. These processes necessitate the reduction of the complex lives of individuals into institutional categories of fit and unfit parents. Categories of neglect or bad parenting, or terms such as best interest, appear at first glance to be concepts utilized by experts who know without question what they mean. These categories and terms are, in fact, vague and poorly delineated; as they are taken up by different actors and move across the complex junctures of distinct institutions, they are given shape through the assumptions and the meaning assigned to them by individuals acting in the name of institutional authority. As such, I have argued that the broad latitude of these terms and categories become sites where the proclivities of individual actors are solidified into abstract government action.

In this sense, each individual operates within his or her own institutional constraints, which are sometimes distinct, but often overlapping. Yet each of these settings—the county child welfare offices, the FFA social work offices, the courtroom—are shaped and constrained by their own policy and protocol. However, for social workers and legal actors, rarely are their pathways guided by clear institutional practice. Rather, they rely on their discretion, their intuition, and their interpretation of legal code and agency policy. This is not because their institutions' protocols call for clarification, but because the nature of their work defies easy routinization. These actors operate within limits, but those limits are loose, unclear, and ever shifting. Institutional constraints do much more to delineate what cannot be done than what actions should be taken. And within this uneasy framework these actors meet at uneven junctures, sometimes operating in collaboration, sometimes speaking past each other, sometimes constraining others' choices. They rarely work within the same frames or employ similar sets of material experiences on which to base their assumptions and assertions. It is for these reasons that these institutions come together to create such a complex, entangled apparatus, one where different actors and agencies intersect and overlap in unexpected ways.

Each child welfare case was both radically unique and reflective of a broad and deep trend, which equated the removal of children from low-income families of color as in those children's best interest. Immigration policies and child welfare law came together in ways that positioned undocumented and non-U.S resident Latina/o families as vulnerable to the removal and, ultimately, the adoption of their children. Yet child welfare was also a space that denied the delineation between citizen and non-citizen, and deemed these distinctions irrelevant to the welfare of a child and to whether or not a judge could rule to dissolve legal bonds between family members. If we are to understand how citizenship, race, and narratives of worthiness shape the boundaries of belonging in this contemporary moment, it is imperative that we pay attention to such spaces as the gaps and fissures at the intersection of immigration and child welfare policy, as I have attempted to do throughout this book, in order to attend to the possibilities and limitations produced in the mess of these entanglements.

NOTES

Introduction

1. All names of organizations and individuals, with the exception of public figures and public agencies, are pseudonyms.

2. In fact, the Child Welfare System refers to a broad web of agencies and actors; see Figure 1, in Chapter 1.

3. See Boehm (2012: 129–30) for an analysis of how Mexican families, in particular, face restricted rights regardless of their legal status.

4. Other large twin border cities, such as El Paso and Ciudad Juárez, maintain a greater degree of social, political, and economic exchange. Payan (2010) and Peña (2007) describe examples of cross-border collaboration among Texas government officials and local residents. The collaborative efforts that do exist in Tijuana and San Diego focus largely on environmental issues and are, for the most part, extragovernmental coalitions (for a discussion of some failed government attempts in Tijuana and San Diego to resolve air and water pollution, see Proffitt 1994). For a discussion of how environmental collaborations occur without accompanying forms of formal governmental collaboration, see Sparrow (2001), and for a discussion of twinned U.S.-Mexico border cities through the framework of both intimacy and separation, see Yeh (2016: 67).

5. The Border Industrialization Program, instituted in 1965, promoted the economic development of the Northern Mexico border region through the implementation of special tax laws that enabled non-Mexican corporations to establish factory-based production in Mexico as long as goods were shipped back into the United States for assembly. This led to the explosion of maquiladoras in Northern Mexico and contributed to the population boom in Tijuana over the last few decades of the twentieth century. One aspect of its aim, largely unsuccessful, was to provide increased employment in Mexico in an effort to reduce Mexican migration into the United States. For a discussion of these dynamics, see Lorey (1999).

6. See, for example, Durand and Massey (2003:234).

7. See, for example, Zavella (2011), Stephen (2007), Abrego (2014), Hirsch (2003), Hondagneu-Sotelo and Avila (1997), and Parreñas (2005) on the complexities of transnational families exceeding nation-state boundaries and constructing a sense of belonging to multiple sites that impact family formations, gender relations, and economic instability.

8. Wessler (2011), who conducted a national research project on the interaction between immigration enforcement and child welfare, which overlapped with my research period, was

similarly denied access to speak with social workers by the San Diego County Child Welfare system, although he found other public agencies quite open to his project. See Wozniak (2001) for similar obstacles to research within the public child welfare agency in Connecticut, where her research took place.

9. D. Webster et al. (2016), *CCWIP Reports*, retrieved May 27, 2016 from University of California at Berkeley California Child Welfare Indicators Project, http://cssr.berkeley.edu/ucb_childwelfare.

10. For further discussion of the DREAM act and the youth referred to as the DREAMers, see Nicholls (2013), Gonzales (2016), and Orellana and Johnson (2011).

11. For a discussion of the concept of a broker/translator, and the role translation plays in allowing certain objects to be constructed in particular ways at particular moments, such that the translation process is implicated in the production of the objects themselves, see De Vries (2002) and Nuijten (2004).

12. See also Cohen's (1998) ethnography of Alzheimer's in India, which works to denaturalize processes of categorization by asking not what categories themselves mean, but why and how particular categories come to matter in a given context.

13. See Carr (2010b:20) and Agha (1999, 2005) for a discussion of register, "a recognizable, if specialized, linguistic repertoire that can include technical terms or acronyms, specific prosodic practices, and nonverbal signs such as facial expressions or gestures" (Carr 2010b:20).

14. For a consideration of the movement of a text across contexts as a transformational process, where one must attend to "what the recontextualized text brings with it from its earlier context(s) and what emergent form, function, and meaning it is given as it is recentered," see Bauman and Briggs (1990:75).

Chapter 1. "Worthy" Migrants

1. As Ensor and Godziak (2010:2) note, legal binaries such as undocumented/documented, labor migrant/asylum seekers are rarely sufficient to capture the complex experiences of migrant children.

2. This tension is a contemporary global phenomenon, not one limited to the U.S. immigration context. See Empez Vidal (2011:174) for a discussion of the manner in which unaccompanied minors in Spain are labeled simultaneously as lawbreakers and neglected children in need of protection. See also Terrio (2010:83), who notes that French judicial authorities have a vested interest in classifying unaccompanied immigrant minors as criminals, rather than children in need of protection, so as to facilitate their deportation.

3. Ironically, the term "economic," which currently places individuals squarely outside the national "family," was a concept historically rooted in the family form, seen as a mode of "good governance" (Foucault 2009:234; Mitchell 2011:125–27).

4. For examples of press coverage of this issue, see Preston (2014) and Robles (2014).

5. Immigration lawyers use the term "relief" to refer to any legal avenue through which an individual might obtain authorization to reside in the United States. The term is broad enough to encompass asylum claims, those seeking green cards under specific visas, or those

seeking a stay on a deportation order. Employing the term "relief" emphasizes a stay, or release, from the looming specter of detention or deportation and is substantially distinct from the process an individual might go through to apply for a visa or for U.S. citizenship before entering the country.

6. Through a focus on two exemplary cases, rather than a broader survey, I follow scholars who have highlighted the central importance of the singular case, particularly in the realm of socio-legal studies (McKinley 1997; Leinaweaver 2013:93–94).

7. Significant changes in children's detention conditions resulted from a class action lawsuit (*Flores v. Reno*, Case No. CV85-4544-RJK, C.D. Cal. 1996), lobbying by organizations such as Amnesty International and Human Rights Watch, among others, and legislation advocated for by Senator Diane Feinstein, which argued that detained minors' rights were being violated by their treatment in immigration custody and their inclusion in the general "criminal" adult population (see also Amnesty International 2003 for a discussion of these issues).

8. For further discussion of this issue, see Cavendish and Cortazar (2011) and Heidbrink (2014).

9. Much has been written on the racialization of immigrants. See, for example, Chavez (2001), Ngai (2004), and Perea (1997).

10. Chavez (2008:205) notes a similar departure from the discourse of deserving child migrants in the case of "anchor babies" who, in popular discourse, are framed as unworthy citizens who threaten the health and security of the nation.

11. For an examination of the way only particular subjects are made legible as worthy of humanitarian intervention, see Malkki (1996) and Ticktin (2011).

12. As Statz notes in her work with unaccompanied Fujianese minor migrants, "the youth's legal status often depends on the extent by which she is portrayed as a rights-worthy unaccompanied alien child, as opposed to a much-less defensible or pitiable 'economic migrant'" (2013).

13. Zetter (2007) and Vullnetari (2012).

14. Interview with Orphanage Director, Tijuana, March 16, 2011.

15. As I argue elsewhere (Rodriguez and Rodriguez 2016), private foster family agencies were supplemental service providers, and subcontracting was the avenue through which privately raised monies were appropriated to address government absences and gaps in services created by ongoing budget cuts. See Smith and Lipsky (1993) for a discussion of the ongoing privatization of social services, a phenomenon they refer to as a "contracting regime" (43). Freundlich (2003) also addresses this trend in relation to child welfare services and notes that while cost-saving is the ostensible goal, privatization does not reliably lead to cost-reduction or increased efficiency for government agencies.

16. Monthly reimbursement rates were set by federal law, and were made up of a complex intermingling of federal, state, and county funds.

17. Fieldnotes, August 20, 2010.

18. Fieldnotes, July 8, 2008.

19. Although I conducted extensive interviews with Tatianna and was given access to documents from Alba's records that were in Tatianna's possession, I was unable to ascertain

how Alba's presence in Esther's custody had been justified to the social worker without a legal birth certificate or other paperwork demonstrating the relationship between Alba and Esther.

20. Gleeson and Gonzales (2012) make a similar point about undocumented youth in U.S. public schools, a sphere where youth do not face differential treatment due to their citizenship status but are nevertheless set up for profound obstacles and social suffering once they leave that institution with meritocratic ideals that are not sustained in the labor market after graduating high school.

21. Interview with foster mother, February 16, 2011.

22. Notably, charges for child trafficking were never pressed against Esther, either by Tatianna's family or by the U.S. government. Perhaps Tatianna's family did not see this as a worthwhile endeavor, or did not want to implicate their own relative in a child trafficking charge. Why the district attorney did not pursue this issue is less clear.

23. Interview with foster mother, February 16, 2011.

24. Fieldnotes, September 15, 2010.

25. Interview with foster mother, February 16, 2011.

26. Kelly (2006) and Yngvesson and Coutin (2006).

27. Shuman and Bohmer (2007), Camerini and Robertson (2000), Vieira (2015).

28. The extension of rights to noncitizens based on their presence within U.S. territory is referred to by Motomura (2006) as "territorial personhood." As Motomura notes, "territorial personhood" entails minimal rights and protections not the more profound extension of rights that is understood to accompany U.S. citizenship.

29. The TVPRA was most recently reauthorized in 2013 as an amendment under the Violence Against Women (VAWA) provision.

30. For further discussion and a critique of the reach of this provision despite its potential, see Bhabha (2014:155–60), Terrio (2015), and Zatz and Rodriguez (2015).

31. For example, see Terrio (2015) and Junck (2012).

32. As I describe in Chapter 3, SIJS has been fairly accessible for foster children within San Diego. However, as Zatz and Rodriguez (2015:142–44) note, this remedy is applied unevenly across regions, a circumstance that has led advocates to attempt to move SIJS-eligible youth to regions where judges are known to grant SIJS more often. Terrio (2015) and Heidbrink (2014) also note the troubling way that SIJS severs kinship ties by foreclosing pursuit of reunification with parents and by denying a SIJS applicant the right to petition for the citizenship of their family members even after that child becomes a naturalized citizen.

33. For an analysis of the ways in which adoptive parents and families struggle to frame their children as explicitly "not immigrants" both in legal and policy language and in everyday discourse, see Dorow (2006). For further discussion of the socially constructed distinction between adoption and migration, see Rastas (2009) and Hubinette and Tigervall (2009).

34. Leinaweaver (2013) and Yngvesson (2010).

35. For an elaboration of this argument, see Briggs (2012).

36. Importantly, not all parents are equally equipped to adopt internationally, and adoption must be understood as embedded in social, economic, and citizenship privilege.

37. Prior to the tenure of the director who was managing the orphanage at the time of my research, children over the age of ten were transitioned to another Tijuana orphanage equipped

for older children. The main barriers were space concerns as well as the lack of staff the director deemed necessary to monitor older children, particularly around concerns of sexual activity. Many children ran away from the orphanages to which they were transferred, and expressed their unhappiness at being sent away from what felt to them like "home." For this reason the director was working to expand the orphanage's capacity to retain older youth when possible.

38. Fieldnotes, Tijuana, September 30, 2010.

39. The director himself told me that staffing was one of the most challenging issues he faced as director, and it was clear that tension over orphanage policies and practices ran in both directions.

40. Fieldnotes, Tijuana, September 30, 2010.

41. Ibid.

42. However, see Kanstroom (2012) for a provocative analysis of the growing numbers of deportees who live internationally but who were raised and acculturated in the United States.

43. The voluntary removal policy was not specifically for minors. Adult migrants were also driven to the border and released each day. Many of them relied on homeless shelters in Tijuana or lived on the streets while they waited to make another attempt to enter the United States.

44. Importantly, the Obama administration framed the detention and deportation of unaccompanied minors as a form of "protection," though that specific term was not used, arguing that these actions might deter other unaccompanied children from pursuing a perilous journey north. See, for example, Linthicum 2015, for press coverage of this issue.

45. It is important to note that both Alba and Tommy were young children at the time of this research, and that their lack of legal documents would certainly have raised different obstacles later in life as they pursued such activities as college education, voting, or employment as adults.

Chapter 2. Belonging and Exclusion

1. Interview with foster father, July 21, 2011.

2. Interview with foster father, July 9, 2011.

3. For further discussion of this issue, see Reich (2005) and Lee (2016).

4. See also Briggs (2002) on the foregrounding of discourses of gender and reproduction in the colonial endeavor and the "importance of thinking of family as an axis of colonialism" (4).

5. Although historians differ on the timeframe of the moral reform and progressive eras, these dates are roughly agreed upon, with the caveat that particular discourses and practices do not everywhere stop and start at discrete moments in time.

6. During this period, U.S. courts drew on the English doctrine, Parens Patriae, to assert their right to intervene in the private sphere of the family for the good of the nation as a whole. For a discussion of the application of this doctrine in the U.S. context, see Schlossman (2005). However, intervention into families was not implemented systematically nor taken up as the primary responsibility of the state during this period.

7. These women took up such projects as a way to stake their own terrain in the civilizing process and to claim a legitimate space in the public sphere, based on their expertise as mothers. They were invested in the production of values that juxtaposed Protestant values with Catholic beliefs, and an impoverished lifestyle with one of relative wealth, primarily around issues of sanitation, hygiene, and diet. For example, see Jacobs (2009) and Mink (1990). Ward (2012) notes that while many large-scale child saving efforts were carried out by wealthy white women, there were also significant child saving efforts spearheaded by Black women, primarily in Black communities. Little scholarly attention has been paid to this aspect of the child saving movement.

8. Many of these organizations in fact grew out of already established Prevention of Cruelty to Animals organizations, illuminating the relative newness of understanding children as in particular need of protection and intervention. Expansion was rapid, with thirty-four separate SPCCs established by 1880 (Gordon 1989).

9. Molina (2006), for example, explores public health campaigns as racialized, national projects in relation to Mexican families in Los Angeles during the late twentieth and early twenty-first centuries.

10. Quoted in Fraser and Gordon (1994:309).

11. See Katz (1989) for a discussion of the discourse surrounding poverty in the United States as primarily a moral discourse about deservedness. See Platt (2009) for an in-depth analysis of the child saving movement.

12. The Canadian Truth and Reconciliation Report, not yet released in full at the time of this writing, represents the first public statement from the Canadian government explicitly characterizing boarding schools for Aboriginal children as "cultural genocide" (Austen 2015).

13. For an analysis of this shift in the context of New South Wales, see Read (1981:22).

14. Although the 1935 Social Security Act is most widely known for the benefits it provided for retirees, the act was in fact broadly concerned with social welfare, including child protection, maternal welfare, aid to the blind, and unemployment, among other provisions.

15. It is also noteworthy that social workers, like nuns, are supposed to experience a "calling," rather than a pragmatic interest in their "profession."

16. See also Donzelot (1979).

17. For example, see Jacobs (2009) and Gordon (1989).

18. The urban immigrant communities often described child savers as "child snatchers," and stories of charity workers scouring urban neighborhoods for children they deemed neglected by their mere presence on the street were commonplace (Gordon 1999:10–11).

19. There is a substantial literature on the politics of child removal in these three nations. Fournier and Crey (1997) discuss child removal as a form of cultural genocide, and Armitage (1995), Jacobs (2005), and Haebich (2000) approach child removal as an assimilation strategy for the production of modern, Christian citizens.

20. For a critique of social workers' discretionary decision-making in relation to the Indian Child Welfare Act, see Briggs (2012:83).

21. As Kanstroom (2012:223–24) notes in the context of immigration law, while international law is not binding for U.S. judicial decision-making it nevertheless plays an influential role and can serve as justification for judicial rulings.

22. Hearst (2012), King (2009), and Fonseca (2002).

23. *In Re Juvenile Appeal*, 455 A.2d 1313, 1319 Conn. 1983, cited in Dalrymple (2006:144). Importantly, Dalrymple asserts that these three principles are considered unequally, with the parents' interests typically being given the most weight. Further, Dalrymple notes that the application of the "best interest" principle is "highly discretionary" (144).

24. Signed into law in 1997, the Adoption and Safe Families Act (ASFA, Public Law 105–89) was controversial for providing cash incentives meant to encourage states to increase their adoption rates.

25. See Mnookin (1973) for an early discussion of concerns about the varied application and interpretation of this principle and Schneider (1991) for a similar critique in the context of family law.

26. This sense of children as unable to act in their own "best interest" is frequently addressed through the use of CASAs, as described in Chapters 1 and 3.

27. See Zatz and Rodriguez (2015:89, 95) for a critique of similar cases.

28. See Golash-Boza (2012) for a lengthy critique of this conundrum. She states, "Immigration policies that lead to family separations force people to choose between their legal citizenship right to territorial belonging and their human right to form a family" (212). See also my discussion of these issues in Rodriguez (2016).

29. For a detailed discussion of this issue, see Wessler (2011).

30. These barriers are discussed in further detail in Chapter 3.

31. These are not the only barriers that characterize these circumstances. As I discuss in Chapter 3, the lack of resources for facilitating cross-border reunifications, negative perceptions of Tijuana social services, the impracticality of border crossing for Tijuana-based family members, and a whole host of other issues constitute serious obstacles to reunification.

32. The facts of this case remain unclear. Because there are special provisions for Cubans to regularize their immigration status, it would be unusual for Isabel's father to be deported. It is possible that Isabel's father had permanent residence status but was being detained for some criminal activity. Unfortunately, Corinne was hired after Isabel's father had been removed from court proceedings. Her best guess was that he had been involved in some serious crime, but she did not have additional information to confirm or contradict the little information contained in the file. Because many social workers are relatively unfamiliar with immigration law, the social workers on this case may not have known enough about the particular status of Cubans to question these decisions.

33. While the impacts of detention and deportation on family separation are by no means limited to Latina/o or racially marginalized families, the differential application of immigration law is profound. Although I did not work with any white families whose child welfare case involved deportation, a colleague, Ella, who was pursuing research in San Diego detention centers during my fieldwork period told me a story of a woman who had four felonies on her record. It was only after the fourth felony that she was detained and in the process of expulsion from the United States. Ella noted that the woman had come to the United States at age two; she was now forty-seven, with a teenage daughter. I asked Ella how it was possible that she got to four felonies before being put in removal proceedings and Ella smiled, saying, "Well, she is from the UK." In this way, detention and deportation practices were understood

by social workers, families, journalists, and policy makers to be primarily aimed at immigrants of color from particular sending nations.

34. The San Diego Child Welfare Agency did eventually collaborate with the Tijuana social service agency, DIF, to provide services for this family as the case progressed. However, the initial court report submitted by the county social worker on Miguel's case stated that she was unable to provide intervention services, saying, "The Agency was not able to provide the family with any services to prevent the need for intervention since the family does not reside in San Diego." Providing intervention services in Tijuana may very well have allowed the social worker to support the family without removing Miguel from his parent's custody.

35. The decision to remove an infant at birth due to drug exposure is one of the most straightforward and least contested instances of removal child welfare services enacts. It is contested primarily in circumstances where the mother believes the tests results were in error or where she was unknowingly given a banned substance. Drug exposure is also one of the few reasons infants are removed at birth, as most other allegations of neglect or abuse do not occur at this young age.

36. For further discussion of this issue, see Motomura (2011) and Zatz and Rodriguez (2014).

37. In making this assertion I follow the work of Mongia (1999) and Molina (2014:147).

38. Importantly, Yablon-Zug's (2011) interpretation of the application of "best interest" recenters the state in a manner that is at odds with a family-centered, and some would argue, child-centered, interpretation.

39. Medi-Cal, the state of California's version of Medicaid, provided free or subsidized health care to low-income adults and children.

Chapter 3. Working the Gap

1. The prohibition against legal reentry after a deportation can range anywhere from five years to a lifetime ban, depending on the initial cause of deportation. Although I was unaware of the length of Lucas's father's ban, even five years would be long enough to remove him from consideration as a reunification option for Lucas, unless Lucas was to live permanently in Mexico.

2. See Zavella (2012) for a discussion of how United States immigration policy since the 1986 Immigration Reform and Control Act (IRCA) has fallen short of attending to the needs of contemporary family formations and the ways current immigration legislation, particularly post-9/11, has engendered the increased separation of families through detention and deportation actions. See also Golash-Boza (2012).

3. Herzfeld (1992) describes a similar example involving Jehovah's Witnesses in Greece who were denied the ability to renew their residency documents, documents necessary for acquisition of mandatory state-issued identification cards. In this sense, they were "being forced by the law at one level to break the law at another" (92).

4. Coutin makes a similar argument in relation to the field of deportation studies: "If, by demarcating the exceptional and the prohibited, deportation simultaneously produces the

normal, then examining the boundaries that deportation establishes sheds light on the contours of the citizenry" (2014:7).

5. Dependency law is the judicial system that guides the implementation of child welfare policy.

6. See Figure 2 for a diagram of the agencies involved with adjudicating immigration cases. However, few of these agencies were mentioned with any frequency by my interlocutors who were not immigration lawyers. Social workers, advocates, and parents generally spoke about ICE agents, immigration judges, and lawyers, and very occasionally about the Office of Refugee Resettlement and their federal foster care program.

7. Non-U.S. citizens facing removal proceedings were not guaranteed legal representation. Because RLA had limited resources, they chose to focus on the groups of non-U.S. citizens whom they believed were most likely to win immigration relief.

8. Fieldnotes, March 3, 2011.

9. Derivative citizenship refers to citizenship acquired through a parent or other qualifying relative. Although it was a rare occurrence, some detained children were discovered to have a U.S. citizen parent they were unaware of, and through this relationship the child could become a citizen (or assert already existing status as a citizen) by procuring the necessary documents with the help of an immigration lawyer.

10. San Diego lawyers and advocates I interviewed saw SIJS as an incredible resource for foster children already in the dependency system; one lawyer described SIJS for these children as a "virtual slam dunk." However, lawyers faced tremendous obstacles obtaining SIJS for children who were not already in state custody, particularly for those children in immigration custody or in liminal spaces such as homeless shelters. Further, as Jackson (2012) notes, the reach of SIJS is severely curtailed by a lack of knowledgeable social workers and lawyers who can recognize SIJS-eligible children. See Heidbrink (2014) for a discussion of the obstacles to SIJS implementation for unaccompanied minors and the consequences of this policy in terms of the legal separation of families.

11. The other commonly used pathway for foster children to regularize their status was through adoption by U.S. citizen parents. This was the path Alba took, as discussed in Chapter 1. The advantage of SIJS was that it was available to children before exiting the foster system through reunification or adoption, and was not contingent on adoption by a family with U.S. citizenship.

12. See Chapter 1 for a more in-depth discussion of these provisions.

13. Fieldnotes, March 3, 2011.

14. Investigators conducted interviews with parents, minors, and other involved adults in order to gather the information lawyers needed to shape their goals in the courtroom. Although lawyers occasionally conducted such interviews themselves, they were limited in their ability due to inordinately large caseloads. A substantial percentage of San Diego dependency court investigators were former county social workers who brought their own expertise with the dependency system to their investigative work.

15. Fieldnotes, March 3, 2011.

16. Luz mentioned the figure "less than forty" because RLA collaborated with another San Diego organization, Pro Bono Lawyer's Guild (PBLG), which contracted with the county child

welfare agency to handle up to forty citizenship cases for foster children. RLA was poised to take on any cases over that limit. To date, however, PBLG had never been over that limit and typically had fewer than thirty cases at any one time. PBLG lawyers confirmed to me that they could handle many more cases than they were receiving from the county agency.

17. There are legitimate concerns about the potential misuse of such data. However, many advocates felt the benefits outweighed the risks. When I spoke with Lucinda, a lead attorney at San Diego Children's Lawyers, the law office that represented minors and parents in the San Diego dependency court, she estimated that roughly 10 percent of the cases the office saw involved some sort of citizenship or immigration issues.

18. As Zatz and Rodriguez note (2015:90), despite Child Welfare social workers' best intentions, the agency is simply not equipped to deal effectively with complex immigration issues.

19. Fieldnotes, March 3, 2011.

20. Interview with a CASA, February 9, 2011.

21. For further discussion of the consequences of the absence of documents or misalignments between individuals and their legal documents see Shuman and Bohmer (2007), Yngvesson and Coutin (2006), Navaro-Yashin (2007), and Kelly (2006).

22. Fieldnotes, April 8, 2011.

23. Fieldnotes, March 3, 2011.

24. This was similarly a problem for older youth living on their own in homeless shelters. State courts were likely to see these youth as currently "safe from abuse," however precarious and temporary their situation might be, and to refuse to take jurisdiction because of the lack of a threat of imminent danger. State courts also resisted taking jurisdiction over older teenagers, assuming they would not be able to successfully intervene before age eighteen. See also Terrio (2015).

25. Bhabha's (2011) analysis of stateless children raises similar concerns. Speaking broadly about policy trends impacting stateless children, Bhabha writes that, "After they are identified as victims of trafficking, trafficked children without legal immigration status (de facto *stateless*) are not as a rule considered for forms of long-term protection such as asylum but instead tend to be repatriated 'home,' even where home is a place where retrafficking is likely and caring family is nonexistent" (21).

26. Fieldnotes, March 3, 2011.

27. For example, see Pallares (2014), Zavella (2011), Schueths and Lawston (2015).

28. Interview with a dependency lawyer, April 19, 2011.

29. Fieldnotes, November 15, 2010.

30. Case law at the state level has repeatedly found that immigration status should not constitute the grounds for custody determinations or the termination of parental rights in family courts. For a discussion of these rulings at the Appellate and State Supreme Court level, see Thronson and Sullivan (2012). However, this does not bar dependency judges from making such rulings. Practice differs widely across the nation in terms of how immigration issues are considered in dependency courts, as judges hold vastly different interpretations of the broad concepts, such as "best interest of the child," that drive their custody rulings. In San Diego County, where I conducted my research, judges were expected to ignore immigration

status in the courtroom in an effort to avoid possible discrimination. For an in-depth discussion of the different ways that immigration status interacts with dependency court procedures and rulings, see Thronson (2005).

31. Interview with a Court Appointed Special Advocate, February 9, 2011.

32. Interview with a dependency judge, March 10, 2011.

33. Ibid.

34. Interview with a former San Diego County social worker, April 8, 2011.

35. For a general discussion of the way barriers to services for undocumented individuals vary widely based on the expertise and commitment of the social worker, see Ayón (2009), and for further discussion of the way child welfare policy and practice in regard to undocumented parents varies widely from one regional office to another, see Wessler (2011).

36. Fieldnotes, March 14, 2011.

37. See Briggs (2012:83) for a discussion of the discrepancy between social workers' actions and dependency law in her consideration of the history of flagrant violations of the Indian Child Welfare Act.

38. See Kleinfield (2013) for a case in the Bronx involving a judge's outrage at a social worker who misrepresented details of a case, stating, in an effort to promote the adoption of the two youngest daughters, that the mother had missed over half the visits with her children in a period when she had not in fact missed a single one.

39. Interview with a dependency lawyer, April 19, 2011.

40. For example, see Butera (2010), Wessler (2011), Zatz and Rodriguez (2014:100).

41. For a discussion of this issue, see Wessler (2011).

42. In this case, Angélica, the adoptive mother, had negotiated an open adoption with her son's birth mother—they exchanged photographs and had a visit about once a year. Because the father had not been present during the adoption proceedings, he had not similarly negotiated these terms. However, Angélica explained that due to his unreliability and the fact that she believed him to be involved in criminal activity, she would have been unlikely to agree to an ongoing relationship even if he had been present, other than perhaps the exchange of photographs.

43. Social workers and dependency lawyers and judges often used the term "willful abandonment" without attention to the degree of "will" involved, as in the case of detained or deported parents.

44. Fieldnotes, November 15, 2010.

45. It is important to note that dependency law does not allow for much of a middle ground; at the end of a dependency case parents typically either regain full custody of their children or have their parental rights terminated. Adoptive parents can elect to maintain some visitation or communication with biological parents or extended family but are under no legal obligation to do so. At the time of this research, county social workers often encouraged adoptive parents to commit to as little communication with biological families as possible, arguing that it was far easier to choose to allow more contact later than to attempt to limit it in the future. This perspective on "closed" adoption is counter to current private adoption philosophy, which has moved away from an erasure of the children's history and has taken the position that open communication, the retention of cultural and historical particularities of a

child's origin, and transparency are in the "best interest" of the adopted child's healthy development. This was distinct from an earlier position that argued for treating an adopted child "as if" they were a "natural" child. For a discussion of this shift, see Yngvesson (1997) and Modell (1994).

46. Social workers told me that children over age eight were at risk of being unadoptable, as were children of color. "Unadoptable" did not mean these children were ineligible for adoption, but that they were unlikely to meet the criteria adoptive families outlined for a child they were willing to adopt. For these children, social workers most vigorously pursued placement with extended family.

47. See, for example, Newton et al. (2000), Doyle (2007).

48. Interview with a CASA, February 9, 2011.

49. Fieldnotes, April 8, 2011.

50. All formal communications between U.S. and Mexican social service agencies were supposed to go through the International Liaison Office in San Diego, an arm of the San Diego County child welfare system. This office was also the official channel for San Diego County social workers who required information from the Mexican Consulate. Many advocates and social workers, including Jaime, bemoaned the lengthy time process this formal mode of communication often took and frequently pursued unofficial, alternative methods for cross-border communication.

51. During 2010–2011 when I conducted the majority of my research, the wait time at the border was prohibitive to conducting daily business in a timely manner. Providing that you were not pulled over for further inspection, crossing from San Diego to Tijuana could range from anywhere from five to forty-five minutes, while a return from Tijuana to San Diego regularly ranged from 1 1/2 to 4 hours. The acquisition of a Sentri pass, attainable for both United States and Mexican citizens based on an extensive background check and a number of fees, could reduce the border crossing time from Tijuana to San Diego to as little as fifteen minutes. However, the Sentri pass required that all passengers in a vehicle were pass holders, thus limiting the use of this timesaving option.

52. For an in-depth study of legal activism in relation to immigration policy in the United States and France, see Kawar (2015).

53. Interview with a dependency lawyer, April 19, 2011.

54. Numerous media reports have also noted undocumented parents' expressed desires to bring younger children with them should they be deported, but to leave older children already immersed in the U.S. school system in the care of relatives or guardians in order to increase the perceived opportunities for their future (Associated Press 2011).

55. See Ferguson and Gupta's (2002) approach to state-making.

Chapter 4. Decisions, Decisions

1. There is a substantial literature exploring the temporality, materiality, and profound impact of institutional files on the workings of complex agencies. See, for example, Bowker (2005), Hull (2003), and Harper (1997).

2. This feeling of powerlessness was felt by most foster family agencies in San Diego County and was not particular to Esperanza.

3. Agency files could technically be subpoenaed if a child welfare case ever went to trial, and Corinne noted this as another pressure she felt to make sure the notes were complete and accurate. However, Corinne did not believe this had ever occurred in Esperanza's history.

4. Agency files for foster parents included documentation of the initial screening and application process and evidence that they continued to meet home inspection requirements and maintain such certifications as CPR training.

5. As I discuss in further detail in Chapter 5, accusations of abuse and neglect were frequently filed against foster parents by biological parents. Although instances of abuse and neglect certainly do occur within the foster care system, social workers interpreted many of these claims as the result of frustrated biological parents, unable to express their anger at the social worker who held power over the custody of their children, and lashing out at foster parents instead. Esperanza's parent training discussed the likelihood of these accusations and encouraged foster parents to remain calm in these circumstances and to give biological parents a sense of respect and control by asking them to give recommendations about what their children liked to eat, how they liked to dress them, and other small aspects of their children's lives.

6. It was rare that claims of abuse in foster homes were found to be true—perhaps because abuse in foster homes was infrequent, or perhaps because abuse in general, particularly involving very young children, was quite difficult to prove. Investigators often were faced with ambiguous or nonexistent physical evidence and few uninterested witnesses. In this way, social workers approached abuse investigations in foster parents' homes as procedural protection for the agency, showing they had taken the necessary precautions. Ironically, the very sort of investigation that had led to the removal of a child, in this case was reframed as "going through the motions" to satisfy an irate biological parent.

7. Interview with Foster Family Agency Director of Recruitment, July 6, 2011.

8. Ibid.

9. See Scherz (2011) for a discussion of this issue.

10. Ayón et al. (2010:274) document Mexican parents' sentiment that child welfare decisions in their Southern California agency were shaped profoundly by whether their social worker liked them or not. This sentiment was supported by comments these parents received from service providers who encouraged them to take care to get along with their case workers.

11. Fieldnotes, August 18, 2010.

12. Thanks to Celina Callahan-Kapoor for this particular formulation.

13. Fieldnotes, April 25, 2011.

14. Judges each typically received the file for their cases the night before the hearings and would hear about ten cases between the hours of eight and noon, with the afternoon session, which lasted from one to four, reserved for trials, appeals, adoption hearings, and other lengthier processes. Judges handled enormous caseloads. Unfortunately, I was unable to determine accurate caseload numbers for San Diego dependency court judges beyond getting a basic sense of their weekly number of hearings. A 2005 survey of California dependency

judges stated that this number was very difficult to determine based on constant fluctuation. The survey asked judges to provide a range of the number of open cases assigned to them and found that, "of the 42 judicial officers with a full-time dependency caseload who responded to this question, 25 estimated a caseload of more than 800 cases, and 11 estimated a caseload between 300 and 800" (Administrative Office of the Courts 2005:94).

15. Although a dependency court judge must authorize the removal of a child and determine that this action had sufficient grounds, this determination is often made after a child has already been removed. In this way, the county social worker has broad authority to enter a home and take a child into custody, with law enforcement support if necessary. This is a manner in which the authority of the social worker is made manifest, as well as a circumstance that conflates the authority of the social worker with the authority of the police.

16. As Sarat (1990:346) notes in the context of welfare recipients, officials "claim authority to say what the law is and what the rules mean."

17. For an extended discussion of how social worker expertise is constructed through appeals to scientific objectivity, see Swartz (2005).

18. For a critique of this dynamic, and the way in which social workers make decisions about children's placement and custody without, in the eyes of foster mothers, knowing the children at all, see Wozniak (2001).

19. Cases for county social workers were typically organized in relation to the primary parent, usually the mother. So a set of four siblings with the same mother would be counted as a single "case," though the children could very well be in different custody arrangements and with different needs.

20. Interview with a dependency lawyer, August 5, 2011.

21. Although most FFAs had an official preference for hiring licensed social workers, and a very few had a requirement that they would only hire social workers with a Master's in Social Work (MSW), individuals with counseling degrees, such as the Marriage and Family Therapy degree that Corinne had, were technically eligible for these positions.

22. Fieldnotes, FFA Monthly Meeting, December 8, 2010.

23. Fieldnotes, September 7, 2010.

24. The term "alleged" is applied to a man who names himself as a child's father, or is named as such by that child's mother or other relative. The father remains "alleged" until a hospital birth certificate naming him is produced, or until a paternity test is conducted. And although incarcerated parents have the legal right to be given reunification services, particularly if their prison release date is within twelve months of the child's entrance into the foster care system, this is not common practice for incarcerated fathers, although it does occur on occasion. More often, incarcerated fathers are contacted primarily for the purpose of determining whether they have any relatives with whom the child might be placed.

25. Parents are typically given six months of services to demonstrate their ability to make progress toward reunification. Most parents are given a six-month extension after this period, and reunification in less than six months is very unusual. It was expected that most parents would then be given a third extension, constituting a total of eighteen months, before either being reunified with their child or the judge moved forward with the termination of parental rights. This is, however, an optimistic time frame, as the average time in care for a foster child

was 28.6 months, as of 2005. Adoption and Foster Care Analysis and Reporting System (AFCARS), http://www.acf.dhhs.gov/programs/cb/stats_research/afcars/tar/report13.htm.

26. Fieldnotes, July 11, 2011.

27. Interview with a foster father, July 9, 2011.

28. Fieldnotes, February 14, 2011.

29. There were strict regulations governing the space necessary for a foster child, including the number of children who can sleep in a given bedroom, and the number of dresser drawers that must be made available for a child's clothing and belongings. Estela and Hernan's home described above met that standard. For this reason, Corinne could not deny the family their foster care license. However, she could and did resist placing a child with them by calling all other available foster families first when trying to find a foster home for a child.

30. Fieldnotes, June 8, 2011.

31. Fieldnotes, September 27, 2010.

32. Fieldnotes, October 20, 2010.

33. The reunification plan was a document drafted by the county social worker that laid out the requirements that parents must meet to regain custody of their children. This might include attending parenting or anger management classes, securing stable housing or employment, or other similar requirements. Although the reunification plan was supposed to be constructed through a collaborative discussion with the biological parents of the child, this was not always the case. Parents did have to sign the plan, however, and failure to do so was interpreted by the agency as a lack of interest in regaining custody of the child in question.

34. For a detailed historical discussion of women's negotiation of domestic violence situations, see Gordon (1989).

35. Corinne was the Esperanza social worker who managed this case and worked closely with Taylor and his foster parents, Anna and Josie. The county social worker, Krissy, was in charge of working with Taylor's biological parents and determining the case plan and his parents' progress, as well as making recommendations to the court about Taylor's placement and pending reunification with his parents. Anna and Josie, as Esperanza foster parents, were expected to report any concerning incidents or issues to both Corrine and Krissy, although both social workers understood that they were under Corrine's direct supervision.

36. Separate attorneys represent children and their parents in dependency court hearings, an issue I elaborate in Chapter 3.

37. Importantly, while the judge had embarrassed Krissy, and was likely to scrutinize her reports and ask more questions in relation to her future recommendations, that was the extent of judicial oversight. See Sarat (1990) for an analysis of how welfare social workers and legal actors may check each other's practices but are ultimately part of the same apparatus, working toward similar goals.

38. Fieldnotes, November 8, 2010.

39. Interview with a CASA administrator, February 4, 2011.

40. Anna was later cleared of any wrongdoing. However, accusations of foster parent abuse, while sometimes well founded, were also tactics used by biological parents as strategies for resisting their replacement by foster parents and their subsequent framing as "bad" families.

41. "Compassion fatigue" is a term used to describe a reaction to the secondary trauma experiences of social workers, nurses, psychologists, and others who work on a regular basis with traumatized clients. Compassion fatigue theory suggests that workers become less empathetic over time as a reaction to the ongoing feelings of hopelessness and despair they face in their work. See Bride and Figley (2007) for an introduction to a special issue of the *Clinical Social Work Journal* focusing on the issues of compassion fatigue and strategies for understanding and ameliorating this issue.

42. "Family maintenance" is the term used to describe the act of providing support services to a family, such as therapy or financial subsidies, rather than removing a child from the home.

43. Fieldnotes, May 19, 2011.

44. Fieldnotes, October 15, 2010.

45. A child can, of course, be returned to the custody of an out-of-state parent, provided that a local child welfare agency to the parent can determine that there is no concern about her home or ability to care for her child. Although I was unable to confirm the details of this case, I assume that there were concerns regarding the mother's ability or interest in custody of her son as the reason that this avenue was not pursued.

46. Fieldnotes, May 19, 2011.

47. Ibid.

48. Interview with a dependency lawyer, April 19, 2011.

49. Murray (2004:5) notes, "A common complaint about the current financing system is that the vast majority of dedicated federal funding—Title IV-E Foster Care and Adoption Assistance—can only be accessed once children have already been removed from their biological families. That is, they support children on the 'back end' of abuse and neglect. The more flexible funding that is available for prevention, reunification, and permanency services—that is, the "front-end" services, funded primarily through Title IV-B—is relatively limited and, as discussed above, is subject to the annual appropriations process."

50. For a discussion of the way the United States maintains a reduced social safety net through its reliance on families to shoulder the burden of the care of dependents such as children, elderly, and others who would otherwise be the responsibility of the state, see Briggs (2012: 263–66).

51. Interview with a dependency lawyer, April 19, 2011.

52. Fieldnotes, December 7, 2011.

53. The requirement for the state to provide medical coverage for foster children is wrapped up in their responsibility as the "custodial parent" for a child. This is an interesting priority in that any of these children could have gone without medical coverage due to their family's impoverished or undocumented status, making child removal one avenue through which children can access the medical care they require.

Chapter 5. Intimacies

1. Fieldnotes, January 27, 2011.

2. Although my focus is not on the "economic," I take an approach similar to Wilson (2004:198) who sees the "intimate" as "an umbrella term to allow for the exploration of 'private' issues in 'public' economic spaces."

3. Fieldnotes, August 20, 2010.

4. Collins and Mayer (2010:115) make a similar argument about mothers receiving welfare services having to give up their personal freedoms, such as the right to choose their preferred employment goals and accept the "tutelage of the state" as a condition for receiving aid. See also Lee's (2016) analysis of the child welfare system in New York City, *Catching a Case*.

5. Although it is indisputable that children of color are overrepresented in the foster care system, the majority of foster children in San Diego foster care are white. Racial privilege and prejudice certainly play a role in social worker and parent interactions, as much of this book describes. However, a white parent does not necessarily stand out as a privileged parent in the child welfare system. The removal of children from upper middle-class and upper-class homes is rare indeed, and social workers often noted these sorts of cases to me as standout cases. Only two such cases appeared during my research. The second case, not recounted here, involved Tijuana-resident parents who achieved their wealth through drug trafficking.

6. Fieldnotes, November 15, 2011.

7. See Mehan (1983) for a discussion of how professional versions of a story are authorized to overlay versions in the context of determinations about special education services for elementary school students.

8. Fieldnotes October 2, 2010.

9. Tough's (2008) Chapter 3, entitled "Baby College," describes the way instructors negotiate these tensions with young parents in Harlem.

10. Fieldnotes, July 17, 2008.

11. Ibid.

12. It was so common for parents whose children have been removed to lack their own vehicle that county social workers routinely brought bus passes with them to their first meeting with the family.

13. Interview with a foster mother, August 11, 2008.

14. Fieldnotes, August 12, 2010.

15. Fieldnotes, December 8, 2011.

16. Interview with a foster family agency recruitment director, July 6, 2011.

17. Fieldnotes, December 28, 2010.

18. Interview with a foster mother, March 2, 2011.

19. Ibid.

20. Ibid.

21. Torticollis is a condition where a child's head is twisted relative to the torso. An infant born with this condition typically develops it due to the position while growing in the womb, in utero muscle damage, or loss of blood to the fetus's neck.

22. Interview with a foster mother, August 11, 2008.

23. Interview with a foster mother, March 2, 2011.

24. Fieldnotes, September 10, 2010.

25. Fieldnotes, June 15, 2011.

26. Although 21 referrals is a remarkable amount of child welfare attention to receive prior to the removal of children, it was not unusual for parents to have had numerous

investigations that did not result in the state taking custody of their children. This was often because claims were "unsubstantiated," meaning sufficient evidence of abuse or neglect could not be found by the investigating social worker, or the evidence that was found did not constitute a "threat of imminent danger."

27. Fieldnotes, August 12, 2010.

28. Fieldnotes, February 18, 2011.

29. See Wozniak (2001:70) for a scathing critique of the damage done to foster children when social workers did not transmit important case details, such as a history of sexual abuse, to foster parents who felt that they then inadvertently re-traumatized these children through such regular daily habits as a bath.

30. Leinaweaver (2013:33) makes a similar observation in the context of foster and adoptive homes in Spain.

31. Fieldnotes, July 19, 2010.

32. Fieldnotes, August 30, 2010.

33. The term "legal orphan" refers to a child who has no legal guardian. This situation occurred when parental rights were terminated, or parents were deceased, before a new guardian had been appointed. In these cases, the state government via child welfare services acted as the child's legal guardian. Social workers and dependency court judges acting in this capacity were routinely asked for permission for such things as participation in school field trips or sleepover parties.

34. Fieldnotes, October 29, 2010.

35. As mentioned above, Abrams Children's Home was the main receiving center in San Diego that provided temporary shelter to children who had been removed from their homes. Children at Abrams were housed in small dorms, separated by both gender and age, causing further trauma for siblings, like Michael and Miriam, who had been together throughout their experience within the foster system. Although Abrams was highly regarded as a safe and loving place for children, child welfare policy required social workers to attempt to place children directly into a relative or foster home—Abrams was meant to be a temporary fallback option only.

36. Fieldnotes, December 10, 2010.

REFERENCES

Abourezk, James. 1977. "The Role of the Federal Government: A Congressional View." In *The Destruction of American Indian Families*, ed. Steven Unger, 12–14. New York: Association on American Indian Affairs.

Abrego, Leisy. 2014. *Sacrificing Families: Navigating Laws, Labor, and Love Across Borders*. Stanford, Calif.: Stanford University Press.

Administrative Office of the Courts. 2005. *California Juvenile Dependency Court Improvement Program Reassessment*. http://www.courts.ca.gov/documents/CIPReassessmentRpt.pdf.

Agha, Asif. 1999. "Register." *Journal of Linguistic Anthropology* 9(1–2): 216–19.

———. 2005. "Voice, Footing, Enregisterment." *Journal of Linguistic Anthropology* 15(1): 38–59.

Alston, Philip. 1994. "The Best Interests Principle: Towards a Reconciliation of Culture and Human Rights." *International Journal of Law and the Family* 8(1): 1–25.

Amnesty International. 2003. *Unaccompanied Children in Immigration Detention*. New York: Amnesty International.

Armitage, Andrew. 1995. *Comparing the Policy of Aboriginal Assimilation: Australia, Canada, and New Zealand*. Vancouver: University of British Columbia Press.

Associated Press. 2011. "Immigrants Fearing Deportation Make Plans for Kids." *New York Times*, October 9.

Austen, Ian. 2015. "Report Details 'Cultural Genocide' at Schools for Aboriginal Canadians." *New York Times*, June 3, A7.

Ayón, Cecilia. 2009. "Shorter Time-Lines, Yet Higher Hurdles: Mexican Families' Access to Child Welfare Mandated Services." *Children and Youth Services Review* 31(6): 609–16.

Ayón, Cecilia, Eugene Aisenberg, and Pauline Erera. 2010. "Learning How to Dance with the Public Child Welfare System: Mexican Parents' Efforts to Exercise Their Voice." *Journal of Public Child Welfare* 4(3): 263–86.

Bartholet, Elizabeth. 1999. *Nobody's Children: Abuse and Neglect, Foster Drift, and the Adoption Alternative*. Boston: Beacon.

Bauman, Richard and Charles L. Briggs. 1990. "Poetics and Performance as Critical Perspectives on Language and Social Life." *Annual Review of Anthropology* 19: 59–88.

Benda-Beckmann, Franz von, Keebet von Benda-Beckmann, and Anne Griffiths, eds. 2013. *Spatializing Law: An Anthropological Geography of Law in Society*. Cornwall: Ashgate.

Benda-Beckmann, Keebet von. 2002. "Globalisation and Legal Pluralism." *International Law FORUM du Droit International* 4(1): 19–25.

Bhabha, Jacqueline. 2011. "From Citizen to Migrant: The Scope of Child Statelessness in the Twenty First Century." In *Children Without a State: A Global Human Rights Challenge*, ed. Jacqueline Bhabha, 1–39. Cambridge, Mass.: MIT Press.

———. 2014. *Child Migration and Human Rights in a Global Age*. Princeton, N.J.: Princeton University Press.

Boehm, D. A. 2008. "'For My Children': Constructing Family and Navigating the State in the U.S.-Mexico Transnation." *Anthropological Quarterly* 81(4): 777–802.

———. 2012. *Intimate Migrations: Gender, Family, and Illegality Among Transnational Mexicans*. New York: New York University Press.

Bowker, Geoffrey. 2005. *Memory Practices in the Sciences*. Cambridge, Mass.: MIT Press.

Bowker, Geoffrey and Susan Leigh Star. 1999. *Sorting Things Out: Classification and Its Consequences*. Cambridge, Mass.: MIT Press.

Brenneis, Don. 2004. "A Partial View of Contemporary Anthropology." *American Anthropologist* 106(3): 580–88.

Bride, Brian and Charles Figley. 2007. "The Fatigue of Compassionate Social Workers: An Introduction to the Special Issue on Compassion Fatigue." *Clinical Social Work Journal* 35(3): 151–53.

Briggs, Laura. 2002. *Reproducing Empire: Race, Sex, Science, and U.S. Imperialism in Puerto Rico*. Berkeley: University of California Press.

———. 2012. *Somebody's Children: The Politics of Transracial and Transnational Adoption*. Durham, N.C.: Duke University Press.

Butera, Emily. 2010. *Torn Apart by Immigration Enforcement: Parental Rights and Immigration Detention*. New York: Women's Refugee Commission.

Butler, Chris. 2009. "Critical Legal Studies and the Politics of Space." *Social and Legal Studies* 18(3): 313–32.

Cabot, Heath. 2014. *On the Doorstep of Europe: Asylum and Citizenship in Greece*. Philadelphia: University of Pennsylvania Press.

Camerini, Michael and Shari Robertson, dirs. 2000. *Well-Founded Fear*.

Carr, Summerson. 2010a. *Scripting Addiction: The Politics of Therapeutic Talk and American Sobriety*. Princeton, N.J.: Princeton University Press.

———. 2010b. "Enactments of Expertise." *Annual Review of Anthropology* 39: 17–32.

Cavendish, Betsy and Maru Cortazar. 2011. *Children at the Border: The Screening, Protection, and Repatriation of Unaccompanied Mexican Minors*. Washington, D.C.: Appleseed.

Chang, Helen. 2003. "My Father Is a Woman, Oh No! The Failure of the Courts to Uphold Individual Substantive Due Process Rights for Transgender Parents Under the Guise of the Best Interests of the Child." *Santa Clara Law Review* 43: 649–98.

Chavez, Leo R. 2001. *Covering Immigration: Popular Images and the Politics of the Nation*. Berkeley: University of California Press.

———. 2008. *The Latino Threat: Constructing Immigrants, Citizens, and the Nation*. Stanford, Calif.: Stanford University Press.

Clarke, Kamari Maxine. 2009. *Fictions of Justice: The International Criminal Court and the Challenge of Legal Pluralism in Sub-Saharan Africa*. New York: Cambridge University Press.

Clifford, James. 1997. *Routes: Travel and Translation in the Late Twentieth Century*. Cambridge, Mass.: Harvard University Press.

Cohen, Lawrence. 1998. *No Aging in India: Alzheimer's, the Bad Family, and Other Modern Things*. Berkeley: University of California Press.

Collins, Jane L. and Victoria Mayer. 2010. *Both Hands Tied: Welfare Reform and the Race to the Bottom of the Low-Wage Labor Market*. Chicago: University of Chicago Press.

Collins, Patricia Hill. 1998. "It's All in the Family: Intersections of Gender, Race, and Nation." *Hypatia* 13(3): 62–82.

Conan, Neal. 2011. "Talk of the Nation." National Public Radio, October 11.

Connolly, Deborah. 2000. *Homeless Mothers: Face to Face with Women and Poverty*. Minneapolis: Minnesota University Press.

Coontz, Stephanie. 2000. "Historical Perspectives on Family Studies." *Journal of Marriage and Family* 62(2): 283–97.

Coutin, Susan Bibler. 2000. *Legalizing Moves: Salvadoran Immigrants' Struggle for U.S. Residency*. Ann Arbor: University of Michigan Press.

———. 2007. *Nation of Emigrants: Shifting Boundaries of Citizenship in El Salvador and the United States*. Ithaca, N.Y.: Cornell University Press.

———. 2014. "Deportation Studies: Origins, Themes, and Directions." *Journal of Ethnic and Migration Studies* 41(4): 671–81.

Dalrymple, Joyce Koo. 2006. "Seeking Asylum Alone: Using the Best Interests of the Child Principle to Protect Unaccompanied Minors." *Boston College Third World Law Journal* 26(1): 131–68.

Das Gupta, Monisha. 2014. "Don't Deport Our Daddies: Gendering State Deportation Practices and Immigrant Organizing." *Gender & Society* 28(1): 83–109.

De Genova, Nicholas. 2002. "Migrant 'Illegality' and Deportability in Everyday Life." *Annual Review of Anthropology* (January): 419–47.

De Genova, Nicholas and Nathalie Peutz, eds. 2010. *The Deportation Regime: Sovereignty, Space, and the Freedom of Movement*. Durham, N.C.: Duke University Press.

De Genova, Nicholas and Ana Y. Ramos-Zayas. 2003. *Latino Crossings: Mexicans, Puerto Ricans, and the Politics of Race and Citizenship*. New York: Routledge.

De Vries, Peter. 2002. "Vanishing Mediators: Enjoyment as a Political Factor in Western Mexico." *American Ethnologist* 29(4): 901–27.

Demian, Melissa. 2015. "Dislocating Custom." *Political and Legal Anthropology Review* 38(1): 91–107.

Donzelot, Jacques. 1979. *The Policing of Families*. New York: Pantheon.

Dorow, Sara. 2006. *Transnational Adoption: A Cultural Economy of Race, Gender, and Kinship*. New York: New York University Press.

Doyle, Joseph J. 2007. "Child Protection and Child Outcomes: Measuring the Effects of Foster Care." *American Economic Review* 97(5): 1583–1610.

Dreby, Joanna. 2010. *Divided by Borders: Mexican Migrants and Their Children*. Berkeley: University of California Press.

———. 2012. "How Today's Immigration Enforcement Policies Impact Children, Families, and Communities: A View from the Ground." Center for American Progress, Washington, D.C., August.

———. 2015. *Everyday Illegal: When Policies Undermine Immigrant Families*. Oakland: University of California Press.

Durand, Jorge and Douglas Massey. 2003. "The Costs of Contradiction: US Border Policy 1986–2000." *Latino Studies* 1(2): 233–52.

Empez Vidal, Nuria. 2011. "The Transnationally Affected: Spanish State Policies and the Life-Course Events of Families in North Africa." In *Everyday Ruptures: Children, Youth, and Migration in Global Perspective*, ed. Cati Coe, Rachel R. Reynolds, Deborah A. Boehm, Julia Meredith Hess, and Heather Rae-Espinoza, 174–88. Nashville: Vanderbilt University Press.

Ensor, Marisa O. and Elzbieta M. Gozdziak. 2010. *Children and Migration: At the Crossroads of Resiliency and Vulnerability*. New York: Palgrave Macmillan.

Fassin, Didier. 2007. "Humanitarianism as a Politics of Life." *Public Culture* 19(3): 499–520.

———. 2011. "Policing Borders, Producing Boundaries: The Governmentality of Immigration in Dark Times." *Annual Review of Anthropology* 40: 213–26.

Ferguson, James and Akhil Gupta. 2002. "Spatializing States: Toward an Ethnography of Neoliberal Governmentality." *American Ethnologist* 29(4): 981–1002.

Flatow, Nicole. 2014. "Judge Who Took Away Immigrant's Baby Said Lack of English Would Cause 'Developmental' Problems." *Think Progress*, March 13.

Fonseca, Claudia. 2002. "The Politics of Adoption: Child Rights in the Brazilian Setting." *Law and Policy* 24(3): 199–227.

Foucault, Michel. 2009. *Security, Territory, Population: Lectures at the Collège de France 1977–1978*. New York: Palgrave Macmillan.

Fournier, Suzanne and Ernie Crey. 1997. *Stolen from Our Embrace: The Abduction of First Nations Children and the Restoration of Aboriginal Communities*. Vancouver: Douglas and McIntyre.

Franklin, Sarah and Susan McKinnon, eds. 2002. *Relative Values: Reconfiguring Kinship Studies*. Durham, N.C.: Duke University Press.

Fraser, Nancy and Linda Gordon. 1994. "A Genealogy of 'Dependency': Tracing a Keyword of the U.S. Welfare State." *Signs* 19(2): 309–36.

Freundlich, Madelyn. 2003. *An Assessment of the Privatization of Child Welfare Services: Challenges and Successes*. Washington, D.C.: Child Welfare League of America.

Gilger, Lauren, Charles Gorra, Josh Haskell, Robin Respaut, and Selly Thiam. 2012. "Adoption Battle over 5-Year Old Boy Pits Missouri Couple Vs. Illegal Immigrant." *ABC News*, February 1.

Ginsburg, Faye and Rayna Rapp. 1991. "The Politics of Reproduction." *Annual Review of Anthropology* 20: 311–43.

Gleeson, Shannon. 2010. "Labor Rights for All? The Role of Undocumented Immigrant Status for Worker Claims Making." *Law & Social Inquiry* 35: 561–602.

Gleeson, Shannon and Roberto Gonzales. 2012. "When Do Papers Matter? An Institutional Analysis of Undocumented Life in the United States." *International Migration* 50(4): 1–19.

Golash-Boza, Tanya. 2012. *Immigration Nation: Raids, Detentions, and Deportations in Post-9/11 America*. Boulder, Colo.: Paradigm.

Gonzales, Roberto. 2016. *Lives in Limbo: Undocumented and Coming of Age in America*. Berkeley: University of California Press.

Gordon, Linda. 1989. *Heroes of Their Own Lives: The Politics and History of Family Violence, Boston, 1880–1960*. New York: Penguin.

———. 1999. *The Great Arizona Orphan Abduction*. Cambridge, Mass.: Harvard University Press.

Haebich, Anna. 2000. *Broken Circles: Fragmenting Indigenous Families, 1800–2000*. Fremantle, Western Australia: Fremantle Arts Centre Press.

Harper, Richard. 1997. *Inside the IMF: An Ethnography of Documents, Technology and Organisational Action*. New York: Routledge.

Hearst, Alice. 2012. *Children and the Politics of Cultural Belonging*. New York: Cambridge University Press.

Heidbrink, Lauren. 2014. *Migrant Youth, Transnational Families, and the State: Care and Contested Interests*. Philadelphia: University of Pennsylvania Press.

Herzfeld, Michael. 1992. *The Social Production of Indifference: Exploring the Symbolic Roots of Western Bureaucracy*. New York: Berg Press.

Hirsch, Jennifer. 2003. *A Courtship After Marriage: Sexuality and Love in Mexican Transnational Families*. Berkeley: University of California Press.

Hondagneu-Sotelo, Pierrette and Ernestine Avila. 1997. "'I'm Here, But I'm There': The Meanings of Latina Transnational Motherhood." *Gender and Society* 11(5): 548–71.

Hubinette, Tobias and Carina Tigervall. 2009. "To Be Non-White in a Colour-Blind Society: Conversations with Adoptees and Adoptive Parents in Sweden on Everyday Racism." *Journal of Intercultural Studies* 30(4): 335–53.

Hull, Matthew. 2003. "The File: Agency, Authority, and Autography in an Islamabad Bureaucracy." *Language and Communication* 23(3): 287–314.

Hulse, Carl. 2014. "Immigrant Surge Rooted in Law to Curb Child Trafficking." *New York Times*, July 8, A1.

Jackson, Kristen. 2012. "Special Status Seekers: Through the Underused SIJS Process, Immigrant Juveniles May Obtain Legal Status." *Los Angeles Lawyer* 34: 20–22.

Jacobs, Margaret. 2005. "Maternal Colonialism: White Women and Indigenous Child Removal in the American West and Australia, 1880–1940." *Western Historical Quarterly* 36(4): 453–76.

———. 2009. *White Mother to a Dark Race: Settler Colonialism, Maternalism, and the Removal of Indigenous Children in the American West and Australia, 1880–1940*. Lincoln: University of Nebraska Press.

Junck, Angie. 2012. "Special Immigrant Juvenile Status: Relief for Neglected, Abused, and Abandoned Undocumented Children." *Juvenile and Family Court Journal* 63(1): 48–62.

Kanstroom, Daniel. 2012. *Aftermath: Deportation Law and the New American Diaspora*. New York: Oxford University Press.

Katrandjian, Olivia and Angela Hill. 2012. "Illegal Immigrant Fights for Custody of Young Son." *ABCnews.com*.

Katsulis, Yasmina. 2008. *Sex Work and the City: The Social Geography of Health and Safety in Tijuana, Mexico*. Austin: University of Texas Press.

Katz, Michael. 1989. *The Undeserving Poor: From the War on Poverty to the War on Welfare*. New York: Pantheon.

Kawar, Leila. 2015. *Contesting Immigration Policy in Court: Legal Activism and Its Radiating Effects in the United States and France*. New York: Cambridge University Press.

Kelly, Tobias. 2004. "Returning Home? Law, Violence, and Displacement Among West Bank Palestinians." *Political and Legal Anthropology Review* 27(2): 95–112.

———. 2006. "Documented Lives: Fear and the Uncertainties of Law During the Second Palestinian Intifada." *Journal of the Royal Anthropology Institute* 12(1): 89–107.

Kerber, Linda K. 2007. "The Stateless as the Citizen's Other: A View from the United States." *American Historical Review* 112(1): 1–34.

King, Shani. 2009. "U.S. Immigration Law and the Traditional Nuclear Conception of Family: Toward a Functional Definition of Family That Protects Children's Fundamental Human Rights." *Columbia Human Rights Law Review* 41: 509–67.

Kleinfield, N. R. 2013. "The Girls Who Haven't Come Home." *New York Times*, July 7, MB1.

Kunzel, Regina. 1993. *Fallen Women, Problem Girls: Unmarried Mothers and the Professionalization of Social Work, 1890–1945*. New Haven, Conn.: Yale University Press.

Latour, Bruno and Steve Woolgar. 1986 [1979]. *Laboratory Life: The Construction of Scientific Facts*. Princeton, N.J.: Princeton University Press.

Lee, Tina. 2016. *Catching a Case: Inequality and Fear in New York City's Child Welfare System*. New Brunswick, N.J.: Rutgers University Press.

Leinaweaver, Jessaca. 2013. *Adoptive Migration: Raising Latinos in Spain*. Durham. N.C.: Duke University Press.

Linthicum, Kate. 2015. "7,000 Immigrant Children Ordered Deported Without Going to Court." *Los Angeles Times*, March 6.

Lorey, David. 1999. *The U.S.-Mexican Border in the Twentieth Century: A History of Economic and Social Transformation*. Wilmington, Del.: SR Books.

Lovelock, Kirsten. 2000. "Intercountry Adoption as a Migratory Practice: A Comparative Analysis of Intercountry Adoption and Immigration Policy and Practice in the United States, Canada and New Zealand. *International Migration Review* 34(3): 907–49.

Malkki, Liisa. 1994. "Citizens of Humanity: Internationalism and the Imagined Community of Nations." *Diaspora: A Journal of Transnational Studies* 3(1): 41–68.

———. 1996. "Speechless Emissaries: Refugees, Humanitarianism, and Dehistoricization." *Cultural Anthropology* 11(3): 377–404.

McKinley, Michelle. 1997. "Life Stories, Disclosure and the Law." *Political and Legal Anthropology Review* 20(2): 70–82.

Mehan, Hugh. 1983. "The Role of Language and the Language of Role in Institutional Decision Making." *Language and Society* 12(2): 187–211.

Merry, Sally Engle. 1988. "Legal Pluralism." *Law and Society Review* 22(5): 869–96.

Michaels, Ralf. 2009. "Global Legal Pluralism." *Annual Review of Law and Social Science* 5: 35.

Mink, Gwendolyn. 1990. "The Lady and the Tramp: Gender, Race, and the Origins of the American Welfare State." In *Women, the State, and Welfare*, ed. Linda Gordon, 92–122. Madison: University of Wisconsin Press.

Mitchell, Timothy. 2002. *Rule of Experts: Egypt, Techno-Politics, Modernity*. Berkeley: University of California Press.

———. 2011. *Carbon Democracy: Political Power in the Age of Oil*. Brooklyn: Verso.

Mnookin, Robert. 1973. "Foster Care: In Whose Best interest?" *Harvard Education Review* 43(4): 599–638.

Modell, Judith. 1994. *Kinship with Strangers: Adoption and Interpretations of Kinship in American Culture*. Berkeley: University of California Press.

Molina, Natalia. 2006. *Fit to Be Citizens? Public Health and Race in Los Angeles*. Berkeley: University of California Press.

———. 2014. *How Race Is Made in America: Immigration, Citizenship, and the Historical Power of Racial Scripts*. Berkeley: University of California Press.

Mongia, Rhadika. 1999. "Race, Nationality, Mobility: A History of the Passport." *Public Culture* 11(3): 527–56.

Morton, John. 2011a. *Civil Immigration Enforcement: Priorities for the Apprehension, Detention, and Removal of Aliens*. U.S. Department of Homeland Security, U.S. Immigration and Customs Enforcement. March 2 (initially released June 30, 2010).

———. 2011b. *Exercising Prosecutorial Discretion Consistent with the Civil Immigration Enforcement Priorities of the Agency for the Apprehension, Detention, and Removal of Aliens*. June 17. Washington, D.C.: U.S. Department of Homeland Security, U.S. Immigration and Customs Enforcement.

Motomura, Hiroshi. 2006. *Americans in Waiting: The Lost Story of Immigration and Citizenship in the United States*. New York: Oxford University Press.

———. 2011. "The Discretion That Matters: Federal Immigration Enforcement, State and Local Arrests, and the Civil-Criminal Line." *UCLA Law Review* 58: 1819–58.

Murray, Kasia O'Neill. 2004. "The Child Welfare Financing Structure." Pew Charitable Trusts, August 2.

Navaro-Yashin, Yael. 2007. "Make-Believe Papers, Legal Forms, and the Counterfeit: Affective Interactions Between Documents and People in Britain and Cyprus." *Anthropological Theory* 7(1): 79–96.

Newton, Rae, Alan Litrownik, and John Landsverk. 2000. "Children and Youth in Foster Care: Disentangling the Relationship Between Problem Behaviors and Number of Placements." *Child Abuse and Neglect* 24(10): 1363–74.

Ngai, Mae. 2004. *Impossible Subjects: Illegal Aliens and the Making of Modern America*. Princeton, N.J.: Princeton University Press.

Nicholls, Walter. 2013. *The DREAMers: How the Undocumented Youth Movement Transformed the Immigrant Rights Debate*. Stanford, Calif.: Stanford University Press.

Nuijten, Monique. 2004. "Between Fear and Fantasy: Governmentality and the Working of Power in Mexico." *Critique of Anthropology* 24(2): 209–30.

Orellana, Marjorie Faulstich and Sarah Jean Johnson. 2011. "'Anchor Babies' and Dreams Deferred: Public Discourse About Immigrant Children and Implications for Civic and Educational Rights." Program on International Migration, UCLA International Institute, UC Los Angeles.

Padgett, Tim. 2009. "Can a Mother Lose Her Child Because She Doesn't Speak English?" *Time*, August 27.

Pallares, Amalia. 2015. *Family Activism: Immigrant Struggles and the Politics of Noncitizenship*. New Brunswick, N.J.: Rutgers University Press.

Parreñas, Rhacel. 2005. *Children of Global Migration: Transnational Families and Gendered Woes*. Stanford, Calif.: Stanford University Press.

Pathak, Zakia and Rajeswari Sunder Rajan. 1989. "Shahbano." *Signs* 14(3): 558–82.

Payan, Tony. 2010. "Crossborder Governance in a Tristate, Binational Region." In *Cities and Citizenship at the U.S.-Mexico Border: The Paso del Norte Metropolitan Region*, ed. Kathleen Stuadt, César Fuentes, and Julia Monárrez Fragoso, 217–44. New York: Palgrave Macmillan.

Peña, Milagros. 2007. *Latina Activists across Borders: Women's Grassroots Organizing in Mexico and Texas*. Durham, N.C.: Duke University Press.

Perea, Juan. 1997. *Immigrants Out! The New Nativism and the Anti-Immigrant Impulse in the United States*. New York: New York University Press.

Platt, Anthony. 2009[1969]. *The Child Savers: The Invention of Delinquency*. New Brunswick, N.J.: Rutgers University Press.

Preston, Julia. 2014. "Migrants Flow in South Texas, as Do Rumors." *New York Times*, June 17, A1.

Proffitt, T. D. 1994. *Tijuana: The History of a Mexican Metropolis*. San Diego: San Diego State University Press.

Rabin, Nina. 2011. "Disappearing Parents: Immigration Enforcement and the Child Welfare System." *Connecticut Law Review* 44(1): 99–160.

Rastas, Anna. 2009. "Racism in the Everyday Life of Finnish Children with Transnational Roots." *Barn* 19(1): 29–43.

Read, Peter. 1998[1981]. *The Stolen Generations: The Removal of Aboriginal Children in New South Wales, 1883–1969*. Surry Hills, NSW: Department of Aboriginal Affairs.

Reich, Jennifer. 2005. *Fixing Families: Parents, Power, and the Child Welfare System*. New York: Routledge.

Robles, Frances. 2014. "Fleeing Gangs, Children Head to U.S. Border." *New York Times*, July 10, A1.

Rodriguez, Jason and Naomi Glenn-Levin Rodriguez. 2016. "Refashioning Inequality: Child Welfare at the U.S.-Mexico Border and NGOs in Bodhgaya, India." *Ethnos* (January 8): 1–22.

Rodriguez, Naomi Glenn-Levin. 2016. "Translating 'Best Interest': Child Welfare Decisions at the U.S.-México Border." *Political and Legal Anthropology Review* 39(1): 154–68..

Rodriguez, Nestor and Cecilia Menjívar. 2014. "'Crisis' Label Deflects Responsibility for Migrant Children." *Houston Chronicle*, August 26.

Rose, Deborah Bird. 2004. *Reports from a Wild Country: Ethics for Decolonisation*. Sydney: University of New South Wales Press.

Santos, Boaventura de Sousa. 1987. "Law: A Map of Misreading. Toward a Postmodern Conception of Law." *Law and Society Journal* 14(3): 279–302.

———. 1995. *Toward a New Common Sense: Law, Science and Politics in the Paradigmatic Transition*. London: Routledge.

Sarat, Austin. 1990. "'The Law Is All Over': Power, Resistance, and Legal Consciousness of the Welfare Poor." *Yale Journal of Law and the Humanities* 2: 343–79.

Scherz, China. 2011. "Protecting Children, Preserving Families: Moral Conflict and Actuarial Science in a Problem of Contemporary Governance." *Political and Legal Anthropology Review* 34(1): 33–50.

Schlossman, Steven. 2005. *Transforming Juvenile Justice: Reform Ideals and Institutional Realities, 1825–1920.* DeKalb: Northern Illinois University Press.

Schmidt, Susan and Jacqueline Bhabha. 2008 "Seeking Asylum Alone: Unaccompanied and Separated Children and Refugee Protection in the U.S." *Journal of the History of Childhood and Youth* 1(1): 126–38.

Schneider, Carl. 1991. "Discretion, Rules, and Law: Child Custody and the UMDA's Best-Interest Standard." *Michigan Law Review* 89(8): 2215–98.

Schueths, April and Jodie Lawston, eds. 2015. *Living Together, Living Apart: Mixed Status Families and U.S. Immigration Policy.* Seattle: University of Washington Press.

Shahar, Ido. 2013. "A Tale of Two Courts: How Organizational Ethnography Can Shed New Light on Legal Pluralism." *Political and Legal Anthropology Review* 36(1): 118–37.

Shuman, Amy and Carol Bohmer. 2007. *Rejecting Refugees: Political Asylum in the 21st Century.* New York: Routledge.

Simons, Abby. 2013. "Immigration Status Not a Factor in Custody Battle, Minnesota Court Says." *Star Tribune*, April 8.

Smith, Steven and Michael Lipsky. 1993. *Nonprofits for Hire: The Welfare State in the Age of Contracting.* Cambridge, Mass.: Harvard University Press.

Sparrow, Glen. 2001. "San Diego-Tijuana: Not Quite a Binational City or Region." *GeoJournal* 54(1): 73–83.

Statz, Michele. 2013. "Strategic Obligation: Cause Lawyering on Behalf of Unaccompanied Chinese Youth." Law and Society Association Annual Meeting, Honolulu.

Stephen, Lynn. 2007. *Transborder Lives: Indigenous Oaxacans in California, Mexico, and Oregon.* Durham, N.C.: Duke University Press.

Stoler, Ann. 2002. *Carnal Knowledge and Imperial Power: Race and the Intimate in Colonial Rule.* Berkeley: University of California Press.

Strong, Pauline Turner. 2001. "To Forget Their Tongue, Their Name, and Their Whole Relation: Captivity, Extra-Tribal Adoption, and the Indian Child Welfare Act." In *Relative Values: Reconfiguring Kinship Studies*, ed. Sarah Franklin and Susan McKinnon, 468–93. Durham, N.C.: Duke University Press.

Swartz, Teresa Toguchi. 2005. *Parenting for the State: An Ethnographic Analysis of Non-Profit Foster Care.* New York: Routledge.

Terrio, Susan. 2010. "The Production of Criminal Migrant Children: Surveillance, Detention, and Deportation in France." In *Children and Migration: At the Crossroads of Resiliency and Vulnerability*, ed. Maria O. Ensor and Elzbieta M. Gozdziak, 79–96. New York: Palgrave Macmillan.

———. 2015. *Whose Child Am I? Unaccompanied, Undocumented Children in U.S. Immigration Custody.* Berkeley: University of California Press.

Thronson, David. 2008. "Creating Crisis: Immigration Raids and the Destabilization of Immigrant Families." *Wake Forest Law Review* 43: 391–418.

———. 2005. "Of Borders and Best Interests: Examining the Experiences of Undocumented Immigrants in U.S. Family Courts." *Texas Hispanic Journal of Law and Policy* 45(11): 45–70.

Thronson, David and Judge Frank P. Sullivan. 2012. "Family Courts and Immigration Status." *Juvenile and Family Court* 63(1): 1–18.

Ticktin, Miriam. 2006. "Where Ethics and Politics Meet." *American Ethnologist* 33(1): 33–49.

———. 2011. *Casualties of Care: Immigration and the Politics of Humanitarianism in France*. Berkeley: University of California Press.

Tiffin, Susan. 1982. *In Whose Best Interest? Child Welfare Reform in the Progressive Era*. Westport, Conn.: Greenwood Press.

Tough, Paul. 2008. *Whatever It Takes: Geoffrey Canada's Quest to Change Harlem and America*. Boston: Houghton Mifflin.

Vieira, Kate Elizabeth. 2010. "'American by Paper': Assimilation and Documentation in a Biliterate, Bi-Ethnic Immigrant Community." *College English* 73(1): 50–72.

Vullnetari, Julie. 2012. "Beyond 'Choice or Force': Roma Mobility in Albania and the Mixed Migration Paradigm." *Journal of Ethnic and Migration Studies* 38(8): 1305–21.

Walters, William. 2002. "Deportation, Expulsion, and the International Police of Aliens. *Citizenship Studies* 6(3): 265–92.

Ward, Geoff. 2012. *The Black Child-Savers: Racial Democracy and Juvenile Justice*. Chicago: University of Chicago Press.

Webster, Daniel et al. 2016. *CCWIP Reports*. Retrieved May 27 from University of California at Berkeley California Child Welfare Indicators Project, http://cssr.berkeley.edu/ucb_childwelfare.

Wessler, Seth. 2011. *Shattered Families: The Perilous Intersection of Immigration Enforcement and the Child Welfare System*. New York: Applied Research Center.

Weston, Kath. 1997. *Families We Choose: Lesbians, Gays, Kinship*. New York: Columbia University Press.

Wilson, Ara. 2004. *The Intimate Economies of Bangkok: Tomboys, Tycoons, and Avon Ladies in the Global City*. Berkeley: University of California Press.

Wozniak, Danielle. 2001. *They're All My Children: Foster Mothering in America*. New York: New York University Press.

Yablon-Zug, Marcia. 2011. "Should I Stay or Should I Go: Why Immigrant Reunification Decisions Should Be Based on the Best Interest of the Child." *Brigham Young Law Review* 4: 1139–92.

———. 2012. "Separation, Termination, Deportation: Why Undocumented Immigrant Families Are Losing Their Children." *Boston College Journal of Law and Social Justice* 32(1): 63–117.

Yeh, Rihan. 2016. "Commensuration in a Mexican Border City: Currencies, Consumer Goods, and Languages." *Anthropological Quarterly* 89(1): 63–92.

Yngvesson, Barbara. 1997. "Negotiating Motherhood: Identity and Difference in 'Open' Adoptions." *Law and Society Review* 31(1): 31–80.

———. 2010. *Belonging in an Adopted World: Race, Identity, and Transnational Adoption*. Chicago: University of Chicago Press.

Yngvesson, Barbara and Susan Bibler Coutin. 2006. "Backed by Papers: Undoing Persons, History, and Return." *American Ethnologist* 33(2): 177–90.

Young, Wendy. 2002. *Prison Guard or Parent? INS Treatment of Unaccompanied Refugee Children*. Women's Commission for Refugee Women and Children. https://www.womensrefugeecommission.org/images/zdocs/ins_det.pdf.

Zatz, Marjorie, and Nancy Rodriguez. 2014. "The Limits of Discretion: Challenges and Dilemmas of Prosecutorial Discretion in Immigration Enforcement." *Law & Social Inquiry* 39(3): 666–89.

———. 2015. *Dreams and Nightmares: Immigration Policy, Youth, and Families*. Berkeley: University of California Press.

Zavella, Patricia. 2012. "Why Are Immigrant Families Different Now?" Policy Brief, Center for Latino Policy Research, University of California, Berkeley, August.

———. 2011. *I'm Neither Here Nor There: Mexicans' Quotidian Struggles with Migration and Poverty*. Durham, N.C.: Duke University Press.

Zayas, Luis. 2015. *Forgotten Citizens: Deportation, Children, and the Making of American Exiles and Orphans*. Oxford: Oxford University Press.

Zelizer, Viviana. 1985. *Pricing the Priceless Child: The Changing Social Value of Children*. New York: Basic.

Zetter, Roger. 2007. "More Labels, Fewer Refugees: Remaking the Refugee Label in an Era of Globalization." *Journal of Refugee Studies* 20(2): 172–92.

INDEX

ACKNOWLEDGMENTS

This project could not have taken shape without the help and support of a great number of friends and colleagues. First and foremost, my thanks go to the families in San Diego and Tijuana who shared their lives with me and offered me friendship and support throughout my research. I extend my deepest gratitude to the parents and children who welcomed me into their homes, who fed me, laughed with me, played with me, and spoke frankly with me about the pain and joys of parenting and fostering. I am indebted to the social workers, judges, lawyers, advocates, and orphanage staff who so generously let me into their incredibly busy lives. Special thanks go to the social workers I call Corinne and Alicia; without their openness and willingness to let an anthropologist tag along this project would not have been possible.

I thank the many thoughtful and generous people in my life during my time at UC Santa Cruz. Special thanks go to Don Brenneis for his cheerful encouragement and rigorous academic guidance, and to Patricia Zavella for her generous mentorship, Melissa Caldwell for her careful reading, and Susan Harding for helping me to see my work from a different angle.

Others at UC Santa Cruz guided me at crucial points in the process—Carolyn Martin Shaw saw this project through its earliest beginnings, Mark Anderson and Andrew Mathews provided crucial interventions at key moments, Matthew Wolf-Meyer made navigating the world of academic scholarship as painless and transparent as possible, and Triloki Nath Pandey believed in my abilities from day one. Thanks to Peter Leykam, Carla Takaki-Richardson, and Celina Callahan-Kapoor for being engaged interlocutors and generous readers at various stages. A special thanks goes to my writing buddies—Kendralin Freeman made sure I sat down to work on this project every week, Patricia Alvarez has read almost every page I've written (some more than once) since we began writing, and Melissa Hackman stepped in to save the day in the project's final stages.

My colleagues and students at Hobart and William Smith Colleges have provided a lively environment in which I was able to bring this project to fruition—special thanks to Paul Kehle for helping a scholar carve out time from teaching to get her book written. Funding for this project came from the Fulbright IIE, the Wenner-Gren Foundation, and the UC Mexus. Grant officers in all three foundations provided invaluable support and facilitated the complexities of cross-border research. Thanks to *Political and Legal Anthropology Review*, *Ethnos*, and the University of Washington Press for permission to reprint earlier versions of material here.

The encouragement and affection of friends and family supported me through this lengthy process. To Katharine Callard, Ayala Bassett, and Jes Anderson for asking with genuine curiosity about my project. To my brother Jacob, for understanding. To my Grandfather Abraham, who would have been so excited to read this book, and to my nephew of the same name, for breathing hope into a sometimes bleak world. To my parents for their support throughout my schooling and their belief in my abilities, and to my early mentors Suzanne McCluskey, Maria Tymozcko, and Rachel Conrad for the guidance and inspiration that set me on this path. And to Jason Rodriguez, the steadiest of companions, who has been with me every step of the way.